I
DID IT
MY WAY

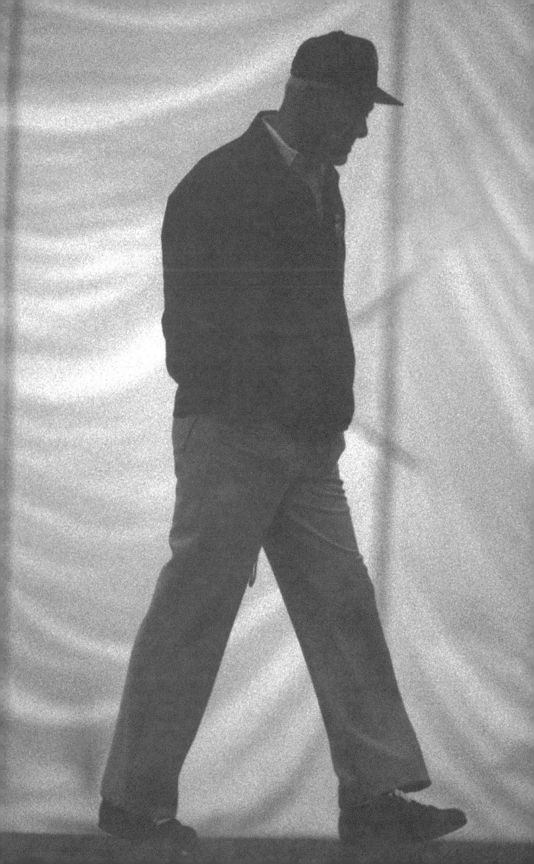

I
DID IT
MY WAY

A Remarkable
Journey to the
Hall of Fame

Bud Grant with Jim Bruton

TRIUMPH
BOOKS

Library of Congress Cataloging-in-Publication Data
Grant, Bud.
  I did it my way : a remarkable journey to the hall of fame / Bud Grant with Jim Bruton.
    pages cm
    ISBN 978-1-60078-786-7
1. Grant, Bud. 2. Football coaches—United States—Biography. 3. Minnesota Vikings (Football team) I. Title.
  GV939.G72G73 2013
  796.332092—dc23
  [B]   2013014880

This book is available in quantity at special discounts for your group or organization. For further information, contact:

    Triumph Books LLC
    814 North Franklin Street
    Chicago, Illinois 60610
    (312) 337–0747
    www.triumphbooks.com

Printed in U.S.A.

ISBN: 978-1-60078-786-7

Design by Sue Knopf

Title page photograph courtesy of Getty Images

To my wife, Pat.
Couldn't have done it without you.

CONTENTS

FOREWORD

BUD GRANT AND I formally met on the first day he attended college at the University of Minnesota, which also happened to be my first day assigned to the Gophers sports beat. But I had first introduced myself to him when he was a member of the Great Lakes basketball team that had played the Gophers at Williams Arena in 1945. Fortunately for me, I got a good introduction from his coach, Weeb Ewbank, who was the basketball coach at Great Lakes and later coached the New York Jets football team in the Super Bowl.

For Bud and me to become best friends seemed unlikely. He was one of the best athletes ever developed at Superior Central High School; I was a rookie reporter who never graduated high school and never went to college. But we hit it off right away. For a good part of four years, we had many of our meals together during the school year and spent a lot of time together.

In the summertime I occasionally drove him to baseball games. Bud was a great athlete. He once pitched two games in one day—at Gordon, Wisconsin, in the afternoon and at Rice Lake in the evening. I traveled with the Gophers football and basketball teams, so we saw each other then, too. When he finished his three-sport career at Minnesota and was ready to graduate, I was running the Minneapolis Lakers. He made his debut with the Lakers on Christmas night, 1949.

His very first basket was from half court, right before the end of the first half. He went on to play on the Lakers' NBA championship team.

Remembering Bud from his football prowess with the Gophers, the place came apart. Anyone who saw him will never forget it. Bud played two years with the Lakers before turning to pro football as a first-round draft choice of the Philadelphia Eagles.

Considering his college career, I think he and David Winfield were the two greatest all-around athletes ever to play for the Gophers. Bud was an All-American football player playing on both offense and defense as a wide receiver and defensive end. He pitched for the baseball team and he was a starting forward on the basketball team. Bernie Bierman, former Gophers coach, once told me that Bud was one of the smartest players he had ever coached and that he didn't recall him ever making a mistake. As a basketball player, he was very physical, and as a Laker he made one of the most important baskets of his career. Bud scored with only seconds to go in a playoff game, sending his team into overtime against Syracuse. The Lakers went on to win the NBA championship that season.

Grant had a reputation of being a very stoic person who wouldn't pull tricks on people, but he was just the opposite. There was the time he put a pet squirrel in my glove compartment when we were driving to spend a weekend at his home in Superior. There was another time, while driving on a highway, when I felt something crawl up my knee, and it was that pet squirrel again.

One year Bud and I went to Bud's home on New Year's Eve and left after midnight to return to the Twin Cities. We had a flat tire and spent part of the night in the car keeping warm while we strategized how we were going to make it home. It all worked out eventually, but it wasn't a good start to the new year for the garage mechanic who helped us out in the early morning hours of New Year's Day. It was just another of our adventures—this time in a car I had borrowed with no spare tire.

The last career I would have thought Bud would pursue was coaching. He never talked about it during his college career. Being the great hunter and sportsman that he is, I always thought he would have a career connected to the outdoors.

He was 29 years old in 1967 when he got the Winnipeg job, coaching the Blue Bombers. Unfortunately, his father died in Pasadena, California, never knowing that Bud got the job. Another secret that few people know is that Bud was the Vikings' first choice as head coach of the expansion team, but he decided to stay up in Winnipeg after taking the job. It turned out to be a fantastic decision, as he coached the team to six Grey Cups, winning four of them, before joining the Vikings.

Many people in the media couldn't understand how we could have a relationship while he was coaching the Vikings and I was a columnist covering the team. The truth is, I wrote several stories—especially about players being added to the team and players being cut—before he released the information to the press. I didn't get them from Bud, but from other sources I had. He understood that I had a job to do, and I understood that he had a job to do. In fact, he favored another writer—a young man named Ralph Reeve, who covered the Vikings for the *St. Paul Pioneer Press*—and likely gave him a lot more tips than he gave me.

I made one great contribution to Bud's long coaching career: I helped him sign Kenny Ploen, a former Iowa All-American who went on to lead Bud's Blue Bombers to several Grey Cups. I had a great relationship with the Iowa coaching staff, especially head coach Forest Evashevski and Jerry Burns, who later became a longtime assistant and then head coach of the Minnesota Vikings. They helped convince Ploen to play pro football in Winnipeg, when he had other plans to become an engineer.

Bud did give me one big scoop when he decided to retire from coaching the first time. He and Mike Lynn asked me to join them on a trip to California. They told me they were going to make a big deal with Al Davis of the Oakland Raiders. I joined them on the plane, and finally they admitted they just wanted me to go to Hawaii with them. They would see Max Winter, president of the Vikings, to break the news to him personally, and I would write the story from there. I broke one of the biggest stories ever to appear in our paper. When Bud decided to come back to coaching, I wasn't as fortunate. The news leaked, and Dark Star, a local media personality, broke the story.

Probably one of the biggest honors of my life was when Bud called me and asked me to be presenter at his induction to the Pro Football Hall of Fame. I never expected that. In my opinion, it was unfortunate that they didn't put him in the Hall of Fame the year before; it could have gotten a lot more local attention, since the Super Bowl was held that year in Minneapolis.

At the Hall of Fame, it seemed as if every honoree cried when they made their speech. I was sitting next to former Dallas head coach Tom Landry, who was a presenter like me, and I made a friendly bet with him that Bud, being as stoic as he is, would not cry. But like others on the platform, he broke down, too. I'll never forget when he remarked what his father would have said had he been there: "The kid made it. The kid made it."

Personally, we have long been close. After many home games, I would be a guest at the Grant home in Bloomington, where his wife, Pat, would cook goulash as good as any cook ever made. After not going to Pat's house for a long time for her special goulash, she kept on insisting that I come over. The night I finally showed up was the last goulash she ever cooked. She went to the hospital the next day and died shortly thereafter. She was an unbelievable mother who raised six great kids and was a perfect wife for a coach, which takes a certain type of person. She will be missed.

Bud's and my relationship hasn't changed much over the years. I often consulted with Bud to get his opinion on various decisions that I had to make. That included buying my home on the St. Croix; he went out and took a look at it and gave it his okay. We still make some trips up to his cabin in Gordon, Wisconsin—which he and a friend originally bought for $100. Today it is a beautiful lake, and there is a second lake that is completely private.

In my career as a sportswriter, I've had a chance to meet thousands of people, but I've never met anybody with the common sense of Bud Grant. That is how he coached—with his common sense. It is how he makes nothing but the best decisions, and that's one of the many reasons I have more respect for him than anybody I know in the world.

—*Sid Hartman*

INTRODUCTION

I SPENT SEVEN YEARS as Bud Grant's quarterback for the Minnesota Vikings, and they were the best seven years of my life. They were certainly successful years. We went to three Super Bowls—and if the stars had aligned just slightly differently, it could have been four or five. But my years with Bud in Minnesota weren't just about our accomplishments on the field; they were important years in making me the man I am today.

During my life, I've been fortunate enough to have been around a lot of great thinkers. I've known some of the most legendary football coaches in history. I've known very successful businesspeople who taught me a lot. Learning from all of them was a great privilege that I have never taken for granted. But I learned more from Bud Grant than from any single person I have ever known. Whenever I wasn't on the field, I made sure I was right there next to Bud, watching him and listening to what he said, learning how he thought and how he saw the world. It was an unbelievable experience.

Bud Grant never did anything halfway. He was a world-class basketball player in college and with the Lakers in the NBA. He was a world-class football player with the Eagles and then in Canada. And to top it all off, he was a great baseball player, too. When he became a coach for the Winnipeg Blue Bombers, all he did was win. When he moved to the NFL in 1967, he took over a struggling franchise and ran it as a world-class organization.

But really understanding Bud is about more than a list of his achievements. It's about who he is—because he is one of the most unique individuals I have ever met. They really broke the mold when they made him! Everyone saw him standing stoically on the sideline during games. He never yelled, never screamed. In fact, he was never demonstrative at all. In seven years, I never heard him chew anyone out, and (what might be the most remarkable thing) never once heard him talk badly about an official on the sideline. And that's in a league where the officials take abuse from everybody (myself certainly included)!

He was always in complete, total control. It didn't matter what the situation was. While others followed their emotions and yelled and screamed, Bud was always quietly thinking. He was always 10 steps ahead of everybody else, and I found that terribly intriguing. When it comes to personality, Bud and I are total opposites—but I knew right away that he was a man I could learn from, so it didn't matter. During my entire career, in both football and in business, my greatest asset has been my ability to think analytically. I got that from Bud Grant. I got so many things from him.

I stayed close to Bud at all times because everything he said just made sense to me. It might be a comment here, a conversation there. Sometimes he was talking to me specifically, sometimes to others, but I always found things to learn no matter who he was talking to. His understanding of coaching and leadership was different from Vince Lombardi's. It was different from Tom Landry's, different from Don Shula's—but it was just as effective, if not more so, than any of them.

One thing I noticed was that Bud looked at things nobody else was looking at. It went way beyond X's and O's with him; if anything, those X's and O's were secondary to everything else.

He also has a particularly uncanny ability to predict the weather. One of my favorite memories was a game against the L.A. Rams.

With the skies still blue, Bud told me that it would storm in the second half—and not just any storm, a big one. "The field's going to be sloppy in the second half," he said, so the time for aggressive play would be right away. We came out extra-aggressive, on all cylinders in that first half, took the lead—and then sure enough, the second half was a mess. But since we already had the lead, we never had to look back. And when it came to practice, Bud also was known to end a little early some days, knowing that even though there wasn't a cloud in the sky at the moment, it would be pouring rain as soon as we'd all gotten inside the clubhouse.

Of all the figures from his period of NFL history, Bud surely stands out. No one else had his team standing on the line at attention during the national anthem. No one else banned heaters from the sideline in subzero temperatures. Bud instilled discipline and smarts in his teams like no one else. He demanded more than any coach in the league and knew how to get us to live up to that high standard. He demanded smart players—team players—and never, ever compromised that.

Being around Bud Grant and getting to know him so well has been one of the greatest privileges of my life. And now with this book, the world has a chance for the first time to really see who Harry Peter Grant really is. It's a rare treat. Enjoy it.

—*Fran Tarkenton*

COAUTHOR'S NOTE

THERE ARE VERY FEW people in sports who are immediately recognizable by only their first name. Mickey, of course, was Mickey Mantle. Willie, Willie Mays. Arnold, Arnold Palmer. And Bud, Bud Grant.

Just the name "Bud" to the sporting public resonates as the man who led the Minnesota Vikings to four Super Bowls. He was the coach, the leader, the general, the mainstay.

Bud was the man on the sideline with the cap, headset, and gray Vikings sweatshirt with the large XL on the front. He was the commander of the Purple, the epitome of success, the cornerstone of excellence.

As a youngster, I had heard about him. He was the former Minnesota Gopher who starred on the gridiron, the court, and the diamond. He won several Grey Cup championships as coach of the Winnipeg Blue Bombers. And then he became the coach of our beloved hometown Vikings.

In 1967 and again in 1971, I was fortunate enough to sign professional football contracts to play for the Minnesota Vikings. I was cut by Bud Grant in both training camps. A friend of mine asked me a while back, "Did you ever think you would work on the autobiography of the man who cut you *twice?*"

Unlikely as it is, the experience has been rewarding. Bud has been absolutely wonderful to work with in every respect. He has been charming, witty, passionate, humorous, and extremely gracious as we worked to capture the totality of his legacy. We have sat for endless hours at his Bloomington home and his lake home in Gordon, Wisconsin.

We have eaten together, fished together, and ridden the trails of his wooded acreage in northern Wisconsin. I have watched Bud clean fish and cook dinner in some of the more interesting moments of this wonderful journey. Each step along the way has been enjoyable, almost as if it were scripted.

Bud has shared with me his utmost private moments and his passion for his family, the outdoors, his menagerie of pets, and life. The stoic, relatively silent figure on the sideline and the television screen has come to life and revealed so much mystery about his life. I am deeply honored that I have the opportunity to help him share his story for the first time.

—*Jim Bruton*

SUPERIOR KICKOFF

I ALMOST MISSED OUT on coaching the Minnesota Vikings to four Super Bowls. I may never have played sports at the University of Minnesota, been a member of the Minneapolis Lakers or the Philadelphia Eagles, or played and coached with the Winnipeg Blue Bombers. I'm only here because of a change of luck, according to my dad.

"Kid," he told me one day, "your mother and I were planning to get married and we had saved $200 for the wedding. I took the money and went gambling with it and lost all but five dollars. Fortunately for you, my luck changed. Had it gone the other way, you might not be here!" Over the years, I have thought about that more than once.

I was born in Superior, Wisconsin, which sits at the western edge of Lake Superior in the northwestern part of the state. Today, the city population is approximately 27,000, about 10,000 less than when I lived there as a boy.

Superior is bordered by two bays—Saint Louis Bay and Superior Bay—and sits within the two rivers—the Nemadji and the Saint Louis. Its neighboring city across the bay is Duluth, Minnesota. The two cities form what is called the Twin Ports and share a harbor, one of the most important on all of the Great Lakes.

Growing up in Superior, our home was down in the low end of the city. Duluth was up above us to the northwest and, of course, in

Minnesota. I used to look up the hill at the city of Duluth, thinking, *That's where the rich people live.* We were what I called the "grubby people" of the area; they were the more fortunate. They lived above us, up there on the hill in Duluth.

My ancestors came from Scotland. There is still a Grant clan there. My mother was a Kielley, which is Irish, so basically I am Scotch Irish, although my mother's mother was a Swede, so there is some Swedish blood in there, too.

The name Grant goes back to the Spanish Armada, and somewhere in there is a little Spanish, too. We didn't keep any records to verify the claims, but I did find out some of our family came from Scotland across Nova Scotia in through Canada. Some journeyed through Wisconsin at Sioux Saint Marie, Ontario.

My dad was born and raised on an Indian reservation in northern Wisconsin called Odanah, which raises the question of whether I have any Indian blood in me. My uncle always called me a "blue-eyed Indian." My heritage never has been very clear to me, but I do remember that my family always had a lot of Indian friends, mostly Dad's. They came to our house from Odanah on a bus or train and visited us often in Superior.

When we lived on 6th Street, I remember they would come and sit on the back steps. My mother would open the door in the morning, and there they were. They never knocked on the door; they just sat there. Sometimes it would scare my mother half to death.

I was never quite sure exactly why they came, but they would always stay to say hello to Dad. To my mind, it seemed as if they came all that distance to get one of two things: either an egg sandwich or a quarter. If my dad was home, they would visit with him, but if he wasn't home, they would be gone—eggs or a quarter, and then off they went. I can remember them sitting on those steps just as clear as if it were this morning.

It's funny how the memory works. Some things of the past just vanish and are lost forever, and others never fade. The geography of

Superior remains instilled in my memory after all these years. There was a 1st Street, a 2nd Street, and a 3rd Street, and as Superior grew, the streets grew. Third Street was the main route from the lake, and that's where the town of Superior really began. Beyond that, toward the water, were the wharfs on 1st and 2nd Streets. In order to move uptown, you had to move up in the street numbers, from 1st to 2nd to 3rd and so on.

I was too young to now remember when my family lived on 3rd Street, but I know where our house was located because I used to run that part of town as a kid. We moved to 6th Street when I was in the first grade.We were more fortunate than many of the other people in town because of my dad's job—he was a fireman. It was during the Depression, and although he never made a lot of money, it was enough for us to live on. He worked hard and had a good reputation around town. I really looked up to him.

My dad was about 5'10", athletic, and took pride in his physical appearance. He used to throw out his chest and take deep breaths. "Do this. It's good for you," he would say. He had an easy way about him that everyone liked. He was also very good at remembering people's names and knew everyone in town. He had a real presence about him and was well liked. When my dad walked into a room, everyone noticed. There was just something about him that stood out. He had a wonderful personality.

When he got to be captain at the fire department he got a uniform, and he was very proud of it because he came from nothing. He liked the status that the uniform carried, and he wore it everywhere. He would go to games, and of course he always got in free with that uniform.

One of the scariest moments of my life was watching my dad get carried out of a building during a fire. It was one of the biggest fires ever to occur in town, at the Hotel Superior in the center of town. It was a spectacular fire that ended up burning the hotel to the ground. The fire started in the afternoon, and I remember spending the entire night on the roof of the building across the street watching it burn. I never will forget it; it was one of the most incredible sights I have ever seen.

It was difficult for the firefighters to get any water to the building because the smoke was so horrific. Dad led the team of firemen who went into the building and was overcome with smoke inhalation. He was very fortunate to come around quickly and turned out to be all right. In fact, he eventually returned to fight the fire.

The whole episode was horrible for me to watch. I will never forget seeing my dad carried out of that building, the fire blazing around him. I cannot begin to express what I was feeling at the time. To see him in danger was devastating.

My father was my hero, but personality-wise, I took more after my mother. She had two brothers about my size, but she was only about 5'5" or so. She came from a poor family and had a very difficult life growing up. Sometimes when she talked about her past, she would cry because things had been so tough for her. But she never complained. She was a very good mother, and I knew she always worried about me. She always wanted the best for me, and I never doubted her love.

I didn't date any girls in high school, and I suspect my mother thought I might be gay. I mean, I *never* dated. I never brought any girls home and never went out. I didn't have a car and spent most of my time playing sports, in the woods, or at the pool hall with my friends. Those were my priorities at the time. There were dances, but I never learned how to dance. My mother was always concerned about that. "Aren't you going to the dance?" she would ask. "Don't you want to see any of the girls? What about the mixer, aren't you going? Why not?" This concerned her, but it was never a concern to me. I had other things to do.

Once a girl gave me a scarf as a Christmas gift. It was about 10 days before Christmas, and obviously the girl wanted a present in return. "What are you going to get her?" my mother asked. I can still hear the question. "I'm not going to get her anything," I told her.

"What do you mean? That's a nice scarf, and you have to get her something," she told me. I said, "Mom, if I get her a present, she will think we are going together or something like that. So because I'm not interested, I'm not going to do it."

Well, my mother went out and bought a present for the girl from me. It's what mothers do, and she was a good mother.

I had two brothers, Jim and Jack, both of them quite a bit younger than me. When I was in high school, they were in grade school. Jim liked the outdoors but was not very athletic. Jack was much younger, so we didn't spend much time together as children.

When our family was able to move up from 3rd Street to 6th Street, that put us about six blocks from the lake. It was a little better area of town. There were railroad tracks near our house that went down to the lake, and I spent a lot of time playing on and around them. The track beds were filled with crushed rocks. I loved to throw rocks and I threw them at everything. I threw at telephone poles, I threw at cans, I threw at bottles in the water, I threw at trees and signs. I bet I spent half of my youth throwing rocks. I walked up and down those tracks thousands of times throwing rocks at anything and everything I could.

As I think back, it is likely the reason I could seemingly throw a baseball forever and never get a sore arm. I built my arm up as a kid throwing rocks. I would carry certain ones, good throwing rocks, in my pocket, so I was always prepared. I made games out of it. I used to toss a can out on a pond nearby and throw and throw at that can, and see how many times I could hit it. Or maybe I would be throwing at a telephone pole and I wouldn't go home until I had hit that pole 10 times in a row. No supper for me until I had hit it 10 times. I threw for accuracy but also for fun. There's no doubt it was a major factor in my later success as a pitcher.

Moving to 6th Street was a big move up in status for our family. Although I suppose we were never really considered poor, the fact was that we really didn't have anything much to speak of. Then again, everybody else we knew was that way too. It seemed that no one really had any of the extras, but we all got along. We had good friends and good neighbors.

As I got older, the Great Depression came—everyone was poor then. When my dad got paid, he didn't get money or a check to cash; he got paid in what was called "script." The city didn't have any money back then, so he and others would take the script, which was basically an IOU, and some of the stores in town would let you buy what you needed with the script. Eventually, the city would come up with the money for my dad and he would pay his bill. The problem was, a lot of the stores didn't take script, so that often made things difficult. But we got by, as did most of the people we knew.

Even though there was always food on the table, I vividly recall a hungry feeling. Maybe it was just being an adolescent, but I was always looking around for extra food. I'd look for anything that might have been left over from meals, things like that. If I could find something, I would eat it. Generally, though, there was never anything left over, so most of my years growing up, I was hungry. My stomach always felt empty.

I had a lot of great experiences growing up, for a kid who never had much to speak of. But then again, I never knew anyone who had much of anything back then. I can recall at the beginning of each week my mother counted out the food on the table. She would have one, two, three, four potatoes and all the carrots and other food all laid out, everything we would eat for the week. When it was gone it was gone. We always ate carefully and never had many leftovers.

She would go to the store and buy just enough to get by. We would get one piece of corn and half of this and half of this and half that. And we rarely had any meat. Later on, at training tables, I got all the meat I could ever want. I rarely eat meat anymore for that reason.

I was always happy, but there were certainly things I just did without. Money never seemed to be a major problem, and it was not something I dwelled upon, but the fact was I never had any. I would try to earn money whenever I got the opportunity, because I never got any money from my parents. Whenever I went anywhere I would walk in the street rather than on the sidewalk because I had a better chance of finding some change.

There was a little corner store in town near where we lived, and I would go there with, if I was lucky, a nickel to spend. I must have been about seven at the time, and I recall being excited about having that nickel. But I would never spend all of it. I would go to the store and spend a long time figuring out how to part with three cents. I always wanted to come home with two pennies' change in my pocket. I remember saving the money even more vividly than the joy of getting that candy.

Later on, I remember it was a big deal when a Bridgeman's Ice Cream Parlor was built in Superior. I love ice cream. After basketball practice I would walk by Bridgeman's and stop for ice cream. Then again, it wasn't just for ice cream; the girls who worked there were from my high school. I would get a malted milk worth a quarter for a nickel and drink that malted milk while I walked home. That was a big thing. I can remember going into the store and first looking around all the seats and on the floor for any loose change.

My dad never had any money either, so it was a huge deal to me whenever I had anything to spend. I guess that's why I was so careful with it: I never knew when I was going to have any money again. I never had anything like an allowance. Any money I had I earned from doing something for someone. On rare occasions, my grandfather would give me a small amount of money. Once in a while, he might give me a quarter, which was huge for me.

Looking back on my childhood, it's hard to determine for sure whether those things I experienced as a kid impacted my life, but I think they did. For example, growing up we lived in very small two-bedroom houses, and we never had enough space. I grew up sleeping on a couch in the main room of the house all through high school.

When I got married, it was very important to me that each of my kids had their own room, because I never had one of my own.

As a kid, we had to make our own entertainment. I remember getting a BB gun when I was around 10 and spending a tremendous amount of time sneaking up on squirrels, pigeons, and rabbits. I would crawl through the weeds, hunting with my gun. A fellow that lived behind us had a chicken coop, so there were a lot of sparrows around all the time, and I would shoot sparrows. Also nearby was a neighbor with a two-story barn that housed pigeons. Sometimes I would sit there for hours waiting for those pigeons.

I also made slingshots. Someone told me once that the best slingshots were made from willow branches. So every time I walked by a willow I would look for the perfect slingshot branch. If I found one, I would make sure to cut it out. With the branch in hand, I would then find an old inner tube from a tire and cut the rubber to attach to it. And I have to say, even to this day, if I see an old shoe, I look at the tongue and think, *Now that would be a great pouch for a slingshot.*

All those rocks I used to keep in my back pocket were perfect ammunition for my slingshot. I got pretty good at using it. Then, when I got the gun, I thought I was a big-game hunter. I went out hunting every chance I could.

That was basically my recreation, except for baseball.

We kids did play a lot of neighborhood baseball. It was the only sport where we could find a place to play. There were no basketball courts in town, and football was not as popular as it is today, so we played baseball. A lot of it was just playing catch, though at times we would play "pepper"—hitting the ball back and forth to one another—if we could find some sort of backstop to keep the ball in play.

One day, when we were playing ball in the streets, the ball rolled into a storm sewer. We were pretty sure we could get it out by raising this huge manhole cover. Well, the cover fell on my finger. I can't begin to explain how much it hurt. My finger was squashed under that cover, and we couldn't lift it again. So I sat there with my finger mangled and hollered at my friend to go get someone to help. It hurt like crazy. I didn't know if it was smashed or broken or what. Luckily, a car came by and a man stopped and lifted the cover.

There was a hospital nearby and the man took me there and the doctors put a little tape on it. They didn't even take an X-ray. They just told me it was likely broken, so they put a couple of Popsicle sticks on my finger to splint it, and that was it. I was shocked. It hurt so bad I thought they would have to cut it off. But I survived. It was a part of being a kid, I guess.

The biggest problem was finding enough kids to play a real game. If there were only two of us, we would be limited to playing catch. If I was by myself, I would throw a baseball up on top of a building and catch it when it came off the roof. I wasn't much for sitting around, so I always seemed to find something to keep me busy.

There were no real recreation departments in town, although on occasion there were some organized neighborhood events. I remember winning a marbles championship once. I was pretty good at shooting marbles. I had coffee cans full of them. But other than that, we kids provided all of the recreation for ourselves.

It is amazing what you can do to entertain yourself when you have nothing specific set up to demand your attention. We didn't have television, and going to the movies was really a big deal. Playing outside was my chief occupation.

The most traumatic thing to happen to me in my life at that time centered around a shoe store in downtown Superior called Kinney's Shoes. When school let out in June, they put a bicycle in the front window. It was a big, fancy bike. I remember it was green, and it had every possible accessory. It was gorgeous. If you bought a pair of shoes at the store, they gave you a number and put it in a barrel. And then before school started in the fall, they would draw a number out of that barrel, and whoever had that number would win the bike. I didn't have a bike, and I can't even begin to say how badly I wanted one. I would walk by that store window a thousand times thinking, *Boy, if I could ever have a bike like that, wouldn't that be something!*

The drawing was scheduled for a Saturday morning. I told my dad that I wanted to be there, I wanted a chance to win the bike. He thought that was okay and said he would take me. This was big. I really wanted that bike. Now, my dad worked for the fire department and his schedule had him working 24 hours on and 24 hours off. So he would get off work at 8:00 in the morning and come home after working 24 hours.

We had to be at the store at 9:00 and I wanted to be sure we got there on time, but there was a problem. Dad always wanted a big breakfast when he got home from work. This was really important to him. He would have bacon, eggs, leftovers, coffee—the whole deal. So on the Saturday of the drawing, Dad got home about quarter after eight. I was sitting there waiting, but he had to eat breakfast. This made me nervous because we had to be there by nine.

I told him, "Dad, we have to be there by 9:00 for the drawing. We can't be late." And I remember him saying, "Well, we'll get there. We'll get there. Don't worry about it. We have plenty of time."

I don't know what happened, but we got there late, about quarter after nine, and the guy from the store came running out and told my dad, "Harry, Harry, where have you been? Where have you been? Your kid had the winning number! I waited as long as I could. Your kid has been walking up and down here all summer long looking at that bike, and now his number is drawn and you're not here! I had to give the bike to someone who was here!"

Well, I just about died right there on the spot. I was absolutely crushed! All this because my dad was late in getting us there. As bad as I felt about losing that bike, I felt almost as bad for my dad. He was devastated. "I mean, what were the chances of winning?" he kept asking.

That was the fall, and by spring I had a new bike. Now, it wasn't that beautiful green bike from the window at Kinney's, or anything like it, but it was a new bike nevertheless. I found out later that Dad had gone and purchased the new bike for me with five dollars down and five dollars a month until he paid for it in full.

If baseball was the most popular sport at the time, then boxing was second. I was a huge boxing fan, and I remember when Joe Louis knocked out Max Schmeling for the heavyweight championship of the world. I used to listen to the fights on our "trusty" radio, which worked about half the time, depending on how you turned it or held it.

I can still remember being at my friend's house, listening to sounds coming over the radio as the legendary fight announcer Don Dunphy voiced the knockdown and the count. "And Schmeling is down," came the call as we listened. My friend and I jumped up in the air and we were hitting one another in our excitement. In the celebration, I got knocked over, hit my head on the corner of a door, and cut it wide open. I bled everywhere; it was quite the mess. Afterward, I went home and told my dad about Joe Louis and what he had done. Louis became my hero, and I gave some serious thought to becoming a professional prizefighter.

It didn't take too long, though, for me to change my vocational dreams. But Joe Louis knocking out Max Schmeling was really something. Had I stayed with my original thoughts on boxing as a career, I suspect the cut from the door corner would have been the least of my worries. I have to laugh at the prospect because not only wasn't I good at fighting, but I had a tendency to get mad when hit, and then I'd throw all caution to the wind—not a good habit as a fighter. But I was a great fan. I used to listen to all the fights I could.

Billy "Kid" Conn was someone I followed. He was a great light-heavyweight fighter who won more than 60 professional fights. He became famous for his fights with Joe Louis. I remember when they went into the service; we waited for almost four years for them to get out and fight.

Conn had almost knocked out Louis in their previous match, so we waited on pins and needles for the big rematch to take place.

Unfortunately, when they finally did fight again, Louis ended it quickly, so it wasn't quite the rematch it was cracked up to be.

I never missed a chance to go to a boxing match when I could. Many of the local Catholic high schools had boxing programs, as did the University of Wisconsin in Superior. Although I didn't participate, the sport fascinated me. I loved the spirit and the passion. Later, I followed boxing at the University of Minnesota and on television on *Friday Night Fights*.

I never went anywhere without a jackknife in my pocket. Really, my only possession was this knife—until later on when I made my slingshots and got my BB gun. I carried that knife to school with me every day, and no one ever said anything about it. We used to play the game mumblety-peg in the schoolyard. It was a great game requiring significant skill, and I got to be pretty good at it.

I wasn't the only one who carried a knife. In fact, most of the kids had one. But I don't recall any danger from them, even though we used to fight a lot as kids. We would have fistfights, get bloody, and be mad at the time. Then, by the next day, it was over. Once I was in a fight in the back of the school at lunchtime when the dean of students came by and saw us. I had a bloody nose and the other kid had a bloody nose, and all the dean said to us was, "Okay, come on now. Go in and get washed up and get to class."

We never had to go to the principal's office. We didn't get referred for a psychological evaluation. My parents didn't have to come to the school. It was simply, "Go get washed up and get to class." It's quite different than it is today. Nowadays, they probably would have had us in for counseling, trying to get to the roots of where our anger was coming from.

I lived on the north end of town for the most part growing up, and my family gradually moved from 3rd Street to 6th Street to 12th Street and finally to 15th Street, which is also known as Highway 2. The highway ran through town and was kind of the dividing line, everything above it being really uptown. By moving up to 15th, you were viewed a little differently. And if you ever got to 21ˢᵗ Street, well, you were the real elite. We never did.

At the time there was a lot of community separation, and we used this in playing baseball against each other. I would call someone in another area and have them get a team together, then we would meet and play them. It's how it all worked. Two teams playing from different neighborhoods in town made it very competitive.

I'd call this guy and he would call some guys and we would play ball. We might not have a full team, but we would play five-on-five or four-on-four or whatever we could do. We just played. There were never any umpires or anyone that officiated the games. We just played.

We found places to play. There were no manicured baseball fields or anything like that. Sometimes finding a good place to play was a problem. We might hit a ball up against a house or through a window, so we had to be careful. In the summer we could use the schoolyards, but during the school year, we had to find other places—church lawns, the courthouse lawn, and so on.

The advantage that we had that kids don't have today is that we had our own rules, and officiated our own games, and we learned how to get along with each other. We couldn't spend our time arguing if we wanted to play. We figured that out rather quickly.

The catcher would call the balls and strikes, and that's just the way it was. If the batter didn't swing at it and the catcher thought it was a strike, then it was a strike. If we argued the strikes and balls, it would cut in on our time to play, so we accepted his judgment.

We made our own schedules, our own rules, and we resolved any problem that arose during the game ourselves. There was no adult there to make the decisions for us; there were no team sponsors. We had to come up with our own baseballs and our own bats. We had no uniforms. We played all the time and we loved every minute of it.

We were 12, maybe 13, and we played for the fun of it. When someone showed up, he went on one team or the other, and we just kept playing continuously. Sometimes we would play all day long.

We each had our own bat and glove. If it broke we put screws in it until we could afford to buy a new one for $2.00. The balls were often taped together with black friction tape to keep them in play. Eventually they wore out, but we always got the most out of everything we used. We didn't have a choice.

We also enjoyed watching games. My dad had a concession stand at the local ballgames. The Northern League had a team in Superior that played against Duluth, Eau Claire, St. Cloud, Fargo, and some other towns in the region. With his job at the fire department and the schedule of 24 hours on and 24 hours off, he had time to do the side job.

Dad ran his stand, and I worked there, too, doing whatever needed to be done. We had hot dogs, candy, and other snacks. I filled pop cases and did all sorts of odd jobs. We rented out cushions for a nickel apiece, and afterward I would pick up the cushions from the stands.

Because of Dad's stand, I was connected to baseball all the time during the season. If I wasn't playing it during the day, I was working for my dad at the games at night or on the weekends. I was around the game all the time, and I loved it.

If someone hit a home run, I would go out and retrieve the ball. I did what a kid did at the ballpark. When I was a little older, if a ball was hit foul over the grandstand, my job was to get it. Sometimes this meant a fight was going to occur because someone had beaten me to the ball and they were going to keep it. But I was motivated. I used to get 50 cents a game for retrieving the foul balls, and I got most of them back.

Sometimes there might be a seven- or eight-game home stand. I wouldn't get paid until it was all over, and then I would get maybe as much as three or four dollars at one crack. That was really good money back then.

Dad would make hot dogs there in a great big kettle. When the games were over and everyone had left, we might still have a dozen or so hot dogs in the kettle. Dad would then take them out, wipe them off, and save them for the game the next day. I ate so many hot dogs as a kid that I got really sick of them. I never, and I mean never, eat hot dogs anymore.

Another food that I never eat is macaroni. My mother was a good cook and she used to make a lot of different kinds of meals, but many of them included some form of macaroni. She also made a lot with white bread. Those are the three things I do not eat: white bread, hot dogs, and macaroni.

Besides playing baseball and working the concession stand, one of the things I used to do was chase rats. Near the railroad tracks and behind our house were storm sewers. The water would run off the streets into the storm sewers and on to Lake Superior. The sewers were about six feet in diameter so you could walk inside them. They had openings to provide for ventilation, and rats would live in these storm sewers. Well, my friends and I used to go into the sewers and go after the rats. One guy would chase them to the end, and some of us would be waiting for them with hockey sticks and—well, you can guess the rest. Some of our group wouldn't go into the sewers with the rest of us. They were too squeamish, probably a little afraid of the rats, I suppose. But we thought it fun at the time.

Later, as we got older, we used .22 rifles to go after the rats in a garbage dump nearby. We would wait for them in the dark and then turn car lights on them and pick them off with our rifles. That was a part of our recreation when we were in high school.

I used to hunt and fish whenever I could. I didn't have a car or any kind of transportation to get out of town, but I used to go as far as I could down the railroad tracks to the outskirts of town. Out there I could fish a little around the lakeshore or go into the woods to hunt.

It wasn't until I got into high school that I had a gun for hunting. At that time I would get on a bus and go to the end of the line. I had a paper route at the time so I would keep my gun in the paper sack. Maybe I would be lucky enough to shoot a rabbit or a grouse or something. I would then put it in my paper sack with my gun, get back on the bus, and go home. It was terrific enjoyment for me. I loved to hunt and especially to be out in the woods. It didn't matter to me if I was alone or with someone else, I just enjoyed being around nature in the outdoors.

I remember one Sunday morning in December, I was 14. I had taken the bus all the way to the end of the bus line to hunt. I ended up shooting four or five rabbits and I put them in my bag and headed home. As I got off the bus, I heard someone yelling, "Extra! Extra! Read all about it." The newspaper had printed an extra edition for people to buy, and I had missed it. I was furious because it was lost money for me.

This particular extra was on December 7, 1941. Pearl Harbor.

I remember that day vividly because from that point on, our life changed. Everything became the war. We got out of the Great Depression and everyone went to work for the war effort.

Even though I was still young at the time, I was smart enough to realize that almost everything centered around the war. Everybody's life changed. One would have to have lived at that time to really understand what was happening in our country and in the world.

The change was dramatic. I was only 14 years old, but I felt it deeply. Our neighbors and some of my friends went into the service. It seemed as if there was nothing else going on at the time. For me, I remember wanting to grow up fast so that I could get into the service and be able to do my part. It was literally all I thought about.

I had friends who were killed in action and others who returned home, many of them wounded. They had been in New Guinea, the Pacific, Africa, and Italy, and they were coming back. We were all united in a common goal: *We have to win this war.* It permeated everything we did. It was not a happy time.

Food was a huge issue during those times as well. There were wartime rations, so we only had so much meat. Because of our limits, hunting became very important. If you were able to get a deer, you had some meat. I remember that it was extremely important to my dad to be a provider for us. I had two younger brothers, so there were three boys in the family to feed and take care of.

Dad would come home from the grocery store and actually puff up his chest with pride. I can still hear him say, "Look what I got here," showing off the groceries. Sometimes we might be fortunate enough to get some extra sugar or some coffee, and that would really be something.

Gasoline was also rationed. We had a stamp that we put on our car that allowed us to buy gas. There was no money. We couldn't just go out and spend money on something. In high school, for example, if someone had a gas stamp, then maybe we could get four or five gallons of gas and be fortunate enough to drive around a little bit, but that was not a common occurrence by any means.

The war brought about tough times. Many families suffered greatly. For us, my mom and dad were always there to care for us kids and were good providers, even during the most difficult of times.

I can remember one year my dad came home one Christmas with a turkey. I can still see him putting this turkey in a pan, standing there with his chest out and saying, "Look what I got. I got a turkey and we are going to have a turkey dinner." I can still see the proud look on his face. It was actually like a celebration for us to have a turkey to eat. We ate it with all of the trimmings that go along with it. We had never been able to afford anything like a turkey before, and now we had one and a big meal to go with it. I looked forward to that meal for days. I finally filled up my stomach, and it sure felt good. This was one day I wasn't hungry.

2

A HAPPY KID

IT WASN'T UNTIL I was in my early teens that we moved uptown. Our house was a three-story brownstone. I didn't find out until much later that Dad didn't buy the house. Instead, he had worked out some sort of a deal through which he would pay rent toward the mortgage each month. I think he paid, in total, $3,500, with $50 per month applied to the overall loan.

Despite the upgrade, the house still wasn't big enough for all of us. As I already mentioned, I had to sleep on a couch for the last three years of high school. Every night I would take my blanket, my sheet, and my pillow out of the closet and into the living room. My bed was right smack-dab in the middle of the room, by the front window facing the street. To this day, I am convinced if I hadn't slept on that couch, I would be three inches taller.

My first job was as a paperboy. I would sell newspapers on Sunday when I was 11, 12, and 13 years old. There was a train from Minneapolis that would stop by Superior on its way to Duluth. About 5:00 in the morning, I would get the papers. I had a red wagon, and I would get as many newspapers as I could into that wagon because I would get a quarter for each paper. I would pull it on 3rd Street and sell the papers out there on the street. I didn't have any customers with subscriptions. Instead, I sold them on the spot to whomever would come along. If there were any left over, I would go door-to-door selling them. "Do you want a Sunday paper? Do you want a Sunday paper?" I'd ask. I'd keep at it until I sold them all.

It worked out for me. I enjoyed being outside, and the work wasn't so bad. The best part, of course, was the money that I earned.

In the winter it was tougher because I couldn't use the wagon. Instead, I had to carry the papers on my back. Winters were brutal in Superior, but it was what made the whole town kind of special. It had its own weather from the lake and its own special sounds. It also had the wind and the fog that came right off Lake Superior.

It seems like we always had some big storm. But the odd thing was, I liked to go outside during the storms. I had a big coat with a full collar and a scarf, and the worse the storm was, the better I liked being outdoors. I was always fascinated by the thought of maybe being lost in a storm. I used to imagine all sorts of things happening. Being out in the cold and wind, I loved to listen to the foghorns. Nowadays we have radar, and those great sounds coming from the lake have for the most part disappeared.

Eeeeeeeeee...nawwwwwwwwwwwwwwwwww...eeeeeeeee...nawwww-wwwwwwwwwwwww! What a great sound that was! It gave you the chills. I loved it. I always felt I could tell where I was by the distance and echo from the great horns. The ships would be coming in and the horns would sound. It was incredible.

We could also hear the locomotives full of coal going up the hill—*chug chug chug chug chug chug.* It would take two or three of those engines to get one of those huge loads up the hill. I remember the sounds of trains on those summer nights so vividly.

Superior back then was a wild town. Wisconsin was wide open for liquor. In contrast, Minnesota had very strict liquor laws. In Minnesota you could only buy 3-2 beer, but in Wisconsin, liquor was there for the taking. As a result, Superior was a very interesting and rowdy place.

When the ships filled with ore and grain came in to Superior, the sailors knew they could go out, get drunk all night long, and visit the whorehouses dotted all along 3rd Street. I don't know exactly how many there were, but I knew of six for certain because I used to stop at every one on Sunday morning with my newspapers.

If you ask anybody from my generation and area he would tell you that 314 John was the biggest whorehouse in all of Superior. Come to think of it, I'm sure you could travel out of the area, all the way to Minneapolis, and they would say the same thing. Everyone knew about 314 John.

When I came to college at the University of Minnesota, there were kids who would go up to Superior for a binge, and many of them would end up at 314 John. It is a two-story building, one of the few in that area. The house is still there. It should be made into some type of historical site.

Despite its reputation, 314 John was one of the places I would go to peddle my papers. The working girls there used to call me "Buddy Boy." I would go to the back door and they would let me in. In the winter they would give me hot chocolate. The girls would be sitting in the kitchen, and I would come in and drink my hot chocolate with them. They would always buy two or three papers from me and always gave me a tip. So of course I would always go to 314 John and get my tip, and hot chocolate in the wintertime, too. I did pretty well at that stop.

Years later, when I was in college at the University of Minnesota, I was on the train from Superior, going back to Minneapolis. I was sitting in the coach section, and a guy came in with two girls and sat down. They sat in front of me, across the aisle.

Now, the fellow who brought the ladies was obviously their "boss," and he left them there and went up to the club car by himself. One of the ladies came over and sat next to me. And she looked at me and said, "Are you Buddy Boy?" I looked at her and said I was. I didn't know what else to say. I kind of remembered her, and I must say she did look a little worn.

And she asked, "Do you remember when you used to peddle papers at 314?" And I said, "Absolutely." I had been about 12, maybe 13, back then, so a few years had gone by. And I said to her, "Are you still in…" "Yes," she said, "I'm still in the business." Because crossing state lines carried a pretty severe penalty for her, she stayed in Wisconsin with her trade. She said she traveled from Superior to Hudson to Milwaukee to Hurley and back.

She also remembered a lot about me and those paper-delivery days. She reminisced about teasing me as a kid and making the hot chocolate in the winter. She told me she had followed my high school and college sports career.

I enjoyed those days at 314 John and being treated so nicely by everyone. I wouldn't call our connection any kind of a reunion, but it brought back memories of people who were very kind to me as I tried to make a buck with my papers. I knew the word "whores" when I was 12 years old, but I recall when I came down to the University to attend college that some guys had never heard the word before. And there I was growing up around them. I mean, of course, from my paper route.

My grandfather owned a tavern. My uncle owned one, too. I have alcoholics throughout my family. My folks were not alcoholics, but they did drink occasionally. Unfortunately, my brothers both became alcoholics later in life. So I had an education about alcohol that many kids never got.

When I was growing up, if someone came to our house to visit, they were always offered a drink. That's just the way it was. I don't mean they would down a whole bottle of whiskey, but a drink was common practice.

I remember going into my grandfather's tavern and being seated on his bar. My dad would be there and always had a shot and a beer—a shot and a chaser, they called it. I would get a shot glass with a little beer in it. So as a little kid I would be sitting on the bar with my dad drinking beer out of a little shot glass. It made me feel like a grown-up.

I remember the patrons coming in and drinking their beers. They would drink away and chew tobacco. There were big brass spittoons on the floor for them to spit in. I also remember the brass foot rail that spanned the length of the bar.

After a patron finished his beer, my grandpa would take that glass, dip it in some water, and put it up on the bar for the next customer. The water didn't help much, because it had been sitting there all day. Now, I can't recall how old I was at the time, but I do remember saying, "Grandpa, give him a new glass!" My life as a kid had its moments, different from most.

One of the experiences I had growing up was with polio. When I was eight or nine years old, my dad noticed that I was limping. Had I been hurt? Was I in pain? I didn't even know I was limping, but he had to find out why. We went to the doctor, and he discovered that one of my legs was shorter than the other, and one of my feet was smaller than the other, too. He told us that I was experiencing the aftereffects of polio. In those days, polio was a murderous disease, a terrible thing to have. He did not know whether or not I was still suffering from it, which was terrifying.

During those days Sister Kenny was a big thing in polio and the treatment for the disease was essentially rest. At least, that was the plan for most who had polio: rest and then massage while at rest.

The doctor my dad took me to was a friend, and I recall him saying to my dad, "Well, it may have to run its course. Rather than follow the plan that Sister Kenny recommends, why don't we just keep him active? Get the kid a baseball glove and let him go out and play. Maybe this won't get any worse, so let's just take a different route and keep him active."

I got some lifts in my shoes for my right leg, and that helped somewhat with the balance. I wore them up to my freshman year in high school.

At the time, I was only eight or nine, still in the development stages of my life. When I was measured, my legs, thighs, and calves were all smaller on my right side. Luckily, because my doctor pre-scribed activity instead of rest, my growth was not hindered by the treatment. They kept measuring me, and eventually my body started to even itself out. The only holdover I have now is that one foot is still bigger than the other—but then again, that is a common trait for many people, so I'll take it.

I was very fortunate because a lot of polio patients do not survive the illness at all. Years later, when I was in the navy at Great Lakes, we were playing a basketball game against Notre Dame in South Bend. While there, we visited a polio ward at the local hospital. We went in to visit the patients who were in iron lungs. This was a Sister Kenny Institute Hospital, full of iron-lung patients. I don't know how many there were, but all we saw was a sea of patients. To see you, while lying on their backs, they would look at you through mirrors.

I felt just terrible for these helpless victims of this horrific dis-ease. I couldn't do anything to help any of them. Sure we could talk to them, but in all reality, what do you say? It was one of the most affecting things I have ever experienced in my life, walking down both sides of the corridor and seeing all of these patients, young and old. It was really difficult to see all of them. I believe it was fate for me that I wasn't in those iron lungs myself. I have always remained grateful for that.

One of the things that I've carried with me since childhood is my nickname, Bud. My real name is Harry, same as my dad. Now, it's hard to have two Harrys in the house. When someone calls out the name Harry, who comes? So my dad would always call me "Kid." I don't ever recall him calling me Harry, even though I am baptized as Harry Peter Grant Jr.

My dad would say, "Hey, Kid, get over here" or "Hey, Kid, do this or that." It was always "Kid" with my dad. My mother, on the other hand, called me "Buddy Boy." Well, over time, Buddy Boy got shortened to Bud, and it has stayed with me. However, in school, it was always Harry Grant. I wasn't Bud full-time until I got to college.

I suppose I could have ended up being called Kid Grant instead of Bud Grant. That was a possibility. Maybe if I had ended up as a boxer, I would have been called Kid Grant. But my mother's nickname for me won out in the end.

I mentioned before what an excellent mother she was to my brothers and me. Her grandfather was from Duluth. He was a decorated Civil War veteran, a Kielley. In fact, he laid out the streets in Duluth at one time. I heard he was some type of engineer, not likely by education but perhaps by necessity.

My mother was raised in Duluth. Her father died when he was 35, leaving behind his wife and five kids. In those days there was no safety net for such an occurrence. What was a family supposed to do when the father died and left behind a large family like that? There was nothing for them, so my mother's mother, my grandmother, turned to prostitution in order to make money and provide for her family.

My mother would often tell stories of being moved from one place to another. Eventually the authorities caught on to her mother's vocation and decided it was not a good environment for the kids to be raised in. So, the children were to be taken away to live in an orphanage.

Obviously, that was very traumatic of course for everyone. Years later, I was fortunate to get to know my grandmother, and she became a very special person in my life. My grandmother was a kind woman, a wonderful cook, and I believe that she did what she had to do; her difficult choice did not define who she was.

My mother had a tough go of it. I don't know all the details, but I do know that once my grandmother realized that her family was going to be torn apart, she made a plea to keep the two boys in the family. The three girls were to be sent to a big orphanage in Owatonna, Minnesota. At the last minute, the family got together and took in the three girls; however, they were divided up and went to three different families.

My mother went to live with her grandparents in Duluth. One might think it was a good arrangement for her, but it wasn't. Her grandmother was a semi-invalid, and my mother became a de facto servant to the family. She had to get up early to do the laundry and other chores. She barely had any clothing, and in the wintertime she didn't have adequate shoes in which to walk to school. It was an arduous existence.

She was around 14 when all of this upheaval began, and she ended up living and working for her grandparents in Duluth for a few years. During that time, my mother and her sisters never saw their own mother, who ultimately lived in Superior. But one day my mother and one of her sisters, along with another relative, decided to go and look for her.

They happened to be walking down 3rd Street on their search. My mother was wearing a coat that she had gotten from my grandmother many years before. My grandmother happened to be on the street and recognized the coat and called out to them. The girls never went back after that.

My grandmother made arrangements for them to live together again. They had a small house in Superior, and for the next three years, Mom and her two sisters all slept in the same bed. But at least they were together again. My grandmother was still working in prostitution, but my mother never wanted to say too much about it. It was a tough time for the girls, who were often scared with strange men coming in and out of the house, but they managed to get through it. And they were able to finish high school.

Later, my grandmother met a tavern owner and they got married. At least I think they got married; I'm not really sure. Joe Gagne, my step-grandfather, drank a lot. I remember being a boy, and my dad would get a call that Joe was home from the bar, drunk and beating up my grandmother. Dad would go over there and make the peace for them and put him to bed. Things just never seemed to get better for my grandmother. She had a tough life.

I really admired her for her resilience. She put up with a lot. She was always very good to me. And she kept up the house for Joe and did what she had to do to make things work. Joe was actually a good-hearted guy. He would give me 50 cents once in a while. But he was like a lot of other people: when he drank, everything changed. To make matters worse, he owned a tavern, so when someone came in and wanted to buy him a drink—well, you can see how that all went for my grandmother and him.

My mother was a rather quiet person, very different from my dad. That's why I say that I am more like her than him. She wasn't the outgoing type but was much more reserved. My dad, on the other hand, was gregarious, great in a crowd. He was a buy-the-first-drink, pat-you-on-the-back, play-cards, play-pool kind of guy. As a matter of fact, he was one of the best pool players in all of Superior. He got to practice a lot working at the fire department, waiting around for the next alarm.

He was also quite an athlete in his day. I can remember going to his baseball games when I was a little kid. He played at the old Hislop Park in Superior. I would be under the grandstand, looking around, and he would be out on the field playing baseball. He also played football with the Duluth Eskimos, which were owned by Ole Haugsrud. My dad couldn't travel with the team since he had a job, so he was only able to play in the home games. Ole, who was very good friends with my dad, later became one of the owners of the Minnesota Vikings.

Dad had a different kind of parenting philosophy, much different from what we see today. He came from a family of four boys. At that time, the conventional wisdom was that you raise boys until they are 16, and then they should be on their own.

Dad was the youngest in his family. When his brothers reached 16 they were put out to find their way in the world. One of his brothers went to Alaska, and he didn't see him again for more than 50 years.

Because my father was the youngest, his job was to stay home and take care of his mother. So he stayed at home beyond 16, while his other siblings had to make their own ways. With his upbringing, he really felt that when you reached the age of 16, you were a man.

With this in mind, I had a lot of freedom. For example, at the age of 15, he let me hitchhike across the country to attend a tryout camp with the St. Louis Cardinals. Quite simply, I told him that I wanted to go to the camp, and he was fine with it. The Cardinals were one of the first of the major league teams to go out and scout younger players; they were well known for this strategy. At that time in professional baseball, there were many more minor league teams than there are today, going all the way down to C leagues and D leagues.

A friend of mine heard about the tryout camp and wanted to know if I wanted to join him to try out. I had just turned 15 and it was in the summer, so I told him I would go with him. Just like that, we set off to hitchhike to the camp, which was being held in Barnesville, Minnesota, just south of Fargo, North Dakota.

Even though I was practically a "man" in my dad's eyes, I can assure you that I knew nothing about anything. I had no idea why the camp was in Barnesville or any inkling at all about what might happen there. I just went along with my friend, who happened to be older. (He was 17.) I thought trying out for the St. Louis Cardinals sounded like a fun thing to do. Who knows? Maybe I would make it.

My mom was apprehensive about the trip, but my dad was fine with it. I figured out the cost for the journey and felt I could live on a dollar a day for food. I saved 10 dollars, and the only money I was given for the trip came from my grandfather, who gave me 50 cents.

We got out of Duluth and headed west. I mean it was not unusual in those days for people to pick up hitchhikers. We certainly didn't impress anybody with the way we dressed, but we still got rides. In one town, I think it was Staples, Minnesota, it started to rain. We were standing under this tree, soaking wet. A lady came out of a house nearby. She brought us in to dry off and fixed us a wonderful fried chicken dinner. I ate enough for two days, and we stayed there until we were warm, dry, and full.

I was so grateful to her for what she did. It was the nicest thing anyone had ever done for me up to that point. Here we were, some wet kids who she had never seen before, and she brought us in and cooked us an amazing meal. It was something, all right. She mentioned to that she had a son in the service and hoped that someday someone would do something nice like that for her son.

We finally got to Barnesville and were standing in line to register for the camp. The kid in front of me was asked how old he was, and he told them he was 16. They turned him away, telling him he couldn't compete because he had to be a minimum of 17 years old. I was next in line, and they asked me how old I was. I stood up straight and tall and proudly told them that I was 17. If I had been in line ahead of that kid, it would have been me who was out and had to head home alone. Fate intervened in letting me try out for the St. Louis Cardinals.

We practiced twice a day for five straight days. We all got evaluated over that time, and we stayed in motel rooms. I think there were at least seven or eight of us in one room. It was pretty crowded, but it was okay. Hey, I was 15—on my own and trying out for a Major League Baseball team, the St. Louis Cardinals. What could have been better?

The other thing I recall is that we were well fed. It was 15 cents for breakfast, lunch was 30 cents, and every night, for 60 cents, I had a hot beef sandwich with vegetables for supper. So for $1.05, I got through the day with my meals. The food was good and plentiful. In my mind, it was worth the trip just for the food. I certainly got my money's worth.

At the end of the five days, we had an intrasquad game. I was the right fielder, and I remember getting a triple in the game. I slashed one down the right-field line and made it to third base. When camp was over, we were all told that we would hear from them later if they were interested.

Once the tryout camp was over, it was time to go home. The kid I had come with was homesick and decided he didn't want to hitchhike back. So, unbeknownst to me, he got some money wired to him from his parents so he could take a bus home. Just like that, I was alone in Barnesville, Minnesota, at 15 years old.

I was growing up quickly. I left in the afternoon to hitchhike back, and soon it got dark. I arrived in this small town about the same time as a train. It was a steam engine, and it had to stop for water. The train had iron ore cars, and I figured it would have to be going east toward Duluth and Superior.

So I climbed up on this hopper near the wheels and was just getting comfortable when a railroad employee called a grease monkey came by, checking the wheels. He told me it was too dangerous where I was sitting and guided me to a boxcar in which he said it would be safe to ride. Night had fallen, and I was all alone in this big, empty boxcar in the darkness.

When the train first pulled out, I sat with my feet hanging out of the boxcar—until I almost got my foot torn off by something the train passed by on the tracks. That scared me enough to get me completely into the car. It was pitch black, and I fell asleep by an open door. I woke up almost falling out of it. Again, scared and alone, I slowly crawled on my hands and knees in total darkness to the back of the boxcar, where I spent the rest of the night.

As morning came, I woke up and had no idea where I was. I looked out and saw a radio tower that looked familiar to me. I was in Superior. I couldn't believe it. I was home with 10 cents left in my pocket—just enough to get to my house on the bus. Here again fate entered my life. After all, I could have ended up in Chicago for all I knew.

I never did hear back from the Cardinals. They probably took a close look at my skinny build and thought I wasn't much of a prospect to play professional baseball. Little did they know, I was still a growing boy. As I think back now, how many 15-year-old kids get to experience anything like that? It was a different time. My dad had not been opposed to me going out on my own. It wasn't that he didn't care, because he did. He just felt that I was responsible and could take care of myself. He trusted me. I grew up quickly and was a responsible kid.

My dad was a big part of my life, especially when I was a kid. To this day, I still have his old football helmet. I keep it in my office at the Vikings complex at Winter Park. He meant a lot to me, and keeping that memento serves as a constant reminder of him.

I feel very fortunate to have had parents who were both exceptional role models. I looked up to my mom and my dad. They were both good, caring people.

I used to watch my dad; what he did in his life always was interesting to me. I learned a great deal by just keeping an eye on him. He started at the fire department as a line-level worker and ended up being the assistant chief. He rose up through the chain of command and earned his ranking.

Dad was always around the guys. Whether it was at the fire station, the bowling alley, or the pool hall, he seemed to be right there in the middle of everything, the center of attention. I know I got my competitiveness from him. He was as good a pool player as there was in town, and he liked to bet. I mean he was a real betting person. And he liked to play cards. He was a good card player, too, so he liked to gamble. He sometimes bet on baseball games, too.

One of the things he would always do was tell those with him, whoever they might be, not to swear around me. "Hey, don't swear in front of the kid", I can remember him often saying. Of course, I could hear him swear when he thought I wasn't listening, but he always made sure to tell the other guys not to curse.

Dad, ever enterprising, also had a bingo stand that he took with him to the county fair. Both my parents would work it, and I would sleep under the stand with the prizes. My mother was always good with numbers, so she would keep track of everything with the stand, the house, and anything related to bookkeeping. Whether it was the bingo stand at the fair and the hot dog stand at the ballpark, it was always my mother who counted the money and paid the bills. Dad had the ideas and my mom handled the books.

I always felt sorry for my mom. She never had anything. She never had nice clothes or pretty things. It was all right for me to walk around without much, but I always felt as if my mother should have had more. She was a good person, a good wife, and a good mother to us kids. She deserved more than she had.

The brownstone house where we lived was tight. We never had an upstairs bathroom—it was in the basement. Mom would have to wash in the sink and then take a bath in an upstairs tub. She never had a place to dress or a nice place to do what women do with their face and hair. She never had her own private place. I always wished she would have had a nice bedroom and a place to dress, something just for her.

Dad smoked, and I absolutely hated it. He used to smoke in the car, and I recall my mother saying, "Harry, put out that cigarette. Bud is carsick." He would open the window and say, "See, the smoke is going out the window. It will be all right." Smoking ultimately killed him at 65.

He smoked hard and never ate well. Sure, he liked those big breakfasts, but they certainly weren't healthy. He would take the bacon grease and wipe it up with his toast and say to me, "Here, have some of this. It's good for you. Take some. It will keep you warm." I'd always refuse it and stayed with my Wheaties.

Growing up in Superior, the lake was a constant presence. I enjoyed Lake Superior. I was raised along the lake and used to walk the beaches. We used to make fires from the driftwood along the shores. When I was really young, around 10, we used to catch smelt with nets. I would bring the smelt home and cook them, or sometimes we would cook them right there on the beach.

The huge Ariel Bridge, which is still operating in Duluth, was another of our favorite places to hang out. We used to sit on the bridge and watch the ships come in. I was pretty good at identifying many of the ships by their superstructure when they were way out on the lake. My friends and I used to play a game to see who could identify each ship first.

In some ways, Lake Superior is a lot like the mountains. It is so big and I really had no access to it. I would get out on it once in a while, but not very often. Instead, I was confined to the beaches along the shoreline. The entire harbor area was a natural harbor, and all sand.

During the war, all the manpower was gone overseas, so I was able to work on the ships when I was in high school. I was big for my age and strong, so I was able to handle a heavy workload. I worked with a grain trimmer and also unloaded the ships when they came in. It was tough, hard work. We would be in the middle of it, with grain up to our knees and wearing respirators because of all the dust we kicked up.

I sometimes even got out of school to work on the ships. They would come to the school and say they needed four or five strong guys to work to get the ship out that night. We might spend 12 hours on a job. I made a little money that way, and that was important.

I always seemed to find ways to keep busy. I would enjoy listening to football games on the radio when I had the chance. Of course, Green Bay had a football team, and they had some terrific players like Don Hutson and Tony Canadeo at that time. Cecil Isbell was another great player for the Packers. In Superior, we used to get the news updates about what was going on with Green Bay.

We also became familiar with the New York Giants because they came to Superior for their training camp before the war. I was just a little guy then, but I spent every single day over at their camp shagging balls and hanging around. I remember they had a player named DeWitt E. "Tex" Coulter, who was a tackle. He was a big man, but I thought he was a mountain. He was about 6'5" and weighed probably about 250 pounds. It's funny to think that that's small by today's standards.

Every day, when he came off the practice field, he would let me carry his helmet. I was maybe nine or 10, and he let me carry that smelly, dirty helmet—I'll never forget it! When I gave it back to him, he always said thank you. That was a huge deal for me. I still remember it like it just happened.

Even though I was out there every day at practice from the beginning to the end, I never for a second thought I would be involved in pro football someday—but my dad did. The Giants' practice field was right next to the baseball field where my dad had his concession stand. The players and the coaches didn't have much to do at night after practices, so they would come over and watch the baseball games. I swear they only came by because my dad would give them free hot dogs.

My dad talked a lot, and he would tell the coach of the Giants, Steve Owen, "Hey, see the Kid there? He is going to play for you guys someday." I was just a little tyke but he would feel my muscle. Maybe my dad was just bragging, or maybe he was prescient. Either way, it made an impact on me; I even mentioned it in my Hall of Fame speech.

The war came, and the Giants didn't come back to Superior for training camp again until many years later. By then I was in college and playing for the Minnesota Gophers. The Giants camp opened before the Gophers started training camp, so I was home for a while when the Giants returned to Superior. My dad, true to form, reminded Coach Owen about me. "Hey, Steve, the kid there is going to play for you someday." Owen looked me over. "Well, he's getting a little bigger, but he's got to put on a little more weight. He's still pretty skinny." Dad replied, "Well, we'll build him up, because he's going to play for you, Steve."

When I got out of school, my dad was positively convinced the New York Giants were going to draft me. It didn't happen. Instead, it was the Philadelphia Eagles who drafted me in the first round. I can't remember who the Giants took.

OUR SCHOOL SYSTEM IN Superior had a junior high school and high school system. It was in middle school that I first got involved in sports. But then I got what I always thought was a big break when they changed the grades around some and put the ninth graders into the high school.

The very best thing about the high school was that they had showers. We never had a shower in our house growing up. Suddenly I could take a shower whenever I wanted. I grew up taking baths and I *hated* it. I took them as infrequently as I could—maybe once a week. I hated it. But in high school, I could take a shower every single day. I loved it and would stay in the shower endlessly.

I went out for football in the fall at age 14 and made the team. I went out for basketball in the winter and also made the team. In the last game of the football season, the coach didn't play me very much. This was unusual to me since I had played on a regular basis the entire season. I wasn't a starter, but I still played a lot. I couldn't understand it. I thought maybe I had played badly and the coach had taken me out for that reason.

My dad noticed it, too. He knew the coach, so he asked him about it after the game. Coach said, "Well, I'm saving him for the basketball season." He didn't want me to get hurt.

I was kind of a skinny 14-year-old at the time and didn't know much. To me this made absolutely no sense at all. And my dad was confused by it, too. Maybe Coach didn't think I was good enough. We never did figure it out. To this day, I don't know the reason. But it obviously had a significant impact on me, because I still think about it from time to time.

Dad loved sports. He couldn't wait for me to get to high school so he could cheer me on. As I mentioned, he was assistant chief, and he used to attend the games with his uniform on. He'd go to sporting events and say, "I'm the fire marshal" so he was guaranteed to get in free anywhere.

We opened the basketball season, and Dad was going to miss the first game. But he called the school office at halftime to ask the score. Whoever answered the phone told him, "Oh, we just went ahead by two points. Your kid just scored two buckets." I got two baskets right at the end of the half that put us ahead in the game. My dad jumped in the car and came right over. He never missed another game after that.

By the second game, I was a starter as a freshman and from then on started every game throughout high school. Unfortunately, that first year, we really didn't have a good team. I think we won only five games during the regular season.

I thrived on the competition and was always ready to participate. In all my years of playing sports, I never missed a game for any reason. In fact, I never missed a day of school or work in my entire life. I guess I just felt it was my responsibility to be accountable. I always showed up, no matter what.

When the basketball playoffs started my freshman year, we were invited, like everyone else. We beat Drummond, much to everyone's surprise; they had an outstanding team. For us, this was a pretty good victory. Our next opponent was Hurley, a ranked team in the state. We beat them, too. Next, we had to play Superior East. I can't remember exactly, but they were either undefeated or had only lost one game all year. We beat them right at the end of the game, and suddenly we were in the state tournament and going to Madison. It was a big deal.

By that point I was an important part of the team and playing every minute of every game. All three of our playoff games had been close to the end and could have gone either way, but it was *us* going to Madison. At the time, I didn't even know what the state tournament was.

When we got to Madison, I couldn't believe it. They had a cafeteria and you could eat as much as you wanted. All you had to do was come in and sign your name. I must have eaten six meals a day.

I was in that cafeteria, constantly eating. I still remember that the food was terrific.

The state tournament began, and we won our first two games. No one could believe it. If we won the third, we were in the finals to play for the state title. They called us the "Cinderella team" of the tournament. Our Cinderella story came to an end when we lost the next game—a heartbreaker—in overtime. We didn't play for the state championship, but we did play for the consolation.

I was a ninth grader playing in the state tournament and never came out of a single game. I played every minute of every game, and they were all close. I was tall, about 6'3", playing a forward position and holding my own. It was quite an experience for me, at the beginning of my sports career.

Later on, when we got home from the tournament, I got sick. Nobody ever said what it was, but I had a fever of 105 degrees. Within a month, my hair began to start turning gray. I always wondered if it was caused by all the eating I did at Madison. I mean, I had never in my life seen food like they had there! With all that food and the showers I could take—well, it was a great time. If my hair changed color as a result, I suppose it was worth it.

I also played baseball in high school. *Esquire* magazine named East and West All-Star Teams composed of players younger than 17. The game was played at Comiskey Park in Chicago. I'm not really sure how the teams were selected, but I made the cut as a 16-year-old and got to go to Chicago. I was a pretty good hitter and played in the outfield, but I also pitched (likely because of all that rock throwing I used to do).

Being selected was a big deal, and my folks came with me to Chicago. I honestly don't think my mother had ever been anywhere outside of the Duluth/Superior area before. I had never been away from home other than that Madison trip for the state basketball tournament and the St. Louis tryout. We took the train there, and I remember sleeping in a berth for the first time ever. We stayed in a hotel, a new experience for me. And in this hotel, they had a shower in the bathtub. I took one of my routine long showers but didn't put the curtain in the tub. Pretty soon, there was a loud knock on the door of the hotel room. Apparently, I had caused some flooding below our room. I didn't have a clue that I should have put the curtain in the tub. I guess that showed what kind of a hayseed I was.

We were in Chicago for three days practicing before the game. In batting practice, I recall hitting one over the fence in Comiskey Park. What a tremendous thrill that was! I also was out practicing my pitching for three days. After throwing more than 100 pitches a day, I was made the starting pitcher.

I was disappointed because I knew as a pitcher I would only play a few innings before they took me out to let someone else come in to pitch. I wanted to play in the outfield so I could play the whole game. I pitched and did okay, but nothing special. My arm was pretty tired by that point.

But for a kid from Superior, it was really special to go and play in the famous Comiskey Park. I remember being in awe of everything. I walked all over—around the outside of the park, in the stands, in the locker rooms, on the field, everywhere. It was unbelievable.

3 THE ARMISTICE DAY BLIZZARD

IT WAS ONE OF the worst storms in our country's history. Nationwide, more than 150 people lost their lives in a horrible blizzard that swept across a 1,000-mile stretch of the Midwest. The deadly storm seemed to come upon us without any warning—and I was caught right in the middle of it.

It was November 11, 1940, and I was only 13 at the time. I loved to hunt, but it was difficult for me because I didn't have any transportation and barely any equipment.

My uncle, my dad's brother, was a barber and owned a little two-chair shop in town. The other barber in the shop was a guy by the name of Phil Cross. Phil was a hunter—not an ardent hunter, but he got out every once in a while. I would go in the shop, and we would from time to time talk about hunting. One day Phil invited me and my best friend at the time, Bill Blank, to go duck hunting with him. It was a great opportunity, so of course I said yes.

Phil had a rather small car, but hey, it was transportation. The day we picked to go was Armistice Day weekend, November 1940. We had no idea at the time that we would forever remember this day and the days following.

We were absolutely thrilled to have been invited. The plan was to stay overnight. We would be traveling about 40 miles from home and staying in a cabin right on the lakeshore of Yellow Lake, near Webster, Wisconsin.

Phil made all the arrangements. We got up early and drove there in the dark. As we approached his place, I recall we had to go down-hill to the cabin. Right behind the cabin were some railroad tracks. We didn't know it at the time, but those tracks may well have saved our lives.

We were all set. I was really anxious to get hunting. We got into a rowboat and went across a bay to a point where there were a ton of weeds, kind of a bog—the perfect place to attract ducks. We set out all the decoys in the lake, hid the boats in the weeds, and stood there waiting for the ducks.

This was all new to me. I had been hunting for ducks before but only in my own way, never like this. I did some hunting on the backwaters of Lake Superior, but I never had decoys, so everything about this whole experience was different for me.

It was a beautiful day. There was hardly any wind. We saw some ducks out on the lake, but they weren't doing much flying. Besides, it was a big lake, and they were pretty far away from us. We got a couple shots off, but that was about it. It didn't matter much to me, because I was just enthralled to be there. We waited patiently for some of those ducks to come toward us.

My friend and I had slept some during the early morning drive, but Phil was tired, so he eventually went back to the cabin. He was going to take a nap, and we planned to meet up in a few hours. I had no interest in going back to take a nap so we stayed on with the ducks. I mean, it was everything I thought it would be and more! Bill and I were having the time of our lives.

We rowed the boat back to where we started and dropped Phil off on the shore. The plan was to meet Phil in the same spot around 2:00 PM. It was only about 10:00 AM, so we had four hours and the lake all to ourselves.

Once we returned to our original hunting spot, we noticed a slight change in the weather. The ducks started flying all over the place, evading a front that was coming in. At about the same time, a northwest wind started blowing.

Just as suddenly, the waves on the lake began to increase. Our decoys were really bouncing around. With all the ducks flying around, we began shooting and actually got a few. I didn't have much of a gun. It was only a single-shot. We would shoot a duck and then have to row out on the lake to get it, and then row back and start over again.

I was having the time of my life, but the weather was really starting to turn on us. The wind was in our faces and becoming more and more severe. Then again, the more the wind blew, the more the ducks flew.

The ducks were swarming like bees, and we were having a terrific time shooting at them. As the wind picked up even more, the temperature dropped and it started to snow. It had actually dropped to about 30 degrees. It wasn't that cold, but we weren't dressed for it; we had left the house that morning dressed for mild temperatures.

With the wind, the snow, and huge waves coming in on us, we soon realized it was time to head back. First we needed to get the decoys before getting back to the cabin and meeting Phil. With a tremendous wind in our face, we could not manage the boat on the lake well enough to pick up our decoys, so we pulled the boat back to shore.

It was then that we realized we were in trouble. The weather had turned downright ugly. We couldn't deal with the wind and snow, never mind the plummeting temperature. It had become a very dangerous situation, and we didn't know what to do.

We knew we could not get back across the lake to where we had come from, because of the conditions. Fearing we could be stuck there, we had to figure out a plan. The wind was really gusting, and with all of the snow we could hardly see anything. We tried to find our way out by walking through this muskeg, but Bill fell into the water and was soaked to his waist. Soon after, his pants froze—then he was miserable. Meanwhile, the temperature continued to drop and the conditions worsened, although it didn't seem possible to us that it could get any worse.

We had gotten a little farther through the bog when Bill said, "I'm going to stay here. My pants are frozen and I can't walk anymore." I told him he couldn't stay there and that we had to keep going.

The conditions were terrible. I figured we had only about 150 yards or so to go to get back to an area where we could navigate somewhat, but it was one step at a time, and we were up to our knees in water.

I kept telling Bill, "We have to keep moving. We have to keep moving!" We went a little farther, and he said again, "I can't go on anymore. I'm going to stay here." I told him, "Look, I'll carry your gun, but we have to keep moving." Bill continued to protest. I wasn't sure what we were going to do next.

Just then, a train came by on the railroad tracks nearby. It blew its whistle and we heard it. We couldn't see the train because the visibility was so poor, but we could hear it. That's how bad it was out there. Fortunately, we knew which way the wind was blowing, so it helped with our direction to some extent.

I said to Bill, "Those train tracks have to be right in front of us." We figured they were about 30 to 40 yards ahead of us. I helped Bill, and we finally were able to make it to the tracks. There was an embankment and Bill was able to get over on the other side, where he was protected from the weather to some extent. We were both soaked and freezing. Had we not heard that train whistle, I'm not sure what might have happened.

Bill waited behind the embankment while I went to get Phil, who was still at our cabin. He was so happy to see me. He had been worried sick about us and didn't know what he should do. Two o'clock had come and gone, and we never showed up. I told him that Bill was waiting by the tracks, so Phil left to get Bill while I made a fire to warm up.

Our shelter was a little framed cabin with a kerosene lamp. I went to start the fire in the stove, but my hands were so cold that I couldn't light the match. So I took the lamp, opened up the stove, and threw it into the burner. By then my hands had warmed up enough that I could light the match. I threw it in and almost blew the roof off the cabin. The exploding fire came right up into my face, and I'm convinced burned my eyelashes right off. I was lucky I didn't burn the cabin down with me in it.

By the time Phil returned with Bill I had a good fire going. But still we had no extra clothes, and Bill and I were soaking wet. Phil had an old pair of waders and we eventually found an extra pair of pants for Bill, so at least we had some dry clothes on.

With the fire, some orange pop, and a half-pint of vodka that Phil had brought with him, we were warming up. We were a little underage for alcohol at 13 but the mixture tasted pretty good to us. I recall Phil told us that drinking it would keep us warm. We didn't argue with him. In an hour we were dry and warm.

We knew we had to get out of there, and that wasn't going to be easy. The snow was waist deep by then. We had to push the car up a hill to get to the main highway, and after a great effort, we finally made it to the top. We were relieved because we thought we were home free. We were wrong.

The snow was deep, and it was very difficult to see out of the windshield. The ice was building up on the windows and the wipers were not doing much at all. It was very slow going. We came around a corner, and in front of us were three cars blocking the road. They were all stuck in a giant snowdrift. We couldn't go any further. I remember wondering, *What are we going to do?*

By then, it was maybe 7:00 or 8:00 in the evening and impossible to move in any direction. We were stranded. We had no choice but to stay there all night in our cars. So there we stayed, dead center in the middle of the road, the blizzard raging all around us.

All of us got together and decided we should get in two cars to save gas and keep warm. Our plan was to run the motors for a period and then shut them off and so forth to preserve our gas. So we went to the first two cars and piled in. There were eight of us, and we fit okay, but it wasn't long before we ran out of gas and had to move to the other two cars. One of the cars was really small, and we were literally sitting on top of each other through the night.

By morning it had stopped snowing, but the wind was still blowing, the temperature had dropped, and the snow was incredibly deep. We were still in the cars, debating what to do next.

No one was dressed for the conditions. I had chest waders on, so it was decided that I would be the one to go and look for help. But which way to go? We were about 40 miles from home and in the middle of nowhere. I had no idea which way to go.

I got out of the car and walked north, into the wind. After about three miles I came to a crossroads where there was a little store. It was one of the old one-pump stations with a convenience store attached. There was a woman who lived there with her small child; her husband was off working somewhere. The woman was extremely kind and very hospitable to me. We had no outside communication. There was no radio, no television, no telephone—nothing. Everything was down due to the storm. No one knew what was going on anywhere.

I was thinking about all the people I had left back in the cars, but there was nothing I could do about it. There was no communication, no one to call on for help. The conditions were far too severe for me to go back and try to get them.

I stayed with the woman in her house all that day and night, and all the next day and night, too. I stayed right in the house. There was nothing to do, nowhere to go, no one to contact. I remember feeling so helpless. I was really worried about Bill, Phil, and the others, and I'm sure they were worried about me.

On the third day of the storm, the weather had cleared but it was so cold you could barely move if you went outdoors. Like everyone else, we were waiting for the plows to come through. Finally, the plow came, and behind the plow were my friends in the car. They were okay! It was nothing short of a miracle, considering what happened to them.

When we had gotten stuck on the road, we had driven around a corner and saw the three cars stuck in the snow. As it turned out, right nearby was a house, but due to the weather conditions, none of us could see it was there. A man lived there with his family. He had just shot a deer the day before and had the deer hung up in his shed behind the house. The house was out of view of the highway, but the shed wasn't. When he went to the shed to cut up some deer meat, he saw the stranded cars. He went down there and brought all of the people up to his house, where they stayed with him and his family for two days. It was a little two-bedroom framed home, so it was plenty cozy; they ate the whole deer. I hate to think what might have happened to my friends and the others if that man hadn't gone out to his shed.

So there Phil and Bill were, behind the plow, and we were reunited. Boy, were we all happy to see each other! Just a short time later, coming down the road from the north behind another plow was a fire engine. And in the fire engine was my dad. We met right there at that little store and rejoiced. I don't think I ever saw my dad so happy.

The reports from the storm were horrific. The conditions had trapped many people on the highway, and there many reported deaths. People had absolutely no warning, no way to prepare for the storm. The day had started out nice and then turned awful very suddenly.

Hunters were stranded in duck blinds, caught up without proper clothing. There were a lot of hunters sitting in their duck boats frozen to death. It could have easily been us.

The toughest time for us was at night, that first night, sitting in the car. The wind was howling and it was rough. We didn't freeze because we had the cars running, but we knew at some point we were going to run out of gas. We all huddled together, trying to stay warm. Other than Phil and Bill, I never saw any of them again.

I remember my dad went back to the place where I had stayed during the storm and gave the woman something—I'm not sure what. I don't know if it was money, but he gave her something for her efforts. She really saved me.

I have gone back to that area several times over the years, but I have never been able to find that exact location where I spent the night. It was a one-pump gas station, but it's long gone now.

It was an incredible event in our country's history. Back then, we had no real weather forecasts. Our only source of predicting the weather was to look to the northwest. Some time later on, a book was written about the storm and the harrowing times people faced that went with the blizzard of November 1940. I guess there were some unbelievable stories of survival and numerous deaths across the path of the storm. We were one of those stories, too. No doubt about that.

The next week we went back to get the decoys and the boat. Of course, it was all plowed out by then. We had to break ice around the lake to get the boat and decoys out, but we were able to retrieve everything. I didn't see Phil much after that. We never went out hunting with him again. I guess he felt responsible. He told my uncle and my dad how terrible he felt about what had happened, even though it wasn't his fault. I certainly don't blame him.

We survived, but the memories of those days and nights in the middle of the infamous Armistice Day blizzard will last a lifetime.

4

INVASION OF ALCATRAZ

I DIDN'T HAVE ANY girlfriends. I was 15, in high school, and a shy kid. Added to which, I didn't have any money. I didn't have any clothes either—nothing fancy, anyway. For a teenage boy with no car, no money, and no clothes, it is rather tough to court anyone. The school had mixers, but I never learned how to dance, so I never went to any of them.

There were two gathering places in town: the drugstore and the pool hall. The guys went to the pool hall and the girls went to the drugstore. Well, sometimes the guys would go to the drugstore to see the girls, but never the other way around. Occasionally someone would invite everyone over to their house for a party, which consisted of mostly eating and hanging around. Now those interested me. If I knew there was going to be a lot of food there and I could get some good stuff to eat, I was in. But for the most part, in Superior, there wasn't any real dating because there was no real place to go.

The closest I came to dating was maybe walking a girl home from the drugstore. Just seeing her to the front steps, and that was it. There was no place to go and no car to go park somewhere. Everything we did was done mostly in groups. I didn't dance. I didn't sing. I didn't play an instrument. I wasn't big in music, and I guess I just had other things to do besides dating.

On Friday nights, I was always tied up playing some sport. In the fall I was occupied with football, in the winter it was basketball, and in the spring it was baseball. During the week I was busy with school, so it was usually Saturday before I could really go out and do anything. For the most part, I kept pretty busy, so I really didn't have any time to think much about girls.

The other reason was that I thought they were a little silly. Girls talked about goofy things. It was always all about who liked who. *"She said she likes you. Do you like her?"* I didn't have time for that kind of stuff. For me, I would rather be out in the country. Sometimes I would take the bus to the end of the line, or often I would ride my bike out of town.

About half the time I went with friends or my cousin, but I was just as happy being alone. We never did anything dramatic. The whole point was just to be out in the woods and away from everything. We might be along a stream trapping minnows or we would be chasing rough grouse or rabbits with our .22 rifles. Even in the winter, we would go out and just walk around in the woods. It was much more interesting to me than anything I could think of doing in town.

In high school, it was mostly sports, no girls, and a lot of work concentrated on the war effort. There were scrap drives and the like. Every day, we woke up with the war on our minds. There were war bonds and there were stamps. You could save your money to buy stamps.

For a quarter you could buy a stamp and put it in a book. It would cost you $18.75 to fill the book, and after the war the book was worth $25. I had one, and it was a big deal.

After I graduated high school, I wanted to go into the service. If you got drafted, you didn't pick where you were going to go. But to avoid the draft you could enlist. At the time, the military would let you leave high school if you had your parents' permission to go into the service. I knew many who left before graduation, when they turned 17. My cousin enlisted in the navy. He went on to make a career out of it and served all over the world. My parents wanted me to graduate first; the war would have to wait.

This may be a terrible thing to say, but I'm going to say it anyway. We all wanted the war to be over, but I didn't want it to end until I had a chance to do my part and serve. I felt an overwhelming obligation to join. I felt as if I *had* to be there.

I never had much interest in doing schoolwork. My main interest in high school was sports, and they were very popular. Our gym was jam-packed for every basketball game. Sports filled a lot of my time, but the military thing was always on my mind.

I looked forward to the games and the practices. It was a big part of my life in high school. It occupied a lot of my time, and I was extremely competitive. I also enjoyed the fact that we had good teams and drew good crowds to our games. Because of the success I had in sports, I was recruited by several colleges and universities. Back then, the recruitment process was much different than it is today.

In my day, most of the recruiting went through the coach. The scouts would tell the coach they would be at the game, and the coach would direct the scouts' attention toward his players. Minnesota was one that ended up recruiting me, but Wisconsin was the primary school to take an interest in me, since most of our games were played in Wisconsin.

I do remember playing Anoka my senior year in high school. Anoka was ranked No. 1 in Minnesota and we were No. 1 in Wisconsin, so it was decided that we should play each other. We played the game in Anoka, after the end of the regular season. I guess it was some kind of a Halloween Festival game or some sort of exhibition. Well, we went over there and they beat us.

One of the players on Anoka was Billy Bye, an exceptional player. Billy and I later became great friends when we were together at Great Lakes.

I was recruited mostly by Wisconsin for all three sports—football, basketball, and baseball—but wasn't seriously entertaining it. I was focused on going into the service after school. Then again, it didn't mean I wasn't interested in college sports, because I was. I followed college football, the great Army-Navy games, Notre Dame, and all the big schools' games. I actually thought at one point that I would like to go to Notre Dame. But it was Wisconsin that had really followed my high school career, keeping in contact with me over the years, mostly by sending me notes and talking to my coaches and parents.

They would send me a note saying something like, "We see you got 29 points in the basketball game the other night. Good luck in your future games." They wanted me to know they were watching me, keeping tabs. They would routinely call my dad, just to reiterate their interest. This was all okay with me, but I knew college would be on hold and take care of itself down the road.

During my recruitment process, some of the Minnesota guys came to Superior and took my mom, dad, and me to dinner. Later on, I went down to Minneapolis and saw the Gophers' coach, Bernie Bierman, at the university, but again, going to college was not a high priority for me. For one thing, I was not a great student.

My trip to the Twin Cities to see Coach Bierman was an interesting experience for me. When I arrived a couple of businessmen picked me up at the train depot and showed me around. We had some lunch and then went over to the athletic department at Cooke Hall to see the coach.

I wasn't impressed with his personality at first. (As it turned out, I really got to know him much better after I was done playing for him.) His coach-player relationship did not get high marks from me. I remember walking into Coach Bierman's office and seeing him sitting there behind his desk. He asked the usual questions, and we talked a little bit and then I left; it wasn't a long meeting at all. The businessmen who had been showing me around town stayed with me, and we went to dinner. After dinner, there was nothing else to do. The businessmen had to be on to other things, and there was no one else I knew there. I would be alone.

Just before we parted ways, we went to a hotel for a press conference. Charlie Johnson from the *Minneapolis Star* was there. After everything ended, Charlie said, by way of introduction, "Well, what are we going to do now?" I didn't know what to say. He continued, "Do you want to go to the Sportsmen's Show?" I had no clue as to what he was talking about. Turns out he had heard that I liked to hunt and fish.

The show was at the Minneapolis Auditorium. I absolutely loved it. It was unbelievable! I was much more impressed by the spectacle of the convention than I was with all of the recruiting attention I had just gotten over at the university. There was Sharkey the Seal and a pool in this building! And Sharkey was jumping in and out of the water. I was fascinated.

We walked around all the exhibits, and I was totally mesmerized by the whole experience. I was in heaven. Charlie was a well-known guy in town. He had a sports column and a good reputation. He turned out to be as good a host, however unwitting, as anyone at U of M. My thinking then was, *If I come to Minnesota, it won't be because of the recruiting efforts that were laid out for me.* It would be because of the Sportsmen's Show. That was what sold me.

As persuasive as the Sportsmen's Show may have been, it wasn't enough to sway me from joining the service. Initially, I had wanted to join the marines, but I changed my mind after some of my friends came back with terrible stories of traveling in boats to New Guinea. They told me about being sick for weeks on end. Well, I would get seasick on Lake Superior, so the appeal of joining the marines wore off. Instead, I entered the navy. I went in right after I graduated. In fact, I didn't even go to our high school graduation.

For me the navy was a better fit. I turned 18 in May, graduated from high school, and by June, I was at Great Lakes in Illinois. I got on a train, and there I was. Now that's a transition.

If I had my druthers, I would say that every young man who turns 18 years of age should go for a stint in the military. I would highly recommend it. You grow up so fast—almost immediately. Today it might be different because of the whole manner of communications. We see the world differently. We see it on a screen and are familiar with what is going on around the world. Back then, you were seemingly separated from everything. Your hometown was your everything. For me, arriving at Great Lakes at 18, my world changed overnight.

When the University of Wisconsin heard that I enlisted, they contacted the Great Lakes Naval Training Center. I would have been going through Great Lakes anyway, but with the help of the Wisconsin athletic department, Paul Brown, the football coach at Great Lakes, heard I was coming.

Brown was a lieutenant commander in the military, but his primary responsibility when I got there was coaching football. The word came to me that I should go out for the football team. Billy Bye from Anoka was also there and was told to do the same. I didn't know Paul Brown, but playing more football appealed to me.

I arrived in June, and the football season started in July. There were no regulations back then. It was football, football, football. Although we were pretty involved in the team, we still had to go through basic training. Let me tell you, it was a wake-up call to be in basic training. You would have about 180 guys in a barracks on one floor and another floor with the same, so 360 guys in one building. There was one big washroom, and everyone was stumbling over one another. There were guys who had never been away from home before, and it was quite the experience. It was like being in one big cuckoo's nest. There was screaming and hollering at night, and some were moved out because they couldn't handle it. It was really hard on a lot of guys.

For me, it was all right. I had been around a lot of guys in locker rooms. But for others, this was tough and they had a hard time with it. My break came from having the opportunity to get out of the madhouse and go to football practice. It wasn't very long before I was able to leave "the zoo" and be assigned to football on a permanent basis. I had completed enough basic training that eventually I was moved to just the football side of things.

Paul Brown had been at Ohio State and would be leaving the next year to coach in the All-America Football Conference in Cleveland. He had some status, and they eventually named the team after him: the Cleveland Browns!

Billy and I were two of the youngest players on the team at the time. We were thrown together by chance and forged a lifelong friendship. Also on our Great Lakes team, we had a huge fullback by the name of Marion Motley. It seemed like every time we had a drill, it was me who had to tackle him. Every single time we lined up for tackling practice, there I was tackling Marion Motley. Later on, he led the National Football League in rushing and went on to become a Hall of Famer. Being matched up against him was not one of my favorite things to do, but it's certainly a badge of honor.

A few years later, when I was playing for the Philadelphia Eagles, there he was again, playing for the Cleveland Browns. He was a great player, but believe me, I had already had my share of him. It was never any picnic.

At Great Lakes, we played a lot of different college teams. We played as an independent squad against some top schools, including Wisconsin, Michigan State, Western Michigan, and Notre Dame. At the time, Army was ranked No. 1 in the country and Notre Dame was No. 3. Army had the great "Mr. Inside and Mr. Outside," Glenn Davis and Doc Blanchard, so they were really a strong team.

By the end of the season, I was starting for Great Lakes and we beat the Irish. I mean, we beat them handily! That felt pretty good. We had a young team, and Paul Brown really knew how to get us ready to play. That was a real highlight of my time there. At the end of the season, Brown had a few of us at a football banquet. There were probably 50 to 60 officers and others there. He showed the film of the Notre Dame game and then introduced all of us. I remember he said some very kind things about me as a player. He said for people to keep their eye on where I went to school because they would be reading about me on the sports pages. I was quite humbled by his remarks.

I have been fortunate to have people in my life who have been of significant influence. Paul Brown was one of them, without a doubt. Another was my high school football coach, Harry Conley. I really listened when he spoke. And although he may have said some things that I didn't fully understand at the time, they did make sense later on.

Harry had been a boxer in addition to playing football. I recall there was this big, tall kid in high school. I guess he was about 6'4", which was very tall in those days. Anyway, one day the kid said something smart back to Harry, sassed him, and Harry went over to him and punched him in the face, knocking him down. Then he said to the kid, "Now get up and get over there and do as you're told or get out of here and don't come back!" I mean he punched this kid right in the face and knocked him down right to the floor! I was impressed. *Everyone* was impressed. Suffice it to say, when Harry Conley spoke, people listened.

He coached both basketball and football at our high school. He was also a very analytical man. He made the game fun, and if you listened to him, you learned the game. He taught you things that made sense. Through the years, not only when I played but later on, as I talked with teammates and others, we discovered we all had a mutual respect for Harry. Players liked him, pure and simple. Just because you play for a coach doesn't mean you have to like him, but with Harry we all liked and respected him.

In high school, we didn't have playbooks or anything like that for football. But at Great Lakes we had Paul Brown as our football coach, and things were quite different. Not only did we have a playbook, but we also had a long list of rules, things we could and could not do. In it there were things I had never even heard of before. I didn't know what an itinerary was! I thought right away that it was really revolutionary and interesting stuff. I was very impressed with

Paul Brown's organization and his way of coaching. We would have meetings and learn techniques. I never had encountered anything even remotely like that in the past. I was enthralled by it all.

One of Brown's assistant coaches was Weeb Ewbank, the future coach of the Baltimore Colts and New York Jets. There were a couple of other good coaches, too. I learned a lot. You learn a lot by just listening, and I listened to each and every one of them. I listened to what they told us to do, and most important, I learned *why* we did certain things. It's a simple fact, but it is easier to do something if you know why you are doing it. If you are told to go dig a hole, that's one thing, but if you are told why the hole is necessary, it makes it a much easier thing to do.

Paul was very, very strict. "Nobody drinks," he told us. That was his No. 1 priority. That, and we were not allowed to gamble. Thankfully, it was not a problem for me. I didn't drink or gamble.

One day we came back after a weekend off and he called us all together for a meeting on the field. He singled out a couple guys on the team and said to them, "Now, it is the opinion of the coaches and myself that you were drinking last night. Now I want you two to get away from me, I want you to get as far away from me as possible, and I want you to get away from me right now!" By that night they were gone, shipped out to California. He made a pretty big point.

I don't know if anyone else on the team had been drinking, but I know this: they must have stopped. He cut those two guys and they were gone, just like that. It was quite a statement. One that I'll never forget. *I want you to get away from me...right now!* Wow, I was impressed!

Paul Brown was a legendary figure in sports, and I admired him from the first time we met. He was a good coach and a good man. He had great organizational skills and was very demanding of his players. He was extremely disciplined and expected the same from his team. Paul was a real innovator, and many of the things he did changed the game. He was the first to call plays from the sideline by sending guards in and out of the game with the plays. No one had ever done that before. Ultimately, he became a tremendously powerful figure in professional football. He refined the passing game with the great Otto Graham as his quarterback and was responsible for many of the things that have since become standard in the professional game.

Looking back on my experiences at Great Lakes, there wasn't much besides sports and training. I didn't have time to do anything else. It was okay with me, because for the most part I enjoyed what I was doing. I played football for only one year at Great Lakes.

After football ended, basketball began. I also played on the Great Lakes team and really learned a lot from that experience. We played some of the big schools, too: Notre Dame, Ohio State, Marquette, Minnesota, Wisconsin, Michigan, and many others. We played 30-something games during the season. With practices and games, it seemed to me as if all we did was play basketball. Our coach was Weeb Ewbank. He might have played some basketball as a student, but he didn't know very much about the game. Weeb was much more of a football expert.

We were not a very good team at the beginning of the season, but we did have a player on our team who had played professionally. His name was Mel Riebe. Mel was a real student of the game, so eventually he took over and handled a lot of things. Weeb gave him some significant responsibilities and we prospered from his knowledge and experience.

By the middle of the season, I was starting on the basketball team and playing in some big games. We played DePaul University at Chicago Stadium in front of 20,000 people. There I was, a punk high school graduate playing against DePaul and the great George Mikan. And we played Notre Dame. We played Toledo. We came to the Twin Cities and played the Minnesota Gophers. We played Wisconsin, Michigan…and all the great teams. I was playing a lot of basketball and really enjoying it. In the process, we beat some pretty formidable opponents.

After playing Notre Dame in football and in basketball, I realized it wasn't the college for me. I saw all the cadets and their uniforms, and I thought, *I don't want to go and put on another uniform and be a cadet.* It just wasn't my cup of tea. Back then, they were much more militaristic than they are today.

It was quite an experience for me to go from little Superior to playing in Chicago Stadium. But one thing I did find out was that I could play with these guys. I realized that whether it was with them or against them, I could hold my own. It was a good experience for me, and I learned how to hold my own as an athlete.

When the basketball season ended, I went out for the baseball team. A sportswriter from Chicago wrote something in the paper about me, something to the effect of, "Keep an eye on Bud Grant. He just finished playing football and basketball and now he is out for the baseball team at Great Lakes."

After the article came out, someone or maybe several people wrote in and said something to the effect of, "Hey, my kid went into the service and he is over in Okinawa. What is this Grant kid doing playing baseball? He already played football and basketball and now he is going to play baseball? What's going on here? Why isn't he overseas?"

Well, that was it for me. I was told, "We can't have this." I was off the baseball team, and within two days I was on a train headed for Treasure Island in San Francisco. That was the end of my sports career at Great Lakes.

Treasure Island was located in San Francisco Bay, within sight of the famous penitentiary Alcatraz. San Francisco was on the other side of the bay, and Oakland was close by as well. The barracks were huge—triple bunks, housing thousands of guys coming and going. It seemed to me like a giant anthill.

I got an assignment with the amphibious forces. They had all this training for small boats and landing crafts. I was an LCI, which meant that I was assigned to landing craft infantry. We were quickly trained to drive a vehicle that would actually go right up onto the beach. It was small enough that we only had a two-man crew aboard. My assignment was to prepare for whatever need there would be for that type of craft. It was 1945 and we were preparing to invade Japan. It wasn't long, however, before the United States dropped the bombs on Nagasaki and Hiroshima, ending the war.

Once the war was over, everyone stationed overseas wanted to come home. Many of the guys had already been there for several years. But in order to get out, you had to earn a number of points, based on a variety of things, that determined your departure date. Those variables were things such as time in the service, time overseas, the number of battles fought, and so on.

As I thought ahead, I figured I was probably going to replace the overseas guys until *my* points got high enough. I was looking at possibly being overseas for two years or more. I wasn't enamored with the prospect. I hadn't joined the navy to see the world; I had joined the navy to win the war and be a part of it, doing my duty. But the war was over.

I was living in a barracks close to where our landing crafts were moored, and one day we heard all kinds of sirens blaring. I wasn't sure where the noise was coming from, but I knew it signaled a problem. It was almost like an air-raid siren, but the war was over so we knew that wasn't it.

This was on May 2, 1946. We were told soon after that the sirens had signaled the beginning of the "Battle of Alcatraz," an incredible escape attempt made by several convicts housed on Alcatraz Island. We were told it was a breakout and that all the prisoners on the island were loose and headed for San Francisco. It wasn't until a little later that we found out those accounts were…slightly exaggerated.

Well, San Francisco was in an absolute panic. We could hear the shooting taking place on the island, since we were not that far away. It was later determined the inmates were holed up inside the cellblocks with weapons and ammunition. The order was given for the marines to go over to the island and take control.

The first guys who went over were just out of boot camp and were not very effective. They were eventually brought back, along with a demand for experienced troops. I was sent over in a contingent that took marines out to the island who had come back from overseas. We came up on the backside of the prison. The marines looked at the situation and fired from land into the cellblocks, again with little effect. They moved in closer and threw in grenades. They went from window to window to window and assisted in driving some of the inmates back into the cellblock. With the number of marines we hauled out there, I think we could have taken Guam.

I had little to do with the marines' work other than driving the boat that brought them to Alcatraz Island. We took one trip and stayed a couple of hours until the riot deflated. We just hung out there until the marines came back to the boat, and then we took them back to shore.

I tell people that I am the only serviceman they know who has a battle star on his American Theatre Ribbon. When you are in the service, a star on your ribbon means you were in a battle. If you were stationed in the States, you wouldn't earn a star because there were no battles fought here. Except for me. I have a battle star on my ribbon. I gave myself one for the "Battle of Alcatraz." Truth be told, it's not official. But it was my only war experience.

I often talk about fate intervening in my life. There have been many times over the years when I believe fate played a significant role for me in the course of things. When I was at Treasure Island at San Francisco Bay, fate became a reality for me again. It was all about being in the right place at the right time.

The war was over, and guys were coming and going from Treasure Island. I expected to be sent overseas in the not-too-distant future. One day I was walking down a hallway and happened to notice a memo posted on a bulletin board. The memo wasn't in a major traffic area of the base. I just happened to be walking by and for some reason glanced at it.

I mentioned before, the point system qualified soldiers' return from overseas service. If you had served a certain number of months and had done certain things or been certain places, you would earn points. And those with the most points would get out of the service first, while those with the least points would get out last. I had no quarrel with that. It was a fair way to do things. However, the memo changed things. It said if anyone was stateside and in a camp or station where discharges were given, and they were registered in an accredited university program, they should be immediately discharged from military duty. Of course, they had to provide proof of the registration. That was precisely what the document said, and I had the good fortune to see it and read it.

It was in the summer and schools were, for the most part, not in session. I called Harry Stuhldreher at Wisconsin and explained to him the situation that I was in. I had copied all of the information down and read it to him. He was the head coach at Wisconsin at the time and told me he would see what they could do about it. The very next day he got back to me, and I was enrolled into some type of music program or something like that. He sent it to me and I had it in my hand when I walked into the office of my commanding officer. I had all of the information necessary to meet the conditions for a discharge, according to the memo.

I remember my commanding officer looked at me and said, "You no good—all these guys have been overseas and deserve to be out, and now you present me with this to get out?"

The fact was, it was the navy that made the eligibility rules. I just complied with them. They had no choice but to follow them. I got the discharge, but it wasn't handled very professionally and it wasn't very pleasant.

My time at Great Lakes and at Treasure Island was over. I had gone through basic training, played some sports, met Paul Brown, and drove the boat to Alcatraz during the infamous riot. It was time for a change. I was out of the service.

Even though it was the University of Wisconsin that got me out of the military, I ended up going to the University of Minnesota instead. The main reason was that it was closer to home. I had been away for some time, and I just wanted to be near my family. It was important to me.

Wisconsin had offered me a car to come there and play football. As long as I was doing passing work, I would have a car—not a new car, but a reliable car. I would also have a job at a sporting goods store in town. In addition, I would get $100 a month and live in a dormitory. At Minnesota, I basically got nothing.

The other strike against Wisconsin was that they wanted me to go out for spring football, too. I didn't want to do that because I wanted to play baseball. At Minnesota, I would be the master of my own fate. I could play football, basketball, and baseball in the spring if I wanted to.

Because Wisconsin had assisted me in getting discharged from the service, it was quite difficult for me to call and tell them that I was going to go to school at Minnesota instead. While I appreciated their assistance with the military, my future was also important. It was a very hard call for me to make, but I had learned a long time ago that procrastination involving a difficult or unpleasant experience doesn't get better with time. Instead of suffering through bad news, it is better just to break it. I employed the same reasoning years later in my coaching career, when it came to releasing players. When I knew what I had to do, I did it quickly.

So I picked up the phone and made the call. It was finally settled. I was home and able to enjoy the rest of the summer before football started in the fall at the University of Minnesota.

5 UNIVERSITY LIFE

WITH THE CALL TO Wisconsin behind me, I had the rest of the summer ahead of me. Back home and out of the service, I had some time on my hands and I decided to go fishing. With my mustering-out pay of about $300 from the military, and armed with a tent and a sleeping bag, I was all set. So I went out in the country, down around Gordon, Wisconsin, where I had been before. I looked for a place to pitch my tent. I thought I might stay a while and look for some land to purchase.

In Wisconsin, everything that goes on seems to happen in a tavern. If you have an art contest for the schools, it will get judged in a tavern. If there is some type of council meeting, it will be held in a tavern. There might be a town hall, but for the most part, the big things and the small things all happen in the bar.

So out in the country, I went to a tavern and asked around about whether anyone had five acres of land they might be willing to sell to me. I was looking to buy the land, put a tent on it, and have a place of my own. One fellow said he had some property that he was willing to sell out by Simms Lake. I didn't know the man, but I soon found he had much more property than I wanted or needed. It was something like 60 acres, with 1,500 feet of lakeshore. All he wanted to do with the land was to cut the pulp on the property. He didn't care about the lakeshore or the land, other than to profit on it.

I had spent $100 of my $300 on a shotgun and another $100 on civilian clothes, so all I had left to my name was $100. He wanted $1,500 for the property, which was well out of my range. He pondered my financial situation for a few seconds and then said, "Well, I sure would like to sell this land to you." I told him I could give him the $100 down and make payments, but he was not interested in that type of arrangement. It didn't look like we were going to make a deal.

Later, I approached a friend of mine who had also just been discharged from the service. He too had some of his pay left. The two of us approached the man with $200—still far from his asking price for the land. He was interested, and suggested that we go to the bank and borrow the balance.

My only collateral was a shotgun. I had no financial experience other than living hand-to-mouth, and I knew my dad didn't have any money to help out either. But I found out that my dad could cosign on the loan because he had good credit and didn't owe anybody anything. It turned out my friend's dad was in the same situation. With a couple of cosigners, the bank loaned us the $1,300.

We bought the property, which I thought was pretty good for a couple of punk kids just out of the military. But then the problem was, how would we pay back the loan? After all, I was only a kid just about to start college.

Well, I found a way. I scalped my game tickets at the University of Minnesota for the next four years. For each home game, the team gave me six tickets. My parents got two, and I sold the remaining four. The tickets were about $3.00 to $3.50 per ticket, and I would sell two tickets for $25. All the games were sold out, so I was able to get premium prices for my tickets.

In addition to my own tickets, I went to the other players, bought their extra tickets for $15, and still sold them at a profit. With my scheme, I was making pretty good money each game. I was now in the ticket-brokering business.

Even though I was able to obtain a lot of tickets, I still had to find a way to sell them. Enter Sid Hartman. Sid remembered me from when I was at Great Lakes and our team came to play the Gophers. He was very interested in the fact that I was coming to Minnesota.

In fact, when I first arrived at Minnesota from Superior that fall, the first person I met was Sid Hartman. My grandparents had a better car than my mom and dad, so they drove me to the campus at the university and dropped me off at Cooke Hall, where the football offices were located.

The only information or direction I was given from the school was to come to Cooke Hall. I had no idea what to do after that. When I arrived, there was no one there to meet me. There were no arrangements made at all.

I had my suitcase in hand and I was walking up the steps of Cooke Hall and there was Sid Hartman, who was going into the building. It was Sid's first day with a beat of his own; he was on the Minnesota sports beat. He had been helping out Charlie Johnson and Dick Cullum and now he had his own column called "The Roundup," which was in the *Minneapolis Times* newspaper. I had no way of knowing when we met on the steps of Cooke Hall that day, but Sid would become my best friend for more than 60 years.

We spent a lot of time together. I love to tease Sid because he has a personality that reacts so well when he is picked on. I mean, it wouldn't be any fun if he didn't react so well. He must have enjoyed my pranks through the years, because whenever he recounts them, he embellishes the stories beyond belief.

Once I threw a dead crow at his convertible as he drove away, and by pure luck it landed in the boot area of the trunk and wedged itself deep inside. Eventually it was found by a service mechanic who was trying to find out why Sid's car had an unpleasant odor. Sid tells the story as if I spent great time and effort hunting crows and then carefully placed the crow in his car so it would never be found. I know on another occasion that Sid had a couple crows fall at his feet when he hit the brake pedal. He is of the belief I had something to do with that, too. Well, I did hunt crows on occasion.

Now, back to the tickets. I had to find a place to sell them. But where was the best place to do it? I was used to being in taverns and bars growing up in Superior, and with Sid's help we found the 620 Club on Hennepin Avenue. There we found people to buy my tickets each week. Every game we played, I was making a couple hundred bucks, so within two years I had enough to pay for the land that I bought.

My friend who I bought the land with had decided to get married, so he needed money. I bought him out and took ownership of the property outright. It took me another two years to pay off another loan, but in the four years that I was at Minnesota, I scalped enough tickets to pay for my land. I still have it today.

Being a landowner was good, except for the fact that when I finished my school obligations and Pat and I wanted to get married, I didn't have the extra cash. So I was broke for another 25 years.

Many people call Sid and me "the odd couple" because we are seemingly so different. Sid was a reporter when we first met, and he didn't have any interests that I had. He didn't like fishing or hunting or much of anything about the outdoors. Added to which, he is seven years older than me—a big difference when we met.

In those days Sid had jet-black hair, and all of his friends from the north side called him "Blackie."

Well, Blackie and I scalped tickets, but there were a couple of other things that cemented. I was always the last one out of the locker room. Most of the guys would take a half shower and race out of the place. Not me. I got full use out of the shower. And the fact was I didn't have any place to go anyway. So I would always be the last one out of the locker room.

Sid found out early on in his reporting career that if you wait until everyone is gone, you get the full attention of the coach. And Sid was always looking for quotes. So he would wait. The other reporters would run in and ask the typical questions, such as, "What did you think of practice today, Coach?" or "Who do you plan to start on Saturday in the backfield?" Sid wasn't interested in the typical patter.

As a result, the two of us were the last two out of the locker room, and we would often go out for dinner together. We got to know each other really well and became great friends. Now, you might think that maybe Sid befriended me so he could get some inside information on the team. But in all the years we have spent together, he never once asked a question of that sort—not one single time. It speaks volumes about his journalistic integrity that in all these years he never once compromised our relationship. His credibility with me has always been impeccable.

The other thing about the early days of our friendship is that I didn't have any money. Sid didn't have a lot of money either, but he did have a job. So most of the time—in fact, almost all of the time—he would pay for supper. That was huge for me.

Sid, Pat, and I often went out to eat together. We didn't go to fancy places, but one of the most memorable places we went to was the Cafe di Napoli. It is a restaurant downtown on Hennepin Avenue. It has been there forever and owned by the same family for so long—a place with a great reputation for Italian food. We could get a huge plate full of spaghetti that would fill me up for 99 cents. Those were the days.

Balancing sports and academics worked out well for me at the University of Minnesota. Again, one of the biggest reasons I chose Minnesota was to play all three sports. At Wisconsin, I figured they were going to give me a scholarship, a car, a hundred dollars a month, a part-time job, and basically run my life—all while telling me that I had to go out for spring football. I liked football, but it wasn't the end-all, be-all for me. I wanted my freedom.

I never envisioned playing football, or any sport for that matter, professionally. I played because of pure enjoyment. In fact, it wasn't until I was in my senior year that I gave professional football even a passing consideration. Back at that time, it wasn't a very lucrative career. I would have been much better off going to work for Cargill or a place like it.

Money for me was always a consideration. There was a time when I went to the athletic department at the university and asked them for help. I was paying for my own room and board with the $75 a month I was getting from the GI bill for my military duty. There I was playing football, basketball, and baseball and getting nothing from the university—no scholarship, no books, no nothing. This was a big problem, because I had to eat!

Eventually they did help get me a job at the Investor Syndicate downtown, moving furniture in the basement. Still, I wasn't getting anything from the university itself. I had to work for it. I would go downtown and move furniture around for four hours or so to make money. I guess I probably made two or three dollars an hour. That was it. It was all I ever got from the University of Minnesota, however indirectly. I had to scrounge the whole time. If it wasn't for the ticket scalping, I don't know what I would have done. It was tough—really tough.

When I was recruited, I was told that I would be staying on campus in a dormitory, Pioneer Hall. Well, when I arrived I was given a different story. I was advised that Minnesota residents would get the first priority for living there, and because I was from Wisconsin, I was out.

I had to find a place to live and eventually found one in the bowels of Memorial Stadium. Hidden inside were rooms. They weren't very nice, but that's where some of us football players stayed.

Football practice was in the late summer, and anyone who knows Minnesota weather knows it is hot and humid in August. I can remember it being so hot and uncomfortable in those rooms. They had no air-conditioning, of course. It was so hot that we would haul our mattresses out onto the football field to sleep at night. It wasn't what I had signed up for—living in the stadium, three bunks high, with just a light hanging down from the ceiling to study. It was far from big league. Overall, it was not a pleasant time for me.

An interesting sidelight to the football team my freshman year: if you looked at the team picture, you would find that 95 percent of the players in that picture were from Minnesota. Years later, when my friend Jim Malosky died, I was looking at a picture of the team with his wife, Lila, and noticed that only a few of us were from out of state; everyone else was from Minnesota. We had one kid from Iowa, one from Montana, Leo Nomellini came from Chicago. Minnesota may have been just across the bay from Superior, but I was from Wisconsin. At that time, every all-state football player from Minnesota came to the university to play football. It was truly a Minnesota team.

There were scholarships given out to players, but not to anyone who had been in the service. I wasn't smart enough to realize that there was still a way to get some money. Some of the players went to someone—I'm not exactly sure who it was, but they got money. They would get 20 bucks here and there. Others would get some cash from one of the coaches, who took care of that kind of thing. I found out later that had I put a little pressure on them, I could have had some extra money, too. But I was a survivor. I always seemed to find a way to make ends meet.

When football started in the fall of my freshman year, there were about 300 players who came out for the team. Every single guy who had gone in the service had come back and turned out for football. It was just that way back then. Bernie Bierman loved the big numbers because that meant there were enough players on the field for fodder.

For me, it was an incredible learning experience. I have to say that I really learned a lot about what not to do as a coach by watching what the coaches at Minnesota did. Frankly, it was a battle of survival for us. We scrimmaged every day of practice. And if you got hurt it was simply, "Get that guy out of here and get the next guy on the field. Find somebody else."

I figured things out early on. Coach was going to get the players down to the number he wanted by attrition. The bottom line was, if you could stay healthy and contribute, you were going to play. You would be on the field, scrimmage, improve, and be a part of things. For the guys who got hurt—well, they were gone. I recall thinking, *Wow, that is an awfully good player to be languishing on the sideline just because he got hurt once.* But that's the way it was.

The daily grind was arduous. We would practice and scrimmage and practice and scrimmage some more. Football is not a fun game to practice. It really isn't. It is much more fun to scrimmage, but the fact was, it was a battle every day. Those who survived would make the team. And that's just the way it turned out. Those who stayed healthy played.

Bernie Bierman had many successful seasons as the head coach at Minnesota. He hired his friends and former players to make up his assistant coaching staff—people like Sheldon Beise, Butch Nash, and Bert Baston. Some of them didn't know anything about football. He only had a couple guys who really knew the game, including Butch Nash, who stayed on as coach for several decades.

We were good because we had good players, but in some respects by the late 1940s the game had passed Bernie by. He was several years removed from the national titles, and we were doing some things that had become outdated. For example, we ran the single-wing offense, which was almost extinct in college football then.

We had a great player by the name of Dick Lawrence who would have been a tremendous T-formation quarterback, but unfortunately we ran the single wing. Still, we had a good team. At the end of the 1949 season, I was named to the All-America Team along with Leo Nomellini and Clayton Tonnemaker.

Football was hugely popular. The stadium was sold out for every game. I remember looking at all those people Saturday after Saturday and thinking, *You know I don't get any of that. I don't a get single nickel out of all those people in attendance.* The thought of this didn't burn a hole in my soul, but it didn't escape my attention either.

I was a good athlete, but I was not a very good student. I didn't like to study and didn't enjoy sitting in class. When I got to Minnesota, I was told that I was already preregistered. "Preregistered for what?" I recall asking. "Well, you are going to be in Phys Ed," they told me. "What's Phys Ed?" I asked." I didn't even know what it was. They just looked at me and said, "Look, you are all set. You're in Phys Ed. You have all your courses ready to go. Don't worry about it." Just like that.

After the war, there was a program offered for servicemen. If you could pass a test covering the freshman courses, you could pick up those credits without actually taking the courses. I was told this would be in place of such courses as English, social studies, and composition. If you passed the test, you got the credits and were automatically given a grade of C. Well, the C grade was good enough for me. Some guys wanted to do better, so they took the full classes, but not me. A C grade was just fine.

My good friend Billy Bye, who was a brilliant student, went in and took the test and told me all about it. He said the test wasn't that tough and he was sure he did well on it. But then, he wasn't like me. He was an A student, so it came easily for him. He started to tell me about the questions, and I didn't like what I was hearing. It might have been easy for him, but I knew it wasn't going to be for me. I was fairly well convinced I wouldn't pass.

Luckily, it worked out. I got the credits, but there was one thing I could never figure out. They never asked for any identification for those taking the test. All you had to do was go in and sign your name. I found that very interesting—interesting enough that Billy Bye actually took the test for me. I appreciated it greatly. And I was especially pleased that in the end, I got a better score than he did!

With all those credits behind me, I began my Phys Ed program. Most of my classes were electives since I had my basics completed. I thought maybe I would become a teacher. Still, I didn't have much of an interest in any of it. And to make matters worse, I had an advisor who hated football players.

One day, in his class, he got all over me for not having my shirt tucked in. It was too short, and I didn't have anything else to wear. I still remember him giving me a really bad time in front of everyone. I wasn't having any of it, so I got up and said, "I'm out of here."

He got really angry. I told him that if I was going to be a teacher, "I won't be treating students the way you do because I don't want my students to think I am a big jerk like your students think of you." That was end of my time in the Phys Ed program. I went into political science instead.

I wasn't a great student, but I did take some classes that I enjoyed. Still, it was tough for me. Along the way, I figured out that if I went to class every day, I would usually do well enough to make it. So I made it a point to always go to class. On the other hand, I knew guys who never went to classes and they still made it.

My problem was I never studied very much. I went to the library a few times, but mostly to escape my ridiculous housing situation in the stadium—there wasn't even enough light to study there. And I am glad I did, because it was at the library where I met Pat, my future wife. We were sitting across a desk from one another and started talking. We ended up going to Bridgeman's for ice cream later in the evening, and the rest is history.

Of all the things that ever came out of the University of Minnesota for me, the very best thing was my wife, Pat. We got married in 1950. Pat was from St. Paul. She worked at Prine's Bookstore on the university campus. She would work full-time for a quarter and then attend school full-time the next quarter. Even during school, she would still work at the bookstore in the evenings. She worked until 6:00 PM, which was the same time that I finished up with football and baseball practices. So, we would meet and have dinner, oftentimes with Sid. We didn't have money, but we enjoyed ourselves. We lived near the streetcar lines, and that worked out for us. I was finally able to afford a car in my senior year at the university.

I never dated at all in high school, so courtship was new to me. It was hard to maintain a relationship because Pat was working, I was playing sports, and both of us were going to school. But from that first night when we met at the library and went to Bridgeman's for some ice cream, we saw each other every week. We always seemed to find something interesting to do. The Campus Theatre was close by, so we often went to a movie. We enjoyed being together. I knew right from the beginning how special she was.

Eventually I moved out of the stadium and was living at a fraternity house. That improved my living situation some. All the while, I was involved in three sports. And every Wednesday night, Pat and I were able to get together for our weekly date night. Oftentimes, these Wednesday dates turned out to be a movie and then a ride to her house and back on the streetcar. We got along well on that basis. Pat and Sid got me through school.

I PLAYED FOUR YEARS of football at Minnesota, and each year, after the football season was over, I would take a week to go deer hunting before the basketball season started. I was playing football in the fall, basketball in the winter, and baseball in the spring. The hunting trip was special because I rarely got the chance to get out to the woods, and being outdoors is absolutely essential to me.

In my junior year, we had a new basketball coach by the name of Ozzie Cowles. I had played previously under Dave McMillan, from whom I really learned a lot about coaching. In my second year under Dave, I was the captain and won the Most Valuable Player award. Under Cowles, things changed. I could tell right away I wasn't one of Ozzie Cowles' guys on the team. He played a slow, deliberate type of basketball, and I was an up-and-down-the-court kind of player. I liked to run, and that was not Cowles' brand of basketball. I wasn't sure what was going to happen.

We had a great team my junior year, but I was not used to the new style and didn't like it. I felt we had too good of a team to play that type of "slowed down" basketball. Cowles had Whitey Skoog as our main shooting guard and Jim McIntyre as our under-the-basket man. My job was to rebound. I have always felt that Coach Cowles never allowed us to play to the best of our abilities. I believe it cost us the Big Ten championship that season.

My senior year started slow, and I played sparingly the first few games. I guess I was supposed to be getting my "basketball legs," having just finished the football season. The other basketball team in town at the time was the Minneapolis Lakers—a professional franchise, and an outstanding team. At about the same time as my troubles began with Coach Cowles, the Lakers lost a key player to injury.

My friend Sid told me he was going to see about getting me into the professional ranks in the National Basketball Association. Sid was actually running the Lakers at that time, while still working in the newspaper business. (He operated under the radar, however, because at the time he was not allowed to do both.)

Max Winter was the team's general manager and was the face man, but the fact was Sid was running the Lakers. He went to the league and told them my situation. He basically said, "We've got a local player—a very popular player in football, basketball, and baseball—who is at the university. We lost a player to injury and we could take this guy and it would help out our team and attendance." Sid did it all behind the scenes and was truly the person who made it happen for me.

As it turned out, I was the very first "hardship case" to enter the NBA. Sid had explained to the league that I was in dire straits. I had run out of my GI Bill funding and couldn't pay my tuition. I appealed to the university, but they wouldn't pay it. I was told there were no provisions to help me out with my tuition or anything else. This was a slap in the face to me. I had played four years of football, played basketball and baseball—and paid my entire way.

I was told, "Well, let's see what we can do. We'll see if we can find some money for you." I didn't like what I was being told and said, "What do you mean find me some money? Just give me a check!" I was told they would look into it for me. They never did.

With the Lakers, I would not be a star player, but I was a name in the Twin Cities, so I might be able to sell a few tickets. So with that, I joined the Minneapolis Lakers professional basketball team, declared a hardship case. Prior to me, in order to play professionally, your class had to complete four years before any player could turn professional. I was granted the first exception to the rule.

I had seen a few games, and although I knew I wasn't going to be any kind of star player, I felt like I could compete in the NBA. Things turned out very well for me almost immediately. There I was, at the University of Minnesota, with no help financially from the school and not among Ozzie Cowles' boys. Then suddenly I left school to join the Minneapolis Lakers. And we won the NBA championship that year! In a very short period of time, my fortunes changed dramatically.

I was paid $3,000 in salary. Coming from no money at all, that was big-time money! I owe it all to Sid Hartman; he made it happen for me. I went from being a nonfactor on the University of Minnesota Gophers basketball team to a world champion.

My mother, Bernice Kielly Grant, as a young woman.

My father and namesake, Harry Peter Grant Sr., in 1934.

Me at six months.

A family portrait in 1939: (clockwise from right) Mother, Jack, Jim, and me.

Top left: Taking my brothers out to hunt.

Top right : A navy man, 1945.

Left: Me and Bob Connelly, right, before we headed off to try out for the St. Louis Cardinals.

Posing with my parents in 1947.

Me and Pat at Osceola during summer baseball.

Modeling as a student at the U of M.

Left: With the Minneapolis Lakers.

Below: The 1950 world champion Minneapolis Lakers.

Left: My first professional football job north of the border: as a player for the Winnipeg Blue Bombers.

Below: Coaching the Blue Bombers, with assistants Joe Zaleski and John Michels.

Manning the sideline at Winnipeg.

Celebrating postgame with players Charlie Shepard and Gordie Rowland.

*Skinning the Tigers: the Blue
Bombers beat the Hamilton
Tiger-Cats in the Grey Cup.*

*With the Grey Cup in
my Winnipeg office.*

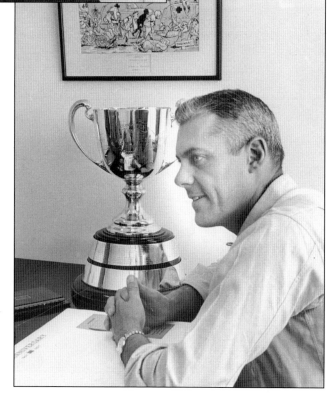

6

GOING PRO

I OWED IT ALL to Sid. It happened so fast that I barely had time to take a deep breath before I was a member of the Minneapolis Lakers professional basketball team. The first game I played in was against the Ft. Wayne Pistons, on Christmas Day 1949. I had a few days of practice with the team and got to know some of the guys on the roster. We had some incredible personnel—players like George Mikan, Jim Pollard, and Slater Martin.

We played our home games at the Minneapolis Auditorium. The Lakers did a good job of attracting fans, because there were big crowds coming to the games. I recall lines of orange school buses streaming in, bringing people in from all over the state and region to see the games.

The Minneapolis Lakers were once the Detroit Gems. I remember the day they became our local franchise. Pat and I drove Sid to the airport. He was carrying a check with him to purchase the Detroit Gems; I think the amount was something like $15,000. He went to Detroit, bought the team, came back home, and we picked him up at the airport that same day. It was just that simple. Suddenly, the Minneapolis Lakers were born.

We had a good team. Both before and after I played, they were a top-echelon club. I was accepted fairly well by the players when I arrived. Actually, I knew most of them already, having met them at various functions while I was a player on the Gophers.

I got off to a rough start with the team. After being with the team and practicing a few days, I went to my future wife Pat's house for dinner and developed food poisoning from some chicken I ate. My first game with the Lakers was the following day and I was up all night, sick as a dog. I was in such bad condition that I didn't know whether I was going to be able to play. The team had already announced that I was going to be making my professional debut on Christmas Day, so I was nervous. I felt absolutely terrible.

I was still really ill when I arrived at the auditorium. The game went almost through the first half and I hadn't been sent in yet, but just going through the warm-ups and sitting with the team was quite the thrill for me. Then, shortly before the first half ended, the crowd started chanting, "We want Bud! We want Bud!" So, just before the half ended, Johnny Kundla, the Lakers coach, put me in the game.

John knew I was sick and had asked me if I could play. I told him I wasn't sure but that I would give it a try. Just before the half ended, the ball came over to me at midcourt, and with only a couple seconds on the clock I put it up and made the basket. My first shot in the NBA with the Lakers was a buzzer beater from midcourt. Well, the house almost came down! Someone could have walked up to me, told me how sick I was, and I wouldn't have believed them. I didn't care; I was floating on air.

I had made one half-court shot in high school and another in college, but nothing had quite the magnitude of this one. It was a terrific beginning. I played a little later in the second half and did all right. I was now officially a member of the Lakers and really excited to be playing professional basketball.

I was really fortunate to have landed on an outstanding team, alongside some great players like Mikan, Pollard, and others. Added to which, we had a fine coach in John Kundla. John was one of the nicest people, just a really good guy. He knew how to keep the team together and did a tremendous job of meshing all the egos of all of his professional athletes. Athletes are very competitive, and in basketball they all want to be on the court getting minutes of action. John always created good balance; he found ways to keep everyone happy and involved.

Coaching in the NBA is extremely difficult. You play so many games in a short period of time and often play the same teams quite a few times during the season. What you say to the team at halftime and before the games can be difficult. You have to be sure not to repeat yourself or your players will stop listening to you. Talking about matchups is okay, but if you get into the same language every game—"Play good defense," "Move the ball up the court," that kind of thing—the repetition will wear players down.

So if there was anything I learned from the schedule we had in the NBA, it was not to say something unless it was worth saying. When you talk as a coach, you have to have something to say and not repeat yourself. And for the most part, I thought John handled that pretty well.

Later on, when I got into coaching, I sometimes found myself at halftime not saying anything at all. It is important not to spout clichés, because they won't work; the players will immediately tune out. If the coach doesn't have something meaningful to say, then he shouldn't say anything.

I had a lot of respect for Kundla. He came out of St. Thomas and did well with the Lakers. I think the team originally wanted to hire Joe Hutton from Hamline as their coach but that apparently didn't work out, so John came and did a terrific job. He was a good choice. He wasn't too much older than some of the players and it was a good fit. We listened to him and respected him. Some of the league's coaches at the time were significantly older, so when John came in, he related to the players very well. Then again, when you win, coaching becomes much easier for everyone.

We had a harmonious team, and there was a lot of local talent on the Lakers. Tony Jaros was an excellent player from Minneapolis and the University of Minnesota, as was Vern Mikkelsen. Joey Hutton was from Hamline. And there was also local favorite "Swede" Carlson. Then with me in the mix, there was an extra bit of hometown flavor.

I want to especially mention one of our most exceptional players. I'll qualify myself by saying one always has to be careful when talking about players. I am always asked, "Who was the best player?" and one just can't really get into that type of conversation. Instead, I like to talk about special players and competitive players rather than who was the best player.

I can say this, however, without any reservation: Of all the sports that I played in and have been around in my life, the greatest competitor I have ever seen was George Mikan. He was a tremendous player and an unparalleled competitor. George was a big man at 6'11", and he was also a heavy man. He was not a graceful player like we often see running up and down the court in today's game, but he could *play* and he never let up. He was as fierce a player that has ever played.

George could get up and down the floor, but it was tougher for him because he was so big. Still, he was in good physical condition. He could run with the best of them and never came out of the game. He would play the whole game! And if the coach tried to take him out, he would get mad. He never wanted to rest or even take a short break in the action.

As a teammate, I had great admiration for him. I knew it was easier for players like me to run up and down the court because we were smaller and lighter. George had to work so much harder just to keep up. I can remember him racing up and down the court, back and forth, and he never seemed to wear out. He played offense and defense, and when things got tough, he wanted the ball in his hands. He would bull his way to the basket, score points, and rebound. He truly did it all.

George Mikan was my kind of guy. His strategy to win was that he would just simply outplay his opponents. He was not the first of the really big men in the league but he was the first of the *great* big men to play professionally in the NBA. There were a lot of big men in the league, but they were not as adept as George was. His competitive drive was greater than any athlete that I have ever seen in any sport, not just basketball.

George would take terrible beatings during the games. In order to try to thwart him, the other teams would put their "hatchet men" on him to try to beat him up during the game. In hockey, these players are called the "enforcers," but in basketball they are called the "hatchet men." And they really went after George. I can recall games in which the opponents would put a guy in and just bang on George every chance they got. The player would end up with four or five fouls and then they would put someone else in the game to work George over. But it never worked; he was just too big and strong for them.

Sometimes he would be black and blue all over from those beatings he took. But he never gave up. When things got worse, he seemed to play even harder. He was without question our best player and almost unstoppable when he had the ball. He was the Michael Jordan of his time. He could literally take over a game single-handedly.

I remember once going to play a game in New York City against the Knicks. Our hotel was right across the street from Madison Square Garden and there was a huge marquee at the arena promoting the game that read GEO MIKAN VS. KNICKS instead of LAKERS VS. KNICKS. The sign was there, for everyone to see, Mikan vs. Knicks! George was that good. You would never see a billing like that today, but back then, George Mikan was the attraction. He filled the arenas wherever he played.

Slater Martin was another great player on the Lakers. He was a great defensive player and did a fantastic job guarding some of the NBA's best, guys like Bob Cousy at Boston. He was a little shorter than six feet tall but he was quick, could shoot the ball, and was a great defender. He would take the toughest small man on the team to guard, and he always did a superb job.

My job on the team was to relieve some of the great players. I would often go into the game and give Jim Pollard a rest. Pollard was also outstanding. Jim was a jumping-jack kind of player. We used to call him "Jumping Jim" Pollard. He would often play against bigger and stronger players so he would wear down and I would go in to give him a breather. My role was to guard his guy and take the fouls instead of having Jim pick up a bunch. I might pick up two or three fouls right away by playing Jim's guy really tight and pushing him around some.

My other role was to play defense and rebound. I could block people out, do some pushing and shoving, because I was not a finesse player. I could also run pretty well up and down the court. But I was not out there to impress anyone with my scoring abilities. I just got minutes and I think I earned respect from my teammates. I made some winning shots from time to time, and for the most part, I think I contributed.

It's interesting to watch basketball today. Compared to us, the players are so much better. I mean, they are just tremendous athletes. And the shooters are so much better! There is no comparison between the players of today and those of 50 years ago, absolutely none at all. Today's players are better in every aspect of the game. Today's game is so much faster and the players are such better athletes—better conditioned and with so much more ability.

Take Michael Jordan, for example. He was an inspiration to young people in the game. Young kids were all saying, "I want to be like Mike." His play challenged the young player to rise to his level, and he made everyone better. The talk was everywhere: *Michael Jordan. Michael Jordan. Michael Jordan.* He brought basketball right to the top of its popularity.

Sure, there were others before him, like Lew Alcindor and Magic Johnson, who were great players, but Michael Jordan was special. For him, it wasn't the conditioning, the weights, that kind of thing, it was his entire persona. That is what inspired people. It increased the pool of players all shooting for the big salaries of today. I was playing on the championship Lakers team and making $3,000 a year. Think about that compared to what players make today. It's unbelievable!

In addition to the increased level of talent, there also have been rule changes that have changed the game and the way it is played. And some of those changes were made because of Mikan. The lane in front of the basket used to be three feet wide; it doubled in size because of George. He used to get in the lane and make it impossible for an opponent to move him out. He would be right under the basket and take control of the game when we had the ball. There used to be some incredible battles under the basket with George, and he usually won out. He was unstoppable under the basket. The league also put in a three-second rule that meant you had to keep moving in and out of the lane. That was also put in place because of Mikan. The rule forbids a player from planting himself under the basket.

George was just as strong a player on defense as he was on offense. He would wait for the other team to come to the basket and then just stuff them. Believe me, it was very dangerous to get in that lane or rush the basket with Mikan in there.

Another development that completely changed the game was the 24-second clock. The rule stated that the team that had possession of the ball had to take a shot within 24 seconds or the ball would be turned over to the other team. This rule really changed the game.

I recall a game we played against the Fort Wayne Pistons. Their strategy against us was basically to hold the ball the entire game. It worked. We chased them around for the entire game. We would have to take fouls in an attempt to get the ball and the game just slowed to a snail's pace. They got ahead and then sat on the ball for the rest of the game, running down the clock. It wasn't much of a game to watch. I believe the final score was a whopping 19–18 in favor of the Pistons. As a result of that game, the 24-second clock was instituted.

The NBA had not raised the baskets, and I felt back then that they should have. Guys like Mikan, Pollard, and Vern Mikkelsen could easily dunk the basketball, no problem. Especially Pollard, because he could really jump. He literally looked at times as if he was flying through the air. If the baskets had been raised some, it would have taken a little more skill for some of the big men to get it in the basket. Back in those days, though, you didn't see guys dunking the basketball like you do today. It was considered "hotdogging" to dunk the ball. Players would do it in practice, but during the game, if you had the opportunity for an easy basket, you would just lay it up.

Today, the slam dunk is expected. It's the entertainment part of the game. I don't necessarily think it detracts from anything. Sure, it is showboating—no question about that—but that's what the fans like to see, and that's okay.

I never was able to quite make the slam dunk. I was able to jump pretty high and could turn the ball over in the air, but I couldn't quite do the actual dunk. Maybe if I hadn't slept on that couch in the front room all through high school, I would have had the extra three inches I needed.

When I played for the Lakers, the home court was a big advantage for the home team, just like it is today. The real hotbeds of basketball out east were in Boston, New York, and Syracuse. We had a tough time beating some of those teams in their cities and they had a tough time beating us in Minneapolis.

I recall playing a big playoff game in Syracuse. They had a better record that year, so they had the home-court advantage for the playoffs. We got beat in the first game, and during the second game we were down two points late in the game and we had the ball. I was in the game at the time, for whatever reason I don't know. Someone must have been in foul trouble or something like that, I suppose. I was pretty good at defense, so sometimes I would be sent in to guard certain players. That might have been the reason. At any rate, we took a timeout with about 15 seconds left to play. The play was called, and we were to run something called a double pick, and then Pollard would take the shot to tie the game. Well, we passed the ball in, ran the double pick, and Pollard came around—but he got the ball and threw it to me. He was supposed to shoot, and instead I had it. I was shocked. I knew there was barely any time left on the clock, so I took the shot and made the basket to tie the game. Syracuse passed the ball in and took an immediate timeout. They had a guy named Al Cervi who was their coach and player. He was their best shooter, and it was on me to guard him.

So Cervi came down the court with the ball after the timeout and I knew him well enough to know which direction he was going. I stayed on him, and he missed a shot. I came up with the ball and threw it down the court to Bob Harrison. He took the shot from midcourt, made it, and we won the game with one second left to play. That was my one major highlight in my NBA career, my one claim to fame as a Laker.

We went on to win the championship, so it was a huge game for us. In one of the games in the finals, I got around 15 points, so I was contributing. I felt like I was really a part of that great Minneapolis Lakers team.

Overall, my time with the Lakers was a great experience for me. The one thing that was really different was the fact that I sat on the bench a lot of the time, something I had never done before. At the University of Minnesota, I played the entire game. The same was true in high school; I just never would come out. But I learned a lot from sitting on the bench; it gave me a whole different perspective on the game. I watched and I learned.

Years later, I remember talking to Bob Knight, the great former Indiana coach, about this very thing, and he said to me, "Well, you could have been a basketball coach." Maybe I could have, because I did study the game, and I got to know it very well. I have always thought Bob to be an extremely bright guy—and obviously he was a very, very good basketball coach. All you have to do is look at his record of wins and championships. Coaching is not easy, but Bob had it mastered.

I think I could have been a decent basketball coach because, watching the game from the bench, I was able to recognize that there are so many parts of the game to learn. Football is different because you can't possibly see everything going on at once. There are lines of players and the sideline and major parts of the game that you cannot see when it is taking place. But in basketball I found that there were invisible avenues that could be utilized to get the ball in to the big men—or spots to shoot from. That was one of the things that Mikan liked about me. As I said, I was not a scorer. I played defense and concentrated on getting the ball to him, and I could do that pretty well. Getting the ball to Mikan was an important part of our team's game plan.

Even when I was on the court, though, I was still watching. And from watching coaches, I picked up more things *not* to do from them than I did things to do. Each coach, no matter how good, taught me something or other about what not to do. Long before making the decision to become a coach, I recall thinking to myself, *Well, I know I don't want to do that.*

I also learned a lot from just watching Mikan. He was so good at maneuvering himself around the opposition. He was a master at getting his man on his backside. If the guy would try to get around him a certain way, he would stretch his arm out and hold the opponent up so he would have to make a big roundabout to get past. I knew if I took two steps in a certain way I could get him the ball, and he would have the guy on a certain shoulder and make an easy basket. This is just one example of a thing I picked up from the bench.

Pollard was one of our big scorers, so when he was in the game, he would shoot. Once in a while he would drop it off to George, but Pollard liked the ball. So Mikan liked it when I came in, because he knew he would be the one shooting, and I would be the one to get him the ball.

Watching from the bench helped me to see the big picture, not just my place in things. I learned about positioning, and how a player could take advantage of certain things at certain times. Being a basketball coach may well have been fun. Who knows? Maybe I would have liked it.

I really enjoyed my time with the Lakers, and getting paid for it didn't hurt either. I was making $3,000 a year—actually more, because we earned another $3,000 from the playoffs. And then I was making money from playing baseball across the state. I think between the two of them I was making about $10,000 a year. I can recall thinking, *Boy, if I can just make this kind of money for the rest of my life, man, I am in clover!*

George Mikan, our star, was making $33,000 a year, over three times what I was making from basketball and baseball—but he was worth it. I'm sure he literally paid his own salary from the crowds he drew in arenas across the country. People came to see George Mikan—and believe me, they got their money's worth.

The Lakers also barnstormed across the state after the season was over. We won the championship and then went on tour throughout the Midwest. I can't remember the names of all of the towns where we played exhibition games, but there were probably 20 or more of them.

We went from Minot, North Dakota, and all across the region. Sometimes we would play a local team, but just as often we would split up our squad and play six-against-six. Or sometimes we might pick up a couple of local players. For our efforts we made $25 per game.

We would go by bus to Milbank, South Dakota, and Devils Lake, North Dakota…Grand Forks and Sioux Falls and so on. We played in these little high school gyms, many with a stage at one end of the floor. Think about that—we were world champions and playing in these tiny school gymnasiums! That would never happen today. But we players enjoyed it. We had a good time playing and the fans were wonderful. Mikan was there with the rest of us and he always put on a great show. He played just as hard with his name on the marquee at Madison Square Garden as he did in the school gym in Milbank, South Dakota.

We still had a really good team the next season. In our final game of the regular season, against Boston, I was in the game right near the end for my defense. With just a few seconds left, I got the ball and was fortunate enough to make the basket. We defeated the Celtics and won the division championship to clinch home-court advantage for the playoffs. I was never a regular player but worked hard and found ways to contribute. Unfortunately Mikan broke his wrist in that game. He was forced to wear a cast through the rest of the playoffs, and that led to our demise.

By the end of the second season I had pretty much determined that I wasn't going to go much further playing professional basketball. I knew I could play at that level, but I was never going to be a great player by any stretch of the imagination. If I hadn't had any other options, I might have stayed with the Lakers and played professionally as long as I could. But I had the opportunity to play professional football—and make a lot more money besides.

I had been drafted in the first round of the 1951 player draft by the Philadelphia Eagles of the National Football League. At the time it didn't really mean that much to me because I was already playing professional basketball. Frankly, I hadn't had much fun playing football. Bernie Bierman was a taskmaster, and I didn't really enjoy the game as much as I did basketball. For me, basketball was fun to play. I loved to run, and there was action all the time. Football, on the other hand, is no fun to practice—especially with a drill sergeant for a coach, like we had at Minnesota. Perhaps because of that, I had no aspirations of becoming a pro football player. But after two years with the Lakers, I felt it was time to give it some consideration.

Even as much fun as I had playing basketball, I never was an *I want to be like Mike* guy, like so many kids of this era who dreamed big about becoming a star. It was not a goal of mine to be a professional athlete at all. After all, I really fell into the job with the Minneapolis Lakers. Being an athlete was simply something I did, and I never really felt a lot of pressure playing, even in the biggest of games.

I just loved playing sports. Over the years, I have talked to a lot of great players in many different sports, and they all had the same attitude about pressure. When the game was on the line, they wanted the ball. I was the same way. The tougher the situation the more I wanted the ball.

I wanted to be the one to take the final shot, catch the winning touchdown pass, or strike out the final batter. I thrived on those situations.

I often played those pressure scenarios out in my mind. We are one point behind, one second to go and I am at the foul line with two free throws. When the game was on the line, I felt I played better. The pressure of playing was what I strived for, and I have been in those situations quite often throughout my playing days, mostly with success.

But there is another important point to be made here, and that is the fact that some circumstances don't always work out for the best. A player has to be able to handle disappointment and losing as well. If you can't handle losing, then you will never be a winner. You lose and you suffer, but it can't be for very long. You have to move on, let it go. Forget about it and think about the next game. I always tried not to dwell on the disappointments, and it's something I steered my players to do, too.

Baseball was my favorite sport to play because as a pitcher I had some control of the game. With the ball in my hand, I felt in control. I liked that part of it. With the other sports, like basketball and football, you have to count on others. But I enjoyed them all, because each had its own unique joys.

But after two seasons with the Lakers, I had to get serious. As much as basketball meant to me, it was not my future. Playing professional basketball was not a glamorous life in those days. You would travel and play and travel and play and never get much chance to do anything else. It was a tough grind.

We traveled by plane, so that was okay, and we would often play in front of huge crowds. Still, I had done that before when I played for Great Lakes, so it wasn't anything new and exciting for me. Playing in some of those big venues for the first time could be a thrill, but returning three or four times in a season, the novelty wore off rather quickly.

Money was also an issue. I got a $500 raise in my second year with the Lakers, but I knew I could make more than that playing in the

NFL. In addition, I was married and had a family, so money became a much bigger consideration. The Eagles had offered me $7,500, but because I was playing with the Lakers I thought I had some leverage in negotiating with them. I was wrong. They didn't feel that way. Then they changed the offer. They said to me they would offer me $7,000 since I hadn't played football the previous year.

I thought I might be able to get them to $8,000 for the season and they wound up cutting me to $7,000. I tried to get them back to the original $7,500, but they wouldn't budge.

In my first year, I reported late to camp because Pat and I were about to have our first child. As a result, I started off on the wrong foot with the team; they wanted me in camp, and I wanted to be with my wife as we awaited our firstborn. They phoned a couple times and eventually told me to report to training camp or not to bother coming at all.

I didn't like that one bit, but I had no choice. I couldn't throw away my job. Grudgingly, I had to leave my wife, who was staying in a cabin in Forest Lake, just north of St. Paul. Within a few days, I was notified that my daughter was born. I later found out that the Eagles had actually received the telegram earlier in the morning but had not told me about it until after supper. It was not a good beginning for my professional football career with the Eagles.

Even though the Eagles had a very good football team, the coaching situation in Philadelphia was in turmoil when I arrived. Even so, they had been winning and had some great players like Steve Van Buren. Chuck Bednarik was their premier player. We had lockers next to each other and he became a good friend of mine. Chuck had been at Penn State, where he had been an All-American. But the thing that I really admired about him was what he had in common with George Mikan: he was a fierce competitor.

When I played defense, he played behind me. On the goal line, he would get down on the line and say to me, "No one gets in between you and I. *No one!*" I can recall one time when we were backed up on our own 1-yard line and a player came through and made it into the end zone by about half a yard. Down under the pile, I could hear him growling, while making some very uncomplimentary remarks to me. Chuck Bednarik did not like to lose, plain and simple.

Chuck had been in the air force and flew 25 missions on a B-24 over Germany as a gunner. He could have gotten out after 25 missions but instead he volunteered for 10 more. He was a tough guy and a great player in the NFL for many years. He was also the last player in the NFL to play both ways, as the center on offense and as a linebacker on defense. He played in the Eagles' championship game against the Green Bay Packers and played every snap. He was some special player! I was fortunate to know him and play with him. We became friends and used to go hunting together from time to time.

Prior to my arrival, the Eagles had been the champions for two consecutive years under Earle "Greasy" Neale. When he left, they hired a coach from Indiana by the name of Bo McMillin. I didn't know him—or anyone else on the Eagles, for that matter—when I arrived for training camp. Shockingly, McMillin got sick during training camp and resigned soon after. I think he had some kind of cancer, but I'm not sure. All I know is that he died rather suddenly months afterward. It was a real blow to everyone.

One of the assistant coaches, Wayne Millner, was appointed as the acting head coach. The team had to do something immediately, so Millner was their guy, but he left very soon after, on September 8. I could see right from the beginning that he was going to have trouble. So there I was, about to have my third head coach in the NFL and the season had barely begun.

Jim Trimble became the new coach. It was a year with a lot of disruption and little productivity. Our first game, we played in Chicago. One of our defensive ends tore his knee up during the game and was out for the year, and I was put in to replace him and got a couple of quarterback sacks. That kept me on the defensive side of the ball, and for the rest of the season I played defensive end and linebacker.

I didn't think either of those roles put me in my best position, since I had always been a wide receiver primarily, but I did what the coaches wanted me to do.

We were in Cleveland against the Browns and there was a guy in the stands that day by the name of George Trafton. He turned out to be a very important person in my life. There is a little backstory here that set things in motion for my departure from the Eagles.

Years ago, when I was finished playing college football, the Winnipeg Blue Bombers of the Canadian Football League had a coach by the name of Frank "Butch" Larson. Larson was from Duluth and had also played at Minnesota. I called him and asked if he might be interested in some sort of a package deal, getting several of us players from Minnesota to come to Canada to play.

I had talked it over with Gordy Soltau, Billy Bye, and Clayton Tonnemaker, and we thought we could all come up to Winnipeg and play in the Canadian league together. Larson thought it was a great idea, but before we could work it out they fired him. So that was the end of that.

So years later, in Cleveland, I ran into George Trafton, the current coach at Winnipeg. Trafton was a Van Brocklin kind of guy. A big man, he had been an All-Pro center for the Chicago Bears. We talked for a while, and I asked him what it would take to get me to Canada to play professionally for the Blue Bombers. "Oh, we would love to have you play for us," he told me. Unfortunately, because I was under contract with the Eagles, the Blue Bombers couldn't have anything to do with me. He told me the only thing that I could do was to play out my option in Philadelphia.

In the National Football League, the player contract was set up so that there was an option on a player for the year after his contract expired. The team could renew the contract by merely writing a letter of intent; it was a real protection for them.

It was my first year playing in Philadelphia and I wasn't too pleased with how things were going. As I mentioned, I was at heart a wide receiver, and they had me playing defense, trying to stop players like Marion Motley, which was a bit like trying to stop a runaway freight train. When I went to sign the next year in Philadelphia, I asked for more money, which I knew I wouldn't get. I told the Eagles that unless they moved me to offense, I would not sign a new contract. I knew I was better than the two players playing ahead of me at wide receiver, even though one had been named the Rookie of the Year and the other was an All-Pro. They told me they would work it out in training camp.

I was given a chance to play offense and ended up beating out both of the players mentioned and became the Eagles' No. 1 receiver. Then, because I had been moved to the offensive side of the ball, they wanted me to sign my contract. But I stalled them some more and told them that I wanted to be sure I was staying on offense. At that time, the league office was in Philadelphia. Bert Bell was the NFL commissioner, and both the league office and the Eagles' offices were downtown. In order to get paid, we had to go to the team office to pick up each paycheck.

When I went to get my first check, I was told that I had to go and see the commissioner. He looked at me sternly. "Son," he said to me, "you have to sign your player contract. You can't go on like this without a contract."

I had talked to a lawyer and knew that I was still under contract from the previous season. What I was doing by holding out was very unorthodox; no one had ever done this before. Most players never really understood how the option worked, but I did. I guess I was posing a threat to both the league and the player contract.

The league office and the commissioner himself insisted I sign the contract. "We know there are issues that you have with the team, but look, you have to sign the contract. That's just the way it is," they told me. They weren't being demanding; instead, they used a kind of fatherly approach in the three different times that I was called there. Finally, it got to the point where they were almost threatening me, telling me that they would not let me play any longer without a contract. I told them, "I already have a contract." I knew it was exactly what the option year was.

The commissioner's office was worried about a precedent being set for other players. And to complicate matters even more for the team and the league, I was having an exceptional season in 1953. In fact, I was leading the league in pass receiving. The conversations continued with the team and they tried everything to get me to sign that contract. It didn't work. I kept my eye on what was going on in Winnipeg. After all, I wasn't very pleased with how I was being treated by the team and the NFL.

I was at $7,000 in Philadelphia and not happy with the money at all. As the season wound down, we were playing Dallas in Philadelphia in the second-to-last game. In the first half I caught 10 passes for 192 yards. We came in at halftime and I was really pleased at how things were going. They were playing a man-to-man defense and I knew I could beat my man every single time—there was absolutely no question about it.

At halftime, Jim Trimble came over to me and asked me if I was aware of the record for most receptions in a game by a receiver. I had no idea, and he informed me the NFL record at the time was 16 passes. I had 10 at the half. He then asked me if I knew the most number of yards that a receiver had ever had in a single game. I again told him I had no idea. He said, "234 yards," and I already had 192.

So, the coach went to our quarterback, Bobby Thomason, and told him, "Look, we have an opportunity here to do a once-in-a-lifetime thing. If Grant catches six passes for 42 more yards, he will set the records." Bobby said, "Good, I'm all for it. Let's do it."

So we went in for the second half. I was covering kicks for the team besides playing wide receiver, so I was out on the field. On the opening kickoff, I got hit below the knee with a helmet and tore my ACL. I was taken out of the game and got taped up but it didn't help.

I was hobbling and in pain. I think I caught one more pass the rest of the game. So much for records.

The next week we were playing the Washington Redskins to determine who would make the playoffs. If we won the game, we would finish in a tie with Cleveland for the division championship, so it was a big game for us. On the other sideline, Sammy Baugh, the great Washington quarterback, was set to retire after the game, so it was a huge game for the Redskins also. And even though my knee was bad, I could still play but had a lot of trouble running.

Near the end of the game, we were down by six points and driving to score. I caught a few passes in the game that were rather insignificant, but I knew I could get open on a pass play down the middle of the field. It was 4th down in the 20-yard line. I ran the pattern and was virtually standing alone in the end zone. The ball was thrown at me and I knew in that instant I was going to catch it and we were going to win the division championship. It was all there, playing out right in front of me. Just before the ball got to me, it hit the goal-post crossbar. In those days, the goal posts were on the goal line, in front of the end zone. The ball hit the crossbar and never got to me. And just like that, we were done.

Every time I think of that play, it transports me right back to that moment. I can see the stadium, the crowd, the action, the throw, and that crossbar. I will never forget it. We were going to win and then we didn't. Just like that, it was over. It was gut-wrenching. Just an inch or so and everything would have been different. There are not many plays that I think about and wish we could do over again, but that was one of them. I still hate that crossbar!

On the train on the way back, I was told to come to the team office the following morning and straighten out my contract. I didn't want to do it. So that night, when I got back to Philadelphia, I called George Trafton. He wasn't home, but I told his wife who I was, explained the situation, and told her it was very important that I talk with him that night. She told me she would tell him to call me.

About 4:00 AM the phone rang at my house; it was George Trafton. "What do you want?" he grumbled. He was half drunk from attending a Chicago Bears reunion in Chicago. I told him, "Well, the season is over and I played out my option. If you are looking for a wide receiver, I'm available."

I told him I was meeting with the Eagles in the morning and I needed to know if he was interested. "What kind of money do you want?" Trafton asked. I told him I wanted $10,000 to play for them in Winnipeg. "You got it," he said. But I had to ask him if he could speak for the team. I needed to know that he had the authority to say he could give me the $10,000. "Yeah, I can guarantee it. I can guarantee it," Trafton said. Going from $7,000 to $10,000 a year was pretty good money back then. I told him I would call him the next afternoon.

The next morning I went to the Eagles' office and met with the team's general manager, Vince McNally. He offered me $8,000. "Wait a minute," I said, "I made the All-Star Team, I'm going to the Pro Bowl, and I led the team in receiving. I deserve more."

They came back with that they could not pay me more than some of the other players, including the receiver I beat out for the position, because he had played longer than me. I argued, "But I'm better than he is." It didn't work. The Eagles general manager wouldn't give in. Our negotiations stalled, and finally he asked me what I wanted. I told him: $11,000. He said, "Well, that will make you one of our highest-paid players," and I said, "Well, I'm one of your *best* players."

I wasn't trying to pat myself on the back; I was just trying to inform him of what I had accomplished for and with the team. The conversation went on and on and ended in a stalemate. All the while, I hadn't told him anything about Winnipeg or my discussions with Trafton. I just walked out of that office, called Tafton, and became a Winnipeg Blue Bomber. I was the first player in the history of the National Football League to play out my option, become a free agent, and leave. Later, other players followed suit.

The odd thing was, the Eagles never called back. I never heard from them again. I could never understand how the Eagles general manager could have just let everything slide like that. He was a nice enough guy and was always very polite in our dealings—I remember he always called me Harry. At any rate, my days as an Eagle were over. It was time to head to Canada.

THE CANADIAN FOOTBALL LEAGUE was allowed only eight American players on their roster, and they paid top dollar for them. When training camp started in Winnipeg, I was in the same situation I had been in during that first Eagles camp. Pat and I welcomed our second child into the world. Only this time I stayed for the birth—and I was only a week late to camp.

In just a short time period, I had gone from playing at the University of Minnesota to the Lakers to the Eagles, and now I was about to begin a new chapter in my life as a professional football player in the Canadian Football League with the Winnipeg Blue Bombers. I had a nice salary increase, a growing family, and a devoted wife and mother to my children. Things were going well, I was happy, and I was looking forward to playing professional football in Canada.

Being raised in Superior, Wisconsin, I never felt that we were very far removed from Canada. We did a lot of trade from Fort William and Port Arthur, now known as Thunder Bay. I worked on the ships unloading grain so I knew what Canadian money looked like and that the differences in exchange favored the U.S. by 5 percent. Canada was not really a foreign country for those of us who grew up in the area. Then again, I didn't know anyone who was actually from Canada, but I was familiar with Butch Larson, who had coached up there.

Today, you read about football and the salaries of the players and it's astounding—some of those guys make an astronomical amount of money. Still, there are the lower-tier players who make the minimum salary, but even that isn't bad compared to the average workforce. In those days, football wasn't nearly the cash cow that it is today. Most players did it to make some good money, but a lot of players worked other jobs when the season was over.

At any rate, I felt it was time to leave the NFL and its salary behind. My friend Gordy Soltau had a little different view. There was a time when we thought it would be great to play together again, but he felt the place to play was in the National Football League, not in Canada. So Gordy went to the San Francisco 49ers and stayed there for his entire career. We never became professional teammates.

I didn't know a lot about Winnipeg at all. After I played out my option with the Philadelphia Eagles, I went to the local library in Minneapolis and got every back issue of the Winnipeg paper they had. I read every single thing I could about their football team. I wanted to become familiar with what was going on not just with football but the city as well. When I got there, they were surprised that I knew as much about the team as I did. I knew all about the players, their history, the area—everything connected to where I was going to be.

At the time, it seemed as if Canada was divided between eastern and western Canada, with really only one road running between the two. The cultures were different, and it really seemed divided. I made a real effort to ingratiate myself to the team and the area.

The coaching situation was in flux. One of the things I learned from the papers was that Trafton was not in the greatest position with management. Indeed, after my first season, it came to a head and Trafton was let go. The new coach was Allie Sherman, who later became head coach of the New York Giants in the National Football League. The general manager was Bill Boivin, and he moved along about two years after I arrived. So it seemed to me that things were constantly changing.

The ownership of the team was akin to the system the Green Bay Packers had, except that it was run by a small committee of people. There was always someone in the group picked to be the "general manager," so to speak, but the team was run more or less by committee, which was not the best way to function.

When I first went up there as a player I was interviewed by the committee. I went to a luncheon to meet the management group; they wanted to take a look at who they had bought. There was no television at the time, so they couldn't watch game film on me; all they knew about me was what they had heard or read.

I could tell right from the outset that this committee knew absolutely nothing about football. There were about a dozen guys, regular businessmen, running the club. None of them had ever played the game so I was at a huge advantage because I could talk football and none of them had a clue if I was credible or not.

As far as hiring went, they were at a disadvantage because they really had no contacts in the States to recruit players. I helped them in this area by recommending some players who I thought could play up there. I had become a source in their midst, a de facto recruiter for the CFL.

The "flood of the century" had hit Winnipeg shortly before I arrived, and the town was digging out. The Red River had flooded the whole town in the spring of that year. It was a real mess, so to prevent that from ever happening again, they built a huge ditch around the town. It took years to complete. The premier of Manitoba, Duff Roblin, was the one who got the project through, despite the fact that it cost millions of dollars; they called it "Roblin's Folly." It's still there today. He had the power and foresight to get it through, and it has saved the city from catastrophe. After the flood receded, the town was in need of some cheering up.

The Blue Bombers, now my team, were very big in Winnipeg. We had a huge fan base. And I really think Canadian football connected the west and east together. It was a huge deal. And of course, hockey was and still is huge in Canada, but back then it was only played in the east. *Hockey Night in Canada* was really big, and everyone, and I mean everyone, listened intently to those games. At the time, there were only six teams in the National Hockey League—the Original Six, as they've come to be known. The Canadian teams were Montreal and

Toronto and the American teams were Boston, New York, Chicago, and Detroit. When Toronto played Montreal, that was huge.

But football was important to the fans, too. We drew about 25,000 fans to each game, and for me it was a tremendous experience. Playing was difficult for me, however, because I played both ways. We played 16 games during the regular season in a 10-week stretch. If we played two games in a week, they were often on Saturday night and Monday night. Then we might get two straight games at home.

When you are playing both ways and playing so many games in that short a time, it can be really tough on your body. Even so, I enjoyed it very much. It was a good move for me and my family to go to Canada. I loved the city of Winnipeg, the people, and enjoyed my teammates.

In my first year as a CFL player I led the league in receiving. The disparity between the American and Canadian player was sometimes huge. Most of the Canadian players did not have the same experience as the Americans. Many had to be "football trained." A lot of them were very good players but they started as professionals very young. Some came as 18-year-olds and played 10, 12, 14 years. For my part, I was fortunate to have had the kind of training I had, as were many of the American players.

I remember two players, both tackles, who were exceptional. They played both ways, so essentially played four positions. Bud Tinsley came from Baylor and lived in Canada year-round. Dick Huffman came from the Los Angeles Rams. Both of these guys in those days were big at 260, 270 pounds. We also had Neill Armstrong, who later coached with me in Minnesota. He played one corner position on defense and I played the other. On offense we both played wide receiver.

Winnipeg had not had a lot of success in previous seasons, but in my first year we went to the Grey Cup championship. Unfortunately, we lost. We didn't go again for the next three seasons, but even though we were not successful, I could sense that the fans' support for the team was growing. The game was becoming increasingly popular across Canada, and I was really encouraged by that.

Allie Sherman didn't have much success coaching us, but of course he did well later on in the NFL. Quite simply, Allie didn't get along very well with the management or the Canadian players. He and I got along because I understood what he was trying to do, but I could see that it was just a matter of time before he would be out of there.

Seemingly every year, the ownership changed and there was a new person in charge. Then they landed on a guy named Jim Russell, who took the reins of the Winnipeg club. Russell was the owner of a car dealership in town. He was a strong leader and was the go-to person in town if you wanted to get something done. Jim didn't know anything about football, but he did know a lot about people. He came in and solidified the workings of the team. Later on, he was the chief architect in helping me get the head coaching job there.

Jim was the kind of guy who was very interested in people. He wanted to know about my family and how I liked living in Winnipeg. He encouraged me to get a job in the off-season and stay there year-round. I liked him and we got along very well, but I was more interested in hunting than I was working in an office somewhere. Plus, I knew that I was going to come back to the Twin Cities during the off-season. He did help my friend Neill Armstrong get a job in town, though.

Jim was different from some of the others who were in charge, in that he had a real desire to mold the team together and make it a winner. He worked hard at putting the pieces in place. My family and I were all living in Winnipeg during the football season, which made it interesting to try to find a place to rent, because we left for the States as soon as the season was over. In the beginning I lived in a one-room apartment until I found a place for my family and me to live. We often found ourselves in a juggling act, trying to secure a decent residence for a few months at a time.

We loved living in Winnipeg. The people were nice and the city was beautiful. The only thing Pat was concerned about was that we would get in there so deep that we would never come back to Minnesota again. Even though the school system in Canada was exceptional, it was very important to her that we raise the kids in Minnesota. (Then, she probably would have been okay living in Philadelphia because she kind of liked it there. I didn't. I wanted no part of it.)

I played in Winnipeg four years, from 1953 to 1956. I was making more money and providing for my family; that was important. Added to which, the Canadian dollar was worth more—and then we got a little playoff money on top of it.

Actually, when we went to the Grey Cup in my first year, I asked the committee what kind of bonus we got for playoff games. The question confused them. They had never given it any thought. I pointed out that there were extra gate receipts, plus the fact we had to play more games, and so on. I reasoned with them we ought to get paid extra for the games we played beyond the regular season.

As it turned out, these discussions led to us players getting extra dollars for playoff games. There was no animosity toward me for bringing it up; it had simply been overlooked. And from that point on, we got bonuses for being in the playoffs. I mentioned that the issue of playoff monies should be in the players' and coaches' contracts. They hadn't thought of that, either.

I wasn't trying to be a troublemaker or stir the pot. Quite the opposite; I was just trying to improve things and make them more fair. I didn't see myself as any sort of pioneer. I just though it was the right way. And it was all accepted by the team and became a reality.

During my fourth season in Winnipeg, Allie Sherman was still hanging on. I had led the league in receiving three of the four years. (The year I didn't, our quarterback had been hurt, which slowed up our passing attack considerably.) We didn't have a very good team. I could see that Sherman was wearing out his welcome, but it was not my concern. I was only 29 years old and knew I had several good years left as a player. My only interest was how to help the team and assist in making them better. Whoever held the coach's clipboard didn't matter to me.

I always kept myself in good physical condition, even during the off-season. Each year I returned with my family to the Twin Cities and played basketball with the Galloping Gophers, barnstorming all around the state. I think there was one February when we played 29 games. I played with former Gophers football players Paul Giel, Bob McNamara, Dave Skrien, and Jim Malosky, among others. Most of those guys had been terrific football players on top of being pretty good basketball players. But the attraction to the fans was the names, not their basketball abilities. They were known because they were great football players. The fans came out to see us and we made 30 to 40 bucks apiece each night. It was good money and kept me in good physical condition for football. (It was fun to play with those guys, many of whom remain longtime friends of mine. Bob McNamara later came to play with us in Winnipeg and I recall in one game he scored six touchdowns. He was a great player and is a great guy!)

The knee injury I had suffered in Philadelphia was healed for the most part, and even though it slowed me down a little, I was still adept at doing what I had to do as a wide receiver and defensive back. I was playing well enough to make the All-Star Team.

The league had an All-Star Game in Vancouver at the end of the season. It was patterned after college's Shrine Football Game in San Francisco, which was very popular at the time. The CFL decided to have the game pit the east and west Canadian teams against each other in Vancouver.

We each made $500 playing in the game, which made it worthwhile for me. The Shriners did all the work in organizing it, so all we had to do as players was show up. Every team had five or six players selected to play in the game, whoever was considered the teams' "best" players.

Well, the game could have gone better. December in Vancouver is damp and rainy and often miserable outdoors. Earlier in the year, in October, the weather was gorgeous, but in the winter, it turned nasty. It was also difficult to play a postseason All-Star Game after we had already played 20 or 21 games during the regular season and playoffs. But the money was good and so was the cause. Unfortunately, the game never really turned out very well because the weather and field conditions were usually bad.

This particular year, my wife Pat had prepared the family for the trip back to Minnesota for the off-season. She left a day before the game, eager to return to the States because we had bought a home in the Twin Cities, in St. Anthony Park, and she was anxious to return to Minnesota to get settled. I left the next day for Vancouver with my All-Star teammates.

The next day, the six of us from Winnipeg went over our packet of instructions for our arrival in Vancouver. I recall looking at our return ticket and noticing that we were not scheduled to return until the Sunday night following the game, which was to be played on a Saturday night. That meant we would be left in Vancouver all day Sunday with a day to kill, just waiting around for our return flight to Winnipeg. It didn't sound like a lot of fun to me.

After we landed, I just happened to walk by the ticket counter, so I inquired about getting an earlier flight back to Winnipeg. I was told there was a morning flight but that it was a full. I asked to be put on a waiting list; they put me on it but cautioned me that there was little chance I'd make it. In any event, I left my name and hotel phone number. In fact, I asked them to put my teammates' names on the waiting list, too. And with that, I didn't give it a second thought.

We practiced several days leading up to the game, and there was nothing significant about the week. Everything was pretty normal in terms of preparation. Game day had arrived and it was time to head to the stadium. I have a habit of never being late, but never being early either. If I am supposed to be somewhere at 10:00, I won't be late—but I won't show up at 9:30, either. I will be there at 10:00.

This was especially true on game day. The last thing I wanted to do was sit on a bus or in an empty locker room just biding my time. I always felt that a bunch of football players who are all revved up to play a game can lose something sitting on a bus. The best way for me to prepare for a game is by sitting in my room. I have always felt very strongly about that—both as a coach and as a player.

So I was in my hotel room watching the clock. I had a few minutes before it was time to leave my room and get to the bus for the game. I picked up my bag and was walking to the door when the phone rang. It was the airline. They said, "Mr. Grant, there is space on the airplane to return earlier on Sunday to Winnipeg if you still want to make the change." In fact, they could accommodate all of us. I told her that was fine and headed out the door, eager to give my teammates the good news.

The next day, we had to all meet around 6:00 AM to return to the airport for the early flight. All of us showed up on time, except for Cal Jones. The rest of us were on the bus, ready to go. I went back into the hotel and called his room. "I'm still in bed, Bud," he told me. "I've overslept and I'm not packed or anything. It's been a long night."

I told him that we could take another few minutes and I would come up to his room and help him get ready. He said, "Well okay, I'll get ready and be right there. You don't need to come up."

A few minutes passed, and still no Cal. I called again. "Bud, I'm back in bed. I have a headache. Just tell them I'm going to stay. Put me back on the first flight." I said I would but told him to check later to be sure he could still get on it. I booked him on the evening flight and we left for the airport.

We landed about noon on Sunday. When we arrived back in Winnipeg, I got word the team wanted to see me at the office before I left for Minneapolis.

By the time I woke up on Monday morning, the news was everywhere. The evening flight from Vancouver to Winnipeg had disappeared. The first thing I did when I heard this was to call Pat at home in Minneapolis. I said to her, "Did you hear the news about the airplane I was supposed to be on?" She had not. "I told her, "Well, the plane that I was originally on has disappeared, but I'm okay. I'm here."

I later learned the manifest for passengers had Bob McNamara and me on the plane. On WCCO Radio, it had already been announced: the flight from Vancouver to Winnipeg was missing and two local athletes, Bob McNamara and Bud Grant, were listed as passengers. Pat had not turned the radio on yet, so she had not heard the news, but her mother had heard it. So while I was on the phone with Pat, her distraught mother was knocking on the door.

I still think about how terrible it would have been had I not yet talked to Pat when her mother came to the house with the horrible news. She almost passed out when Pat told her, "I'm on the phone with Bud right now. He wasn't on the plane!" Again, fate took its course.

We eventually learned the tragic news that the plane had crashed into a mountain and everyone was killed. The entire contingency from Saskatchewan was on the plane, which wiped out any resemblance of the team they once had. Our team lost Cal Jones. He was an outstanding player. He had been an All-American at Iowa, the first black player to win the Outland Trophy as the best collegiate lineman in the country. We were devastated.

THE TRAGEDY OF THE plane crash overshadowed the events of the previous day, when I went to the team offices after returning to Winnipeg. When I got there, I didn't know what to expect. It had been announced at the All-Star Game that the team had fired Allie Sherman, so I figured I was going to be traded or something.

When I got there, I was asked if I had ever thought about coaching. It was Jim's idea, and he was the one who asked me directly. He told me that they had been thinking about me coaching since

Sherman had been fired, and that if I was interested they wanted to talk with me further about the possibilities. I was only 29 years old at the time and I knew I could play for five, maybe six more years, so I was floored. But at least I knew they weren't going to be shipping me out to some other team.

I told Jim and the rest of the committee that I would have to think about it and talk to my wife when I got home. It was kind of a stall on my part, because I had to really give it some serious thought. They wanted me to be a player/coach. They thought that because I got along well with the Canadian players, the American players, and the people in town, I could take on the dual responsibility. I told them that if I was going to do it, I would be a coach only.

The plan was for me was to go home and come back later to discuss it further. But the next day we heard about the plane crash, and that put everything on the back burner. I kept in touch with the team over the next week, but it was another month before I flew back to Winnipeg to meet with the board of directors, about 15 members.

The meeting was at Jim Russell's house. I will never forget it. They all had a few drinks before I got there and were feeling pretty good. When I walked in, the first thing I saw was a blackboard set up in the front of the room. One of the first questions that I was asked was, "Now, if you are coaching our Blue Bombers, how are you going to beat Edmonton?" Edmonton had won the Grey Cup championship so their logical question was, "How are you going to beat them?"

They handed me a piece of chalk. I knew they knew nothing about football, so I went up to the blackboard and put up a bunch of X's and O's and hit them with all the terms about football that I could think of at the time. I said, "Well, we will do this and they will do that, and we will counter with this." It was quite a performance— and I must say it completely blew them away. I knew they were sold.

I talked about our team. I said to them, "I love these guys. I know we can win with them." It was close to being scripted. I told them,

"We can do it!" When I walked out of there, the job was mine if I wanted it.

They offered me the job later that day. I was making about $11,000 as a player at the time, and they offered me a $1,000 raise to coach. "And we will give you a three-year contract as coach at $12,000, $13,000 and $14,000." I looked square at them and said, "Well…I'll tell you what: I'll accept $12,000, but I only want a one-year contract."

I recall them looking at me and sighing in relief but asking, "Why do you want that kind of a deal?" I told them, "Because if I don't like coaching I can still play. If I don't work out or I don't like it, I'll go back to being a player again."

They absolutely loved it. But they also knew as part of the deal, if I was successful, that we would have to go back to the negotiating table anew. To be honest, I had actually given no thought to any of it ahead of time. It just seemed to be the right thing to do at the time.

It's actually something that I have said many times through the years when I have been asked why I did something: "Well, it seemed like the right thing to do at the time." The situation was perfect in Winnipeg. If I worked out as a coach I could stay. If it didn't work out, I could return to being a player. It was a win-win. It was a good deal for them also because they were only committed to me for one year. These were money guys, so for them, this was very good for the organization.

Still, even after signing the contract, I was not sure if I really wanted to coach. I had never given a single thought to being a football coach. Everything was going to have to change for me. My life was going to be different—no doubt about that.

For example, I never wore a tie; suddenly, I had to go and put one on. I'll confess that to this day I still do not know how to tie a tie. Clip-on ties saved me, because every time I went somewhere I had to put on a tie.

Another change was that I had to go out and give speeches. I didn't know how to do that. I had taken a speech class in college, but that was the extent of it; public speaking wasn't even on my radar. Sure, I could talk in a huddle, but before a crowd? I had no experience with that at all.

I had to go out and sell tickets and be the team representative, too. All of it was very different from how my life had been in the past. We had a team general manager and he helped out some, but the reality of all this was it would never be the same for me again.

I recall talking with my dad about the situation when I was first approached about the job. He was living in California. They had moved out there after attending a funeral of a cousin. My parents liked what they saw and stayed permanently, moving to north Hollywood. "You won't believe this, but they have flowers blooming in February," I remember him telling me. From that point on, he was sold. Even so, I'm not sure he was really very happy there. He was never able to regain the job status he had with the fire department back in Superior.

When we first discussed the coaching situation, I remember my dad saying to me, "Why in the world would you want to do that? You are only 29 years old and you can play for many more years."

"How many opportunities do you have to become a head coach?" I asked him.

"Yeah, but you can get fired. As a player, you can play for a long time."

We talked about it at length, and as we talked, I knew he was supportive about it being my decision.

After I had accepted the job and returned home, I told Pat I was going to call my dad to tell him my decision. My plan was to call him first thing the next morning, New Year's Day. I never got to tell him. Dad died New Year's Eve.

He had some bad habits that likely led to his death. He smoked and ate a lot of fatty foods. What he would eat in those morning breakfasts would choke a mule, without question. His diet was horrible.

My father was a great influence in my life, and his death hit me hard. The team had planned to have a big press conference in Winnipeg to announce me as the new head coach of the Blue Bombers, but my mind was somewhere else. They delayed the announcement for a good month before I went up there.

My dad taught me a great deal. He grew up at a time when a boy at 16 years old was a man. I looked up to him and admired what he stood for in life. I often recall thinking how he handled certain situations when I approached things in my own life. We didn't have the same personality by any stretch. He was outspoken, gregarious, the life of the party. Being around him I saw the effect he had on people. He was well respected, forthright, and very competitive. I could always tell how admired he was by the way his fellow firemen talked to me about him. He set an outstanding example for me to look up to in my life. My dad was a man among men.

Wherever we went, it was always, "Hey, Harry! Hiya, Harry!" He was well liked. He always had positive things to say. He was a positive man. It almost seemed like a motto for him. *"Bernice, that is a lovely hat you have on today. Bob, nice shirt and tie."* That was my dad. He was always nice to people and had a way about him.

You can often disarm people by being nice to them. I carried that into coaching. If I was going to talk to a player privately and wanted to make a point, I might say something like, "Well…you had a good practice and you have that concept down. I like what you are doing out there but…" See, now you can make the correction because they are receptive. But you have to set things on a positive tone. My dad taught me that.

I eventually did get up to Canada for the announcement, but I never got to tell my dad I took the job as head coach. He would have been proud. And all my life, I was sure proud of him.

7

GREY CUP CHAMPIONS

A FEW WEEKS PASSED after my dad died before I was finally able to get back to Winnipeg for the press conference. There was nothing unusual about it, although I did hear later that the team's decision had surprised some people, mostly because of my age. I was only 29 years old, and I guess some thought it was pretty young to be the head coach of a professional football team. I thought it was perhaps too young to retire as a player, but I was happy with my decision and ready to get started.

Taking the job also meant the end to my amateur baseball or "town ball" career. I had spent more than a decade with different teams playing in small towns across Minnesota and Wisconsin. It was simply a matter of dollars and cents. I did it for the money. I was also a "hired gun," sometimes making as much as $150 per game as a town team's pitcher. Even though baseball may have been my best sport, I had no desire to sign a professional contract and end up in some small minor league city. It wasn't the route that I wanted to take in my life. Town ball had suited me much better through the years.

In my last game I was playing on Hastings with my good friends Bob and Pinky McNamara. I hit the game-winning home run with two outs in the ninth, laid the bat down, and never picked one up again. It was a lot of fun, and I earned some good money in the process, but coaching became my priority.

Stepping into the role as the head coach of a professional football team was a huge responsibility. In addition to the age factor, I suppose the fact that I had not coached before also raised some eyebrows. In retrospect, I think one thing that made the decision very positive for me was the fact that I had no qualms about permanently moving to Winnipeg. I wasn't a social animal in that I didn't go out and drink with the locals, but I had a good reputation around town, kept my nose clean, and the management of the team liked the contract that I had proposed to them. It was a good fit from the very beginning.

For the press to be skeptical is typical—in its nature, even. Then again, the outgoing coach had not left the greatest impression with reporters, so they were not sorry to see him go. Still, since I had just been a player, they didn't really know much about me or what to expect.

Likewise, some of the players were not sure what to think. *Now you are my buddy and now you are my coach* was the prevailing attitude; they didn't know how to be around me at first. The ownership had first proposed the job as being both a player and coach, which might have eased the transition some, but I felt very strongly that there was far too much work to do as a coach for me to do both.

As it turned out, the transition was quite easy. I had to hire an assistant coach, but that was it for my staff—at the time, we only had one assistant to each head coach. Comparing that to today's teams, it seems almost like make-believe when you consider that some NFL franchises have 20 or more coaches on their staff.

I hired Wayne Robinson, with whom I had played at the University of Minnesota and with the Eagles. Three years my junior, he had been a very skilled linebacker in his playing days. I had simply asked in passing if he had ever considered coaching, and he immediately indicated his interest. That was it.

Over the years, I have been asked many times how in the world anyone can coach a football team with only three coaches. I always tell them the same thing. I have always seen an advantage to it because as a coach you learn to fully understand every aspect of the game.

With me, it was not as difficult a task because I played both offense and defense as a player, several positions on each side of the line. I understood the position responsibilities. Over the years, I had played practically every position, except interior lineman. In high school, I was a quarterback, fullback, and end. In college, I played linebacker, defensive end, defensive back, wide receiver, and tight end. I also had been involved in all aspects of the kicking game; I had been a punter at one time and had also covered kicks. I was confident anywhere on the field and I knew all parts of the game very well. Because of this, I knew what it took to be effective at each of those positions. Wayne was primarily a linebacker, but in college he was also a center, playing both ways.

Initially it was going to be Wayne and me, and I was okay with that, but later I was able to hire a third coach and chose Joe Zaleski. Joe was playing for Winnipeg when I first got there and then went over to Eastern Canada for a while with a minor league team. I was glad to have him, and he was certainly a credit to our team.

I believe strongly that knowing the ins and outs of so many positions gave me an edge. Many head coaches had a much more narrow range of playing experience than I did. Take Allie Sherman, for instance: Allie had been a quarterback, and it was the only position he ever played. Of course, that doesn't mean he couldn't be a successful coach, but I do believe it limited his ability to understand all of the game's nuances.

I felt comfortable talking to players about how to play their positions, pure and simple. Additionally, I felt I had a good relationship with our Canadian players; there was no culture clash between us. Head coaching was uncharted territory for me, and it was going to be interesting, but I was very confident it was going to be a positive experience.

The key to success and winning for any coach is to get the best players. Winning is dependent upon good players. And you will always be a better coach with better players, too. It's just that simple.

I knew right from the start that the first and most important thing I had to do was recruit. There was no free agency at the time. I had to find them, and I spent a great deal of time looking for players in both the United States and Canada. I spent the bulk of my time in the States, mostly because of the greater population. I felt we had to get the very best American football players to come to Canada and play for us, and I worked hard to accomplish that goal.

The most difficult thing in the beginning of my coaching career was releasing players that had been my teammates. Some of them I had played with the previous season, and I knew then they weren't good enough. I knew then that they wouldn't last, but suddenly it was my decision. Letting some of them go was tough to do, but it had to be done for the sake of the team.

A lot of coaches feel that they can outcoach or outthink other coaches. That just is not true. You really can't outcoach someone else, but you can outpersonnel them by putting the right pieces together. I knew I had to find the pieces. So I spent a lot of time with my contacts in the States. I didn't have a huge network, but I knew some people. I kept track of college players and pro players in the States. Even though we could only utilize a small number of American players (because of CFL restrictions we were limited by how many we could carry on our roster), I knew that they were going to be the key to our success.

I didn't know anyone who could help me in Alabama or the other football-rich states in the South, but I did have good contacts in Iowa. I asked myself who they had down in Iowa. As it turned out, they had a terrific quarterback by the name of Ken Ploen. So I started there with Ken and convinced the best quarterback in college football to come to Canada.

At the time, we could compete with the NFL moneywise because we could only have eight Americans on our roster. We could afford to pay the Americans a bigger piece of our pie because we carried fewer of them. I was well aware of this since it was what had gotten me to Canada in the first place.

I wasn't the only one who had gone to Canada from the States, though. Tom Brown, the great Minnesota player and All-American, had a very successful career in Vancouver. Bob McNamara, another Gopher and All-American, did really well in Canada, too. Gophers Mike Wright and Roger Hagberg also did well in Canada. I almost had Paul Giel talked into coming, but he eventually chose baseball. It's too bad; I know Paul would have been an outstanding Canadian football player.

Besides Ken, I was able to convince a few other players from Iowa to join the team—but because of limitations I always had to be very careful in considering what was available. It was important to first determine your needs and then fill those needs with players who you went out and recruited.

One thing I had in my favor was that there were not as many teams in the National Football League back then. The reality was, there were more players available than there were teams. Because of this, there were some teams that let some pretty good players go. I noticed this was especially true of the Philadelphia Eagles when I was with them. There were some players who the Eagles cut that could have been very good players in the Canadian Football League. But at that time, when a player was released, there was really no other place for them to go.

I always felt confident that I could go out and find good players, and I did. I remember getting a couple from Cleveland who couldn't make their championship team but they were very good players for us. NFL teams just couldn't keep everybody.

We signed a great athlete from Northwestern, a quarterback named Dick Thornton. I was able to convince him that he was not suited to play in the NFL but that he had all the right makings for a player in Canada. He was a rushing quarterback who could maneuver all over the field, which was perfect for the larger fields in the Canadian Football League. He could also play defense and turned out to be one of the all-time great defensive backs in the CFL.

In my first year in Winnipeg, I made a lot of changes—especially with our American players. Putting together personnel was what I spent most of my time doing. I felt the rest of it was secondary to getting the right players and the most players. I knew I could look mighty good as a coach as long as I had the right players around me.

It might be hard to believe, but I never developed a true coaching philosophy. I can say again that learning from others what not to do coaching helped me more than anything else. I saw it over the course of my playing career—coaches trying to put their systems in place rather than developing systems suited for the players on their rosters. I have always felt that it is important to work out a system for the talent that you have on the team. I have always coached my teams that way, and many other coaches never understood that.

I felt that I could judge talent successfully. I knew what a football player was. If there is a key to being a coach, the wrong word to use is "coaching." I believe that what you are is not a coach, frankly, but an evaluator of talent. There is always a certain amount of organization necessary, but the bottom line if you are going to be successful is that you better be able to evaluate players. You have to have the instinct and the ability to make the right decisions for the team. A lot of people think coaching is sitting down and constantly strategizing. In my opinion, strategizing is not a great part of coaching. Hard work and knowing what to do and when is it, in my opinion.

I always felt that I could outwork any other coach. If I knew I had to go all the way to El Paso, Texas, to get a player, I would go. I would spend the time it took to get that player. I can recall some great players that I narrowly missed out on, but I always gave it my best shot to get them. There was one kid who was a first-round draft choice of the Washington Redskins. I had convinced him that the place for him to play was in Winnipeg. In addition, I had with me a roll of money. I put the money on the table and said it was his if he signed with Winnipeg. He was poor, and this money looked pretty good to him. I told him I would be back in the morning with the contract all together for him to sign. I left that evening confident he was going to be a Blue Bomber. In the meantime, his roommate called Washington and told them, "Hey, you better do something here, because this guy is going to go to Winnipeg." Well, someone from the Redskins got on a plane and got there before I returned to sign him.

My offer was actually $2,000 more than their original offer to him, but when they heard what I had almost accomplished, they met and ultimately exceeded my offer. If nothing else, I helped make him some extra money. He ended up playing in Washington for more than a decade and was a great receiver for them. His name was Charley Taylor.

Another near miss I had was Alex Karras, a great All-American lineman at Iowa. Alex was an outgoing kind of a guy and was also a wrestler. I knew he had an interest in wrestling, so I got my good friend Vern Gagne, who was a great wrestler and promoter, to come down to Iowa with me. Besides being an outstanding football player, Karras was a good wrestling prospect, too. He had the right temperament for it, and I know Vern liked him. Vern told Karras that he would set a regular wrestling schedule for him in the off-season. That way, he could double the money he would make in football wrestling the rest of the year.

We went to meet him in Chicago, near Alex's hometown of Gary, Indiana. During our negotiations, we met with Alex and his brother. Although Alex liked what we had to say, I could tell right away that his brother wasn't buying it. After we concluded the meeting, I put him on the train to go back home, and just before he left, he told me, "Coach, I'm coming. I'm coming to Winnipeg." He guaranteed it before we parted ways.

It never happened. Alex's brother called the Detroit Lions and they came right away to see him. They really twisted his arm and sold him on Detroit. And just like that, he was gone. Of course, he became a terrific player and was with the Lions for many years. The bottom line was, I came just a hair's breadth away from landing Alex Karras for the Blue Bombers.

Even though I didn't get every player I went after, I was still successful. We got better players than most of the teams in the league because I worked very hard at it every single year.

Our first game with me as the head coach in Winnipeg, we played Edmonton. They had won the Grey Cup championship the year before. We played them at home, and although we lost, the score was very close, which was a real confidence builder. I learned early on that we could play with them. Personnel-wise we could match up with them, and with all the other teams in the league, for that matter.

We won our share of games the first season—enough to make it to the Grey Cup. Hamilton beat us, but we had lost some key players through injury that season.

The second year, we won the Grey Cup. And then we won it again the following year. It was a terrific beginning. Winning the first Grey Cup really validated things for me. I was convinced that we were on the right track. But then we had to keep it going, and I tried to improve every year, because that's what everyone else was doing. Recruiting was still the key ingredient.

My first year as head coach with Winnipeg was 1957. A few years later, in 1961, Max Winter from the Minnesota Vikings called me about the head coaching job there. I knew Max from years ago, when he had been general manager of the Minneapolis Lakers. Max thought he was doing me a favor in contacting me for the job, but I didn't see it that way. The Vikings were a newly formed franchise in the National Football League, and they were sure to have a lot of growing pains as an expansion team. I did not relish the idea of building a squad from the ground up.

I told him, "Max, I've got a good job up here and we have been doing really well." He said, "Well, that's why I'm calling you, because you are a successful coach and—" I cut him off, "But, Max, you are an expansion team and you are going to have a tough time. With all due respect, I'm going to have to stay up here."

I know Max was very puzzled by my decision, but I was happy in Winnipeg, and I had a lot of security. I honestly think he was really shocked that I would pass up an opportunity to coach in the NFL.

I wasn't naive enough to think that I could come back to Minnesota and set the world on fire with an expansion team, especially with the system that was in place for those teams to get players. With the way the league had set up the expansion draft, a new team wouldn't be able to challenge the better teams for many years. The fact of the matter is, no teams gave up any good players to the draft. So the new teams had to draft from a pool of the lowest-caliber players in the NFL, the players on the rosters of the other teams who were left unprotected. Most of the players taken by the expansion teams rarely lasted in the league more than a year or two. I honestly think the NFL was not very fair to those expansion teams.

In the end, I gave Winter's offer some consideration, but I wanted to stay in Canada. I told him to call me the next time they were looking for a coach.

I was happy in Winnipeg and we had a good team. My family had adjusted well and I enjoyed the community and the success of winning. It was also interesting for me to work within the rules of Canadian football, which was quite different from that played in the United States and the National Football League. Canadian football had been around long before the NFL ever began. In fact, 2012 was the 100th anniversary of the Grey Cup, which symbolizes the CFL championship.

In the beginning, Canadians called it rugby football. If you watch closely, you will pick up some of the subtleties that are similar to American football, but the major differences are clear for everyone to see. For example, in Canadian football, there are only three downs in which to make a first down.

As a student of American football, you might say, "How can you do that?" Well, they do it because linemen are a yard off the ball. Because players are a full yard off the ball, it opens up the game. It is a pretty important yard. If you know the snap count, which the offensive players do, you are able to get a running start. It is hard to make up that yard gap on defense, so they give up a yard on almost every down.

The NFL might average maybe three and a half yards on a running play. In Canada it might be four and a half. Defense is really stressed in Canadian football as well, so when a team stops the opponent on three downs, the punting game becomes very important. The average number of punts in a game is much higher in Canada. So with these rules in place, the kicking game is extremely important.

While recruiting, I was always looking for kickers and punters, and I had some great ones over the years. Charlie Shepard was one of the best I have ever seen. He was also a very good running back, so we got two for one with him. Unless you had a Canadian player as your kicker, you couldn't afford to have an American player take up that spot on the roster unless he also played another position.

Another difference between the two games is the field of play. In Canada, fields are longer and wider, and the end zones are 25 yards deep. As such, you could be on the 3-yard line and still throw a 25-yard pass for a touchdown.

Canadian football also has the single point, which can only be scored by the punting team, kickoff team, or field goal team if the kick is missed. If you punt the ball in the end zone, the receiving team has to run the ball out. If they fail, they give up a point. This adds significant strategy to the game.

One of the biggest differences in the game is that in Canada there are 12 men on a team. Most teams play with another wide receiver on offense and another defensive back on defense. Some use an extra running back or tight end.

Another major difference in Canada was we played two more games in the regular season than the NFL. Because of the climate, the season started much earlier. But because the league wanted us to finish up by late November, we sometimes had to play two games in a single week. The playoffs were also different. We had a two-game schedule, and the total points scored determined the winner, and then the best two out of three went to the Grey Cup.

Despite the disparity in rules, the techniques are basically all the same. You use the same football. You have to pass the ball, catch the ball, run with it, and kick it. The tackling and blocking techniques are also similar. Blocking is slightly different because of the space between the linemen on offense and defense. For the most part, though, the Canadian game and the American game are mostly interchangeable. Players don't have to make many adjustments.

When I was in Canada, and later with the Vikings, I wanted the quarterback to be the one to call the plays. In today's game, everything is all scripted. Few quarterbacks ever call their own plays. My guys had a plan for what they would do in given situations and at various places on the field. I never sent in the play on every single down. In certain situations, I might send in a play, but for the most part, I wanted the quarterback to call the play.

Fran Tarkenton always called his own plays. On occasion we might send in a play but it worked for him most of the time to call his own plays. For some quarterbacks, it might not be effective, but for Fran it definitely was. He had the qualities necessary to handle it, the intelligence, the emotional capacity, and the competitiveness. He understood the game. He prepared extremely well and we were on the same page most of the time. We would often talk things over, with each giving input, but in the end, I would usually have the confidence to go with Fran's instinct. The way I saw it, he was the one in the middle of the action.

I GOT TO KNOW John Michels when I was with the Eagles. He was an undersized offensive lineman who had been a collegiate All-American. With players in the NFL getting bigger and bigger, John only lasted a couple of years. But I remembered what a competitive player he was, and I went after him to come with me to Canada.

In his first year in Canada, John was a good player for us. He then went to Texas A&M as a coach. Once I got permission to hire another coach, I went straight after John. He came back with me and we were together for a long time in Canada and later in Minnesota. He was a smart coach, an excellent motivator, and a great person. And to use a Sid-ism, he was a "close personal friend."

Another coach who started with me in Canada was Jerry Burns. Jerry was connected with Iowa and knew my main contact there. He was a great connection for me and got me hooked up with Kenny Ploen, who became our quarterback in Canada for many seasons. Burnsie was a big recruiter in that part of the country and we had a great relationship not only with players, but in talking football, particularly the passing game.

When I started coaching, it was my responsibility to put in with all parts of the game—offense, defense, the kicking game, everything. During that time, Jerry and I talked a lot about football. I would bring him up to Canada in the summer for a couple of weeks as a guest coach and that worked out well for both of us. He would bring his family up, stay at the lake, and work with us on the team. He got some money and he and his family got a little vacation out of it. Through that experience especially, we became good friends. Later on, I was fortunate to bring him with me as a coach in Minnesota.

Everything about living and coaching in Canada had been good for my family and me. The terrain suited me well in my love of hunting and fishing, too. There was no hockey team in Winnipeg, so football was very big. The Blue Bombers gave the fans and community a great outlet. It also brought out the competition between eastern and western Canada as well. At the time, east and west didn't play one another until the championship game. It was often said that football united Canada back at that time more than anything else.

I can remember going to Toronto and the hotels would be full, the streets would be packed with people during the Grey Cup. It was a *huge* event in Canada. It was very rewarding and enjoyable to be a part of it. But one of the things that really bothered me was that the game didn't get enough exposure in the States. I especially found this out when I went to recruit the American players. Some of them would know where the state of Minnesota was but they had no idea where Canada was, let alone what we were accomplishing in Canadian football. This was especially true of players I tried recruiting in the South.

Over the years, I had become more involved in league activities. Through our efforts, we were finally able to get ABC to cover the Grey Cup Championship Game all across the United States. This was great news for us as a league because we would get exposure in America. It would be easier to recruit and really bring up our image. I really felt this was crucial for the league and its future.

The 1962 game was played in Toronto, and as the game started, fog drifted in from the lake. All of the ABC cameras were stationed high above the playing field; they had no ground cameras and no sideline cameras. Once the fog came in, the cameras could not pick up any of the game. Eventually, it was as if the television screens had been completely blacked out. Likewise, the announcers could not announce the game because they could not see from their vantage point. If you were at ground level, like the coaches and players, it was fine. The coverage of the game was a disaster, to say the least.

The league commissioner, who couldn't see a thing from where he was seated, came down to the field and the game was called. On the last play before the game was called, we completed a six-yard pass. But of course no one saw it. As I recall, there were about 10 minutes left in the fourth quarter and we were ahead by one point when the game was postponed until the next day.

It was truly a goofy scenario, one of the strangest of my career. The game was going to give us the exposure we needed, but it was a spectacular debacle. Because of that freak weather, it took a while longer for us to get the kind of attention we needed.

Because of the postponement, we had to leave the field, go back to the hotel, and then come back the next day to finish the game. We had about 16 hours to call the next play—it was second down, four yards to go—and it didn't work. We had to punt. I guess it was too much time! But in the end, we won the game and the championship.

A rather unusual thing occurred the night before one of our other Grey Cup Championship Games. John Michels, our assistant coach, was assigned to do player bed checks. He came to me and told me that he was sure one of our players had a female in his room. I have always felt that bed checks are import to determine if players are physically ready to play the game. I wanted to be sure that no one was sick with the flu or otherwise not feeling well. But we also had rules about conduct, and this was a big one. Having a female in your room the night before a game was a $500 fine—and that was a lot of money back in those days. So I went to the player's room.

I told the player what John had suspected and the player denied it. But It was tough to stick with his denial after I saw the woman standing behind a shower curtain, part of her legs and feet exposed. I told him he had 10 minutes to get her out of his room before I came back to see him.

Rules were rules, and we had fines and other consequences for rule breakers. But it was important to carefully weigh out all of my options. I never wanted to make a decision that was not in the best interests of the player and the team. So when I went back to the room, I told the player that I had carefully considered my options and reminded him of the penalty for such behavior, as stated in his playbook. Additionally I told him that I could not understand how he could do something like that on the very night before our championship game. Now, how do you turn a negative into a positive?

I said to him, "Okay, here is what we are going to do: If we lose the game tomorrow, you are going to pay a $500 fine. If we win, this will all be forgotten." He looked at me and said, "Coach, we are not going to lose tomorrow!" And he was right; by the end of the following day, we were Grey Cup champions.

While we had been very successful in Winnipeg, I still kept track of how the Vikings were doing. I knew Norm Van Brocklin, the Vikings coach, somewhat, and I used to watch some game film at their offices when I had the chance. In the back of my mind, I never had the thought that I might someday coach the Vikings. I was busy doing what I was doing. Not to mention that I had six kids by then and truly enjoyed living in Winnipeg. My life was full, and I had no aspirations of anything else. In 1967, I renegotiated my contract with the Blue Bombers. I planned to stay.

Then, after six stormy years, the Vikings fired Norm Van Brocklin. Meanwhile, my situation in Winnipeg had changed to some extent. The team had a new president; he was an accountant, and I have a theory on accountants. Accountants are people who gather information but don't make decisions. True to my theory, this new guy had been very difficult to deal with during my contract negotiation. He could not make a final decision, and this bothered me. Still, I signed my contract to stay on as head coach.

Shortly after Van Brocklin got fired in Minnesota I got a call from Jim Finks, who had become the general manager of the Vikings. He wanted to know if I would consider the Vikings job. I immediately told the new team president in Winnipeg about the call. He told me, "Well, you can't go anywhere; you just signed a contract." I told him, "Well, this is the National Football League. It's home. And it's a lot more money than you are paying me." The response was, "We are not going to release you from this contract."

When he said that, he only succeeded in making me determined to leave Winnipeg. I told him, "Go back to the rest of the people on the management committee and see what they think about all this."

Well, it worked out and I was released from the contract by the committee. I was free to leave if I wanted to.

There were a lot of things about the Minnesota franchise that felt right at the time. I knew Jim Finks from his days in Calgary. In my last three years in Winnipeg, I was also the general manager of the team. Jim and I had many interactions during that time and were involved in a lot of league matters, through which we got to know each other well.

The timing of this was good. We had been in Winnipeg for 14 years. The kids were getting older. My wife was very active with the family and really wanted the kids to go to school in Minnesota. We had both attended the University of Minnesota.

The call from Finks had come from out of the blue. Van Brocklin's dismissal was interesting, but I hadn't considered they'd be interested in me replacing him. I got Jim's call only a day or so after Norm was gone, so I really hadn't had a chance to give it any thought.

I told Jim when he called that I would need some time to think it over. The plan was for me to come to the Twin Cities to discuss it further. I went to talk with him, and we spent four or five hours going over a variety of things, including the roster of players. If I took the job, he told me that I would have the authority to make the roster changes I thought necessary. From time to time, Jim would say, "You have to get rid of this player. He is trouble," and my response was always, "Yeah, but can he play?" If Jim's response was, "Yes, he can play, but he is trouble," I would say, "Well, let me take care of that. If he can play, I will handle the rest of it. If he can play, we will keep him. We will figure it out and find a way to make it work. If he can play, then it is my job to make it work."

After meeting with Jim, I told him that I would have to talk to my wife. I knew Pat was all in favor of coming back to Minnesota, but I had a good thing going in Canada. I knew that if I took the new job in Minnesota, in a short time I could be out on the street and looking for a job.

Security is one thing, but confidence is something else. You have to have confidence in what you are doing. I was confident that I could make the change with a team that had not been very successful and turn it into a winner.

The decision to leave a very secure position for another, more tenuous one is a very large crossroad in your life. This was a big one for my family and me. I loved living in Winnipeg. It was truly a great place to raise a family. The schools were good, and we were very secure and happy there. The people were absolutely wonderful. They were the nicest people you would ever find anywhere. I suppose the fact that we won championships helped, but they were just great people.

In addition to all of this, the hunting and fishing were really good. All fall, I kept my canoe on top of my car. If I had any free time at all, I would run out and duck hunt or do some grouse hunting. Canada was just perfect for that. I always had a couple of labs that I was working with, and I would take them along with me. I loved to watch the kids playing hockey out in the cold. I can recall many a time being outdoors watching them and wishing I was playing with them, just to keep warm. I used to curl and played in a curling league, which was so much fun. My family and I lived there for 10 years and were very settled and comfortable. All of my memories of Winnipeg are good.

I had the good fortune to be around excellent coaches and terrific players during my 14 years with Winnipeg as a player and head coach. We won a lot of football games together, but it was time to move on.

8

BORDER CROSSING

WE WERE HOME. WE were back in Minnesota. I had a new career as the head football coach of the Minnesota Vikings, the second in franchise history.

Geographically, Winnipeg is not that far from Minneapolis, so it had been easy to keep track of what was happening in the Twin Cities and with the Vikings. I got the local newspaper, so I had a basic idea of how the team was perceived. Having said that, I had no ulterior motive to keeping up on what was going on other than a purely personal interest.

But it was a leg up, because I knew some of the players' names and what was happening with the team in broad strokes. From my conversations with Jim Finks I was aware of some of the growing pains the team had gone through during its initial years as an expansion team.

Even though they were a relatively new franchise, they had acquired some talent, but Finks was not a great believer in how Van Brocklin evaluated that talent. He thought Norm was a very emotional person, and that sometimes led to him making the wrong choice in player selection. For example, without naming names, the team had a No. 1 pick who couldn't play. The guy was picked because Norm had seen the guy play once—but it was against an inferior opponent. Even though the scouts did not think him a good candidate, he was selected as first pick. Over the course of things, it became apparent that he simply wasn't good enough. It fell to me to release him.

Finks understood that some bad choices had been made in the past. I told him that if I brought anything to the Vikings, I felt it was my ability to evaluate players. Jim and I talked a lot about player evaluations, but there was one thing I wanted to make clear from the very beginning: I would have the final say on player matters. To me, this was critical and an essential part of being a head coach. We talked about that a lot and finally agreed that the final say on any draft choice, release, or trade would be my decision. Without that caveat I never would have left Winnipeg. Luckily, he agreed; he would handle all the administrative work and I would handle personnel decisions.

When I got to Minnesota, we went over the entire roster. He had his own opinions about the players, and we talked about each of them. With some of the players, there had been problems. It might have been contract problems, personality problems, performance problems, or something else. How they played, how they lived, trouble they got into—he shared it all with me. I took it very seriously, but it was just as important to me that I had the opportunity to make my own evaluations of each player.

I felt that I was hired to see if they could play football. If a player had a personality problem, it wasn't insurmountable, as long as the latent talent was there. I told Jim to let me worry about that. If they could play, it would be my job to get them to play under certain schemes and rules.

Early on, one of our best players came into the discussion. Jim was saying, "I don't know if we can keep this guy. He can play, but he is into his own thing. He doesn't fulfill his responsibility with the National Guard. In those days, if a person served in the National Guard, he would not be drafted into the military. He had to go to certain meetings and report for camp in the summers. And if he did the things required, he did not have to go into the draft pool and would not be sent overseas. At any rate, this particular player wasn't going to the meetings and I received notice that he was going to be drafted and be gone. It seemed simple to me. "Go to the meetings," I told him.

One of the things I learned a long time ago was never to ask why. Never ask someone the reason for his bad decision. He usually won't tell you, or he won't tell you the truth. There was no sense in asking this player why he had blown off this obligation; there was only finding a solution to the problem at hand.

I went down to the military people and got it straightened out for him. They told me that if he made up his missed meetings he would be back on track and would be released to us. This went on for two or three years. It was always a question whether he was going to play for the Vikings or go into the army. But we managed to keep him in line, and he stayed with us for the long haul. He continued to be a terrific player for us for many years. We became close and still are to this day. I helped him out, and he sure helped the Vikings in return. Today he is in the Pro Football Hall of Fame.

Another one of our great players was a real free spirit. So free, he had decided one year that he wasn't going to sign his contract. He wasn't making a lot of money, but he had received about half of his salary in advances before he even signed. So the team was having a tough time getting him to sign on the dotted line.

Jim Finks and I talked about it, and we agreed that this problem fell into Jim's department, not mine. But still, I did what I could to help. I called the player in and asked him, "Okay, what's the problem?" His response was, "Well, I don't have any money."

He didn't have any money, didn't have a contract, and wasn't going to come to training camp. To make matters worse, the state had taken away his driver's license for traffic violations, so he couldn't get himself to camp if he wanted to.

I asked him, "What if I can get your driver's license back for you? I don't know if I can or not, but if I can, will you report to training camp?" "Yeah," he said. "You get my license back and I will be in camp." I was stepping out of the coaching ranks a little, but in some ways it was just another part of coaching. I had to make sure it got done for the good of the team.

So I set out to get the license back. I went to the State Highway Department or somewhere, I can't recall exactly, and made the case that we had training camp starting and we had to get this player, one of our best, to camp. I was able to convince them that the driver's license should be returned; they granted him a provisional license that allowed for him to drive to work.

That was all it took. And the money issue never came up again. All I know is that it was very important to us to get one of our best players in camp. I would have done whatever I could to make that happen.

Another time I recall Mick Tingelhoff having difficulty with his contract. This was later, when Mike Lynn was the general manager. When Mick left Mike's office he didn't go out the door, he busted it down. I was nearby and saw him fly out of there in a rage. My first thought was, *Now I've got to go and patch that up*. Mick was the nicest, most mild-mannered guy off the field. For something to get him so upset—well, it had to be serious.

Mick was a terrific center for us, one of the best ever to play the game. But if he had been a linebacker, he would have been just as good. He had tremendous talent and instinct for the game. He had incredible field sense. If we ever had an interception, it seemed Mick would make the tackle. He was always our leader in tackles made after interceptions, and on kick returns, too. Mick was as tough and as good a person as there ever was.

Before I settled with the Vikings, I had tried hard to get Mick to come to Canada. I came down to Minnesota once around Christmastime and we talked about it. I told him, "Mick, if we can work it out, you would have to play on both offense and defense." That wasn't a problem for him; he wanted to do it. Unfortunately, we could not sign him because he had a contract in Minnesota, even though he was unhappy playing for Van Brocklin.

AFTER I ARRIVED, SOME thought there might be a transition period with me relearning the American rules. After all, the Canadian and American football games are very different, aren't they? I never saw it that way. To me, they are the same thing. You wear the same equipment. You have the same ball. The only real difference is in the rules, but for the most part, the game is the same. Football is football. Blocking, tackling, throwing, catching, kicking, basically all the same. The makings for a great football player in Canada are the same in the United States, plain and simple.

The kicking game is a big part of Canadian football, and I always took pride in coaching that aspect because it was an important part of the Canadian game. Some coaches in the US didn't look at it that way. I disagreed; even in the American game, it's crucial, because it involves a change in score or possession. It became an integral part of my coaching. I brought it with me to Minnesota, and I'm proud to say that our kicking teams were always outstanding.

The Canadian game always had an appeal for me because of the kicking game and the strategy that went with it. For example, we used a lot of "quick kicks" in the game. We would punt the ball down the field when the opponents would least expect it and it would play an important part in determining field position. In the NFL, the kicking part was not quite as prominent. But I always have felt this part of the game is crucial to winning—especially having the ability to block kicks. I think it worked out.

When I got to the Vikings, there were some solid players on the roster. Before I arrived, I had the opportunity to watch film from time to time, and there was one player who really stood out to me. His name was Bill Brown. Bill was as good a football player as there was in the league at the time. He was not a big player—maybe 5'10" and about 230 pounds—but he was a devastating blocker and terrific ball carrier. One of the things that really impressed me about him was that he was a great pass receiver out of the backfield. For a fullback to catch the football as well as he did was nothing short of outstanding.

So I knew about Brown coming in, and I also knew quite a bit about Dave Osborn. I had looked at him as a recruit for Canada when he was coming out college at North Dakota. I had some connections there and had been down to watch some of their film but noticed that he rarely caught any passes. I asked about it and was told he did not have good hands for catching the football.

In the end, I decided that Canadian football was not suited for Dave Osborn because we threw the football around a lot up there. But I knew about him and his terrific running skills. I also knew that we had to improve his pass-catching ability. That was easier said than done. I didn't have a drill nor did I know of any drills that could teach players how to catch a pass. It is simply one of those things you are born with. I sincerely believe that.

The same can be said for throwing the football. If you can do that well, then that's an innate skill you have. Sure, you can improve upon already good skills with hard work, but the reality is you are either a good receiver or a good passer—or you're not. And Dave Osborn was not a good pass receiver. Or so I thought.

One day he came to me and asked me for advice in becoming a better catcher. I thought about it for a second and told him, "Concentrate." That was a goofy answer, perhaps, but that's what I told him.

To truly understand what happened, you have to know Dave Osborn. He was focused. He concentrated to the point where he became our leading pass receiver one year. And wouldn't you know, he made himself into a fine receiver out of the backfield. And even though he could take a routine catch and make it look spectacular, as if he put forth a giant effort to just come up with the ball, he learned to catch the football.

Dave is the only player I ever coached who got better as a pass receiver by concentrating. He didn't use the proper technique by a long shot, and I would never use his technique as an illustration for other receivers, but it worked for him, and it sure worked for the Vikings.

There were also some veteran players who I knew, guys like Grady Alderman. Unfortunately, there were some others on the team that I knew of, but who I right away knew were not good enough to play in the National Football League. One thing that you learn in coaching is that you never get rid of a player until you are sure that you have one to replace him who is better, or at least as good. Most of the time, you want to improve at the position. But you never want to get rid of a player without having anyone better to take his place. It is a delicate process, and when I came in we gave a lot of thought to replacing the players who I felt were not good enough to help us win consistently. But that transition took time. It took a year or two to get where we wanted to be, and during that time we had to play with guys who I knew we would have to replace.

Another of the important things when coming to a team as the new coach is to be very careful about instituting a lot of rules. Because when you make a rule, you have to enforce it. You will be called on to enforce every rule that you make. It is easy to make rules and to say you can't do this and you can't do that, but you also have to think about the consequences of the changes. The key is to make the ones that are important. I made a few, and I felt I could enforce them.

When I got there, the meeting rooms were all full of paper cups and ashtrays. The players were allowed to smoke and chew tobacco, and they would spit in cups during the meetings. This was pretty foreign to me because I didn't chew and I didn't smoke. So to be in a meeting and see it going on all around me didn't sit right with me. I told the players there would no longer be smoking or chewing in the meeting rooms.

"Mickey Mouse," some of the players called it. Although no one complained to me about it, some didn't like the changes. At first, guys would occasionally play games, trying to hide a cup from me. But I had to put my money where my mouth was and enforce the rule. It took a while, but it eventually became a part of our team culture. And ultimately I was successful in banning smoking from the dining hall, the campus, and the locker room. Back in those days, the players used to come into the locker room to have a cigarette. That was over, too.

I also advised many to quit smoking altogether. We actually brought a doctor in to talk to the team about the health risks of smoking. He had films with him, and stayed with us for an hour and a half supporting my stand. It gave me credibility and I'm sure convinced some guys that they were better for it and the team was better for the players stopping the smoking. Remember, this was the '60s, when it seemed like most everybody smoked cigarettes. Well, we got most of the players to quit. And I believe that in order to make a rule, you have to be able to prove its worth. You have to convince those who must follow the rule that they are doing some good for themselves or the team.

"We are in Mankato, on a college campus, in a dormitory, in the public eye—we can't be smoking," was my message, loud and clear. "We don't want you to present a negative image of yourself or the team, by walking around with a cigarette in your mouth." Today, that may sound strange, but back then it made sense. And in my conscience, I knew I was doing the right thing.

I set the rules, but for the most part I allowed my coaches to be coaches. I hired them for their expertise, so I trusted them to handle it. Though I was always very much involved in the kicking game. Everything done with this part of the game had to come through me.

One of the big tactical advantages I had from Canada was understanding the coverage game. Because of the width of the field, it was harder for defenses to cover the opponent. As a receiver, I loved it because there was a lot more room to run around, and it was easier to find the open spots on the field. As a defensive back, I hated it because there was simply too much room.

I remember one playoff game against Edmonton. They had a really great quarterback out of Mississippi State named Jackie Parker. He had been an All-American and was one of those rollout, play-action quarterbacks. His style really suited Canadian football, but it was very hard on defenses.

At the time, I was playing with Neill Armstrong, who later came to coach with me at Minnesota. Dave Skrien from Minnesota was also playing with us, and so was Billy Bye. We went to the coach with the thought of running a zone defense against them instead of man-to-man. If we did that, we felt we could better control what they were going to do rather than try to cover their receivers man-to-man while Parker ran all over the field.

By using the zone defense, we could roll over on the field with the quarterback and get better coverage. It worked. And in the process, Dave Skrien made one of the greatest plays in the history of Canadian football. The game against Edmonton would determine which team would go to the Grey Cup. They were ahead by one point and had the ball. They were moving down the field and we were having trouble stopping them. I was playing cornerback and told Dave, "Don't cover your man. Let him go and I will pick him up downfield. You stay out in the flat." The plan worked. He intercepted a pass, then threw a lateral to our safety, who ran it in for a touchdown. The score gave us the victory and we advanced to the championship.

When I got to the National Football League, none of the teams were running a zone defense. Jimmy Carr had been an assistant coach under Van Brocklin. When I arrived, I wanted to retain him because he and I saw eye to eye. He thought that a team could be successful with the zone defense.

There were various versions of the zone that didn't incorporate the whole secondary, and he had a lot of ideas. He and I worked together to a great extent on this kind of defense. Jimmy had developed the zone concept to a greater degree than I had in Canada. So between the two us, we came up with the concepts and started to run the zone defense almost exclusively. The Vikings were the first team in the NFL to do this.

With our tremendous four-man pass rush, no blitzing made sense for us. And with Carl Eller, Jim Marshall, Alan Page, and Gary Larsen on our defensive line, we had a great pass rush that limited the amount of time the quarterback had the ball in his hands. Their talents complemented the zone defense perfectly.

If you can get to the quarterback quickly enough and get him to put the ball in the air in, say, three seconds, then the zone works really well. But if you allow the quarterback to have the ball for five seconds, then the zones get so big that the coverage is more difficult. We understood this, and the defensive scheme was perfect for the personnel we had on the team. I think that's why we had so much success on defense over the years.

There's no doubt that our strength back in those days was defense. We had Marshall. We had Eller and Dickson and Larsen. And once we got Page, our pass rush was truly dominating. When we got ahead in the game, we could play it somewhat loose because of our tremendous pass rush.

On offense, we ran the ball a lot. Early on, we did not have a top-flight NFL quarterback. We had some good players at the position, including Bob Berry and Ron Vander Kelen, but not who we needed to win consistently. That's why I went after Joe Kapp shortly after I got to the Vikings.

I had gone to Jim Finks and told him we had to find a great quarterback. The question was, where were we going to find him? I didn't know, but no team ever wins without a great quarterback, so we had to find one somewhere. I told him that I hoped I would remain in Minnesota long enough to find one.

When Joe Kapp's name came up, I really felt as if he could be the one to help us win. Kapp came to us from Canada. He had kind of worn out his welcome in Calgary, went to Vancouver, and was then available. He had been drafted out of California by the National Football League but went to Canada instead, having gotten a better salary. Jim Finks was the general manager at Calgary during that time, so he knew Kapp well.

Money was the factor, and I'm sure that's why he came to Calgary, where Finks was the general manager at the time.

Canadian football was made for Joe Kapp. He could move around well on the field and had a good arm. He even won a Grey Cup in Vancouver. But personality issues had been his undoing. Some of his issues had alienated people, making him available for us to pick him up.

Going in, we knew that we could get him but that we would be lucky to have him for more than a few years. That had been his pattern, so we didn't expect to be any different. Still, Joe was a good quarterback and we could use him with the Vikings.

Knowing he was not the long-term answer at the position, we brought him to Minnesota, and he was immediately the perfect fit. We had a really tough defense, and Kapp was a really hard-nosed football player himself. It was a great match. He was a good guy and he got along well with everyone on the team. We felt we could handle some of the other things that had brought Joe some difficulties with other teams.

Kapp did well for us, but he had an agent, an attorney, representing him. The attorney took the position that the National Football League contract was not enforceable. He made the claim that the contract could not tie a player to one team but could instead go from team to team. So he came to us and said he wanted more money. Joe was smart, but he had a way of putting you right to the wall. If he thought he had one over on you, he would not give in. He had done the same thing in Calgary and Vancouver. So on the attorney's advice, they went to court over the issue. That marked the end of his career with us.

Joe did a great job leading us to the Super Bowl after the 1969 season, but once he was gone we had to find someone else. Following him, we used a combination of quarterbacks—Gary Cuozzo from Baltimore, Bob Lee, and Norm Snead. Those guys stood in for us, but they were by no means the long-term solution we needed. We had to find a quarterback.

One day, Jim came to me and said, "What would you think if we can get Fran Tarkenton to return to the Vikings?" Fran had been with the team in its infancy, but had gone to the Giants the same season I got there. I told him, "Hey, give anything to get Tarkenton." He was the quarterback I knew we needed.

I didn't know Fran personally. I had seen him on film but had never met him. I felt if we could get him we would be in business. He would become our franchise quarterback. Without him, we were already winning a lot of the time because of our great defense. But with Tarkenton, we would win much more. He was just what we needed to run the offense.

We gave up a lot to get him, but he was worth it. I had not even talked to Fran ahead of the trade, but I talked to a lot of people who knew him, including many of those players who had been teammates with him under Van Brocklin.

In New York, where Fran had been, it was a different world. Players there were really under the microscope. I really admire Eli Manning for what he has done in New York. He handles it so well. New York and Philadelphia are just tough places to play. I knew Fran would really prosper back in Minnesota.

I had certainly found coming to the Vikings to be a perfect fit for me. I knew my family was pleased to be in Minnesota. I seemed to fit in well with the Vikings and I got along well with the team ownership. It was very different from Winnipeg, where I had to deal with a committee. Not to mention that every two years the committee would have a new president, so I had to learn how to work with a new person all over again. That wasn't always easy. Especially since the Canadian ownership was made up of a variety of businesspeople who did not have solid football backgrounds.

In Minnesota, the atmosphere was quite different. The ownership group was composed of five people: Bernie Ridder was a newspaperman,

H.P. Skoglund was with North American Life Insurance, Bill Boyer was with Ford Motors, Max Winter had a sports background, and then Ole Haugsrud. Ole was from Superior, Wisconsin, and was the owner of the Duluth Eskimos back in the 1920s. He was there because of a promise from Chicago Bears owner George Halas, who'd dictated that a Minnesota franchise would include Ole. And as it happened, my dad and Ole had been friends back in Superior.

Finks was really the buffer between the ownership and me. I didn't have to deal with them very much at all; Jim did a great job of keeping them at arm's length. No one ever stormed into my office and demanded to know what was going on. I appreciated that.

Finks did an outstanding job as general manager. He was marvelous at keeping the ownership abreast of everything. They were happy with the way things were going and for the most part I didn't have much contact with them at all, other than Max Winter. I had known Max for many years, going back to my time with the Minneapolis Lakers, and we always got along very well. Max knew little about football. He knew the business side of it and knew how things were done in the sporting business. Overall, I was very comfortable with the ownership of the Vikings, and they were always good to me.

One of the critical things for me in Minnesota was to have a good coaching staff, and I always felt I had a good one. Jim Finks was very supportive and really understood what we were trying to do in building up the franchise. When Jim asked me about my coaches, I first told him that I wanted to bring John Michels with me. There was not a better line coach in football, in my opinion, and Jim was completely supportive of me picking my own assistant coaches. He told me that I may want to consider keeping Jimmy Carr (of the zone defense, of course), who had been on the Van Brocklin staff. I also added some wonderful coaches in Bus Mertes and Bob Hollway.

I was humble enough to acknowledge that I knew some things about football, but not everything. So I made a conscious decision never to hire any of my close friends because I felt they knew what I knew about football, and that wouldn't help me expand my knowledge of the game. I had many friends who I played ball with or coached over the years who wanted to come to Minnesota and coach the Vikings. We might have had a good time together, but I just didn't see how it would help us win football games. We were not in this business to have a good time; we were in this business to win football games. I needed to get people to be with me who had different ideas, different concepts, and a different understanding of how the game is played.

Assistant football coaches are very much like accountants. There are lots of them and they are very good at what they do, but they are not paid to make decisions or judgment calls. Instead, they are paid to provide information. They have got to provide the information to the head coach, who in turn makes the ultimate decision.

People perceive coaches as drill instructors, saying, "Okay, let's get out there on the practice field and try this and that." Well, that's just a small part of it. Everything else takes place before you get on the practice field, with the decisions that are made behind the scenes. And to my mind, no one quality is more essential to being a coach than leadership.

In the words of the famous Chinese philosopher Lao Tzu: "A leader is best when people barely know he exists. Not so good, when people obey him and acclaim him. Worse when they despise him. But of a good leader who talks little, when his work is done, his aim fulfilled, they say: We did it ourselves." I always kept this quotation on my desk. It is outstanding advice.

To a lot of people being a football coach is glamorous because you are on the football field and work every day with great athletes. With that in mind, the head coach has to hire coaches who are in it for the right reasons. You can apply this same thought process at any level, from Pop Warner to high school to college and the professional ranks. If they are in it for the wrong reasons, you have problems.

I had contacts in a lot of places and got to know a lot of people over the years. Through these connections I was also able to learn who the good coaches were and who might be a good fit with me in Minnesota. And even though I played in the National Football League for only two years, I still got to know a lot of people. I also made contacts all over the United States while recruiting for Winnipeg.

Jerry Burns was a coach who I got to know through Forest Evashevski at Iowa. He introduced me to Jerry, and it didn't take me long to recognize that he was a good football coach. It is like any other profession: if you are going to hire someone, you have to recognize what they bring to the table. Well, it didn't take long for me to see that Jerry Burns knew football. In particular, he knew a great deal about the passing game.

I felt the same way that I had when I first went into coaching. I knew that I knew something about coaching but there was still a lot that I needed to learn. A good example to make my point came from a meeting that I attended many years back at a coaches' convention. I was just starting my coaching career, and I happened be sitting at a table with four former Green Bay coaches just coming off of a championship season. I was hanging out with them around, trying to get whatever I could from them to help me out. They started discussing concepts and defenses and schemes. To me it seemed as if they knew everything about the game. I mean, these were very intelligent football coaches. I felt like a dunce compared to these guys and the sophisticated things they were talking about. I kept listening and listening to what they were saying. "Well, if you do this and they do this, then you counter with that." They were essentially playing out a game right there at the table. And I just sat there feeling pretty stupid because although I could follow what they were saying, I wasn't so sure that I really understood all of it.

They all knew everything that you could possibly know about football. They were as knowledgeable and as confident as could be. When I left them that evening, I thought to myself, *You know, I don't know anything about football.* Really, I felt so out of place; I couldn't contribute one single thing to their discussion.

Although, as I thought further about the discussions while I walked out, even though I felt like I couldn't come close to their intricate knowledge of the game, I did conclude that I was way ahead of them with other things. They never talked about the concepts of building a team or how to operate one. They never talked about what you should look for in a player. In the end, I felt as if I knew more than they did about being a football coach. Coaching was a lot more than diagramming and executing a play.

Wouldn't you know it, every one of them—Tom Fears, Norb Hecker, and Bill Austin—went on to become a head coach in the National Football League…and not one of them was successful. They all got the big job because they had coached on a good team and were successful in their roles as assistants. They knew all of the X's and O's of the game. But everything they talked about was plastic. A lot of people want to be coaches and become enamored with the game but they often leave out the real importance of organizing and managing.

From my experiences in Canada, I knew what I wanted from a coach in selecting my staff for the Vikings. I was able to get a very good variety of people who had good track records and who met the criteria that I felt was important for our success.

My coaches were smart, good at player evaluations, and understood that organizing and managing people are the keys to success. And with these coaches and a roster of outstanding players, we had some incredible seasons.

9 EARLY VIKINGS

I KNEW I HAD to find the leaders on the team if I was going to be successful. I also had to get them to buy into what I was doing. The first thing I had to do was to establish an image of the team. From what I knew about them beforehand, things were kind of helter skelter. Norm Van Brocklin had been a terrific player and had a flamboyant personality, but from what I understood there was not a lot of discipline on the team. He cultivated a barroom-brawl mentality, and I wanted to change that image completely. I didn't think it was the right way to win football games.

I'd had an outstanding high school coach who commanded respect, and from him I went to Paul Brown, who was a magnificent leader. When they spoke you paid attention. They had something to say and it made sense. I learned a lot from people like that.

The way things had been operating in Minnesota simply wasn't the way I operated. Things had to change. We needed discipline. When I first got to Winnipeg as a player, there was no discipline. We got away with things as players. We were not held accountable for what we did, and I learned fairly early on that you cannot run a football team like that and be successful. So coming to the Vikings as a coach, I benefited from that experience and had a pretty good idea of what needed changing. We were going to clean up our act on and off the field.

Discipline would set the tone for how we practiced, how we prepared for games, and how we presented our team image. This affected everything, all the way down to the way players wore their uniforms.

One of the very first things that caught my attention was the way the players wore their socks. The first time I saw the team come out for a game, I noticed that every player had a different way of wearing them. Some wore them high, some wore them low, and some wore different colors on the inside and outside. There was no uniformity to speak of.

Then and there I made a rule. Everyone's socks had to look the same. White socks were to be worn over purple socks. They were not to be worn halfway to the knee or not down around the ankles. "We have to look alike if we are going to play alike and be a team," I told the players.

I explained it simply and didn't dwell on it. If I would see them before a game, all I had to do was point to their socks and they knew what I was talking about. It was a rule that was easy to enforce.

It was the same when we went out on the practice field. It was not the time for them to fool around, tease each other, or slack off, as they had been used to. I told them, "We will all get dressed and we will all leave the locker room at a certain time. Everyone will know the time. Let's say we set a practice for 2:00. I told the team, "You can do whatever it is that you need to do to get ready, but at 2:00 we will leave the locker room. I will come out from our dressing room and be the last one out of the locker room. And then we will start practice."

I felt it was an important step in restoring order, but some of the players thought it was Mickey Mouse. Either way, the players didn't have much choice. So we would all line up in the locker room and go out together. Some guys like to get out early to stretch. Well, I don't believe in stretching either. I think it is absolutely the dumbest thing I see players do. So I said, "We will line up and all go out together and I will lead the exercising." We brought in an exercise routine. I didn't want some players working hard at the exercises and others loafing through them, so everyone did them together.

One of the things we did when I first got there was get what we called an Exer-Genie. We used it in Canada and had some success with it. It was a machine with ropes on it that used resistance training. With this equipment, I could watch the players using it and observe that everybody was doing it at the same level. It allowed me to spot pulled muscles and watch energy levels and other measurable things. For a number of years we used this for our warm-ups. When it seemed to lose effectiveness, I went to what we called ups and downs. "Up. Down. Up. Down." After three or four minutes of that everyone was really stretched out and ready to go and no one got hurt doing it.

This routine would work up a little sweat, and the best part was I could easily see if anyone wasn't following the routine because they all had to get down and get up at the same time. I kept my players on their toes, varying the time of those exercises. If it was a good day, we might cut it short or I might do it longer if I thought they needed more. So that took care of any of the nonsensical kinds of things that we saw taking place during on-field warm-ups. In five minutes or so, we were ready to begin practice. It wasn't hard work at all, but it was productive work. It was very different for a lot of players when we started, but ultimately they bought in to the program.

ONE OF THE THINGS that I got from playing, coaching, and living in Canada was the whole concept of the national anthem. I thought "O Canada" was a terrific national anthem. When it played, everybody sang; here in the States, that's not always the case. I thought about the differences between us and Canada. In the United States, they only play the national anthem, for the most part, at sporting events. In Canada it is played everywhere, all the time, for all different kinds of occasions. With this in mind, I wanted our team to evoke its respect for our country. When our national anthem was played, the team would stand at attention. I thought it would set an example around the league, and maybe it would give us a little pride, too.

We practiced lining up properly for the anthem during training camp. I would say, "You have got to put your feet on the sideline. You have to hold your helmet in your right hand. You cannot have your chinstrap hanging down. You have to tuck it in or hold it in your hand. And you have to look at the flag. Now, you don't have to sing, but if you want to sing that will be all right. You might learn something about the song. And you can't be shifting around. You have to stand still. You can't be rocking with the music, you can't be fidgeting or scratching your ass—you have to be still. You can't be chewing gum either."

I continued, "Look, I'm old school on this. I happened to have been in the service during the war. I believe in our country. I believe in our national anthem and I believe in respect—respect for our country and respect for our flag. Now, you don't have to feel like I feel, but you do have to act how I act."

Then I made Carl Eller our sergeant at arms. I said to him, "Carl, you are going to be our inspector general." Carl had been in the military, so he knew what was expected. I said to him, "You get everyone in line and make sure we all do it properly." He would go up and down the line while we practiced, making sure everyone was doing it the right way. He wouldn't allow jittering or looking for airplanes flying overhead. He took on his role in fine fashion.

I wouldn't do this at every practice, but we did do it twice a year, every year. I had a strategy with it. We would practice standing for the anthem on days that they figured we would be doing wind sprints at the end of practice or something else I knew they didn't like to do. I would say after practice, "Well, today instead of the wind sprints, we are going to practice standing for the national anthem." They were all for it then. And when the rookies came in, the veteran players would teach them how to do it.

Soon after, I started getting letters and comments from people, especially from people from my vintage who had served in the military. They thought our team's behavior was great. Not all the fans got to see it, though; some television stations would go to a commercial so the fans watching never saw the anthem. I didn't like that one bit.

I recall one time we were playing in Buffalo and I guess they didn't have a commercial to show, so we were on television for all the viewers to see, standing at attention for the national anthem. I remember it was snowing, a really wintry day in Buffalo. I told the players, "Okay, we are all going to wear the outdoor capes when the anthem is played or none of us will wear them." Well, some wanted to wear them and some didn't, so I told them, "When they play the national anthem, throw the capes off and stand at attention. I don't care if it is raining or snowing or what. This we will all do the same." And we did.

We were on one side of the field and Buffalo was on the other, and the cameras caught both teams during the anthem. It provided quite a contrast. Buffalo was all huddled up, half were barely standing, some not even paying attention, some with capes or helmets on, others not. The contrast was stark, and people reacted.

I got a ton of letters from fans praising us for our respect for the flag and country. The league office got a lot of letters also. I learned later that there were people upset because what we did was a disservice to Buffalo. We made them look bad, unpatriotic even. The league heard about it, and because of what happened, the commissioner's office sent a memorandum suggesting that all teams utilize the "Vikings formation" during the playing of the national anthem.

Well, to a lot of coaches, this was an affront. I'm sure they thought, *Here we are, we're trying to win football games and now we have to spend our time on this Vikings formation, or whatever they call it?* Needless to say, it didn't go over very well around the league with the other teams. I remember the Bears came here to play once when Mike Ditka was their coach. He had been getting a lot of heat because he was sort of a nonconformist anyway. He wasn't very happy about any of it. I told our players that because of the publicity this was getting, I would guarantee them that when the anthem was played, they would be on camera. The cameraman would go right down the line. I said, "Sing if you want to, or just mouth the words." Well, that is exactly what happened. We were on film everywhere.

Then we had another incident before a nationally televised game. The timing sheet we were provided had the national anthem being played before we got out on the field. This was different from past games; we had always been on the field when it was played at home.

I told the network people that we wanted to be on the field for the anthem, and they said, "Well, we aren't going to televise it anyway, so it doesn't matter." I told them it mattered to us; their schedule was not going to work for the Vikings. The producers went back to the brass in New York, or wherever these decisions are made. They told me it was a no-go; I had to follow the script. They wouldn't buck what their network told them to do.

It was getting interesting. I told them, "Look, you do whatever you want to do, but if you are not going to play the national anthem, then we are going to line up and sing it ourselves before the game."

"You can't do that," they said.

"Yes we can, and we will," I shot back at them. "And you know what else? Every single person in the stands is going to stand up and sing it with us."

I was having a little fun with them, but they didn't know it. They were going absolutely nuts. Word leaked out about what we planned to do, and it became chaos. Then I got a call from New York, the big bosses. I told them the same thing I'd told the local network. In the end, we reached a compromise. The anthem was played—with both teams on the field—but it was not televised live. Instead, they played it later in the broadcast.

I think I got a telegram or letter from every service organization in the country. It was unbelievable. And I guess NBC got absolutely bombarded. People from all over the country contacted me. We had made our point, and even our players took pride in what we set out to accomplish. The pride had returned to our team and our players, and it carried over into other arenas. *"Hey, spit your gum out." "Hey, stand up straight. This is how we do things around here."* It meant something to the players.

It was a little thing with a big impact. And above all else, it brought us unity. You only have so many things you can do to bring an entire team together, and this was one that mattered.

IN DEVELOPING MY OWN coaching philosophy, I took a page from my early days as a player. When you come in at halftime, what do you tell your team? What does the coach say? The last thing I ever wanted to do was give them empty words. So without ever giving it much thought, when it became my time to say something to the team, if I didn't have anything new to say, I said nothing. I was never a rah-rah sort of guy. If I found a little hook, something that was insightful to our situation, the team would listen. If I said the same old thing, they wouldn't.

Occasionally I might tell them something like, "You must have eaten the wrong thing at the pregame meal because you have no energy out there. Let's pick up our energy level." Or maybe I would go over our penalties and make some adjustments. At times, but not at all often, I felt the need to call down a player.

I didn't do it very often, but I recall a game we played in Cleveland when our safety made a foolish mistake just before halftime. Cleveland had a receiver who raced to the end zone to catch a long pass. The ball was badly overthrown—there was no chance to complete the pass—but our safety leveled the Cleveland receiver with a clothesline tackle. It was a very flagrant foul that gave the Browns the ball on our 1-yard line, after which they scored a touchdown.

In my mind, that was discipline gone out the window. Going into the locker room, I had plenty to talk about with the team. I was steamed. I told the player, "First of all, that was not very smart. You knew the situation; there was no need to do that. I am going to do something I have never done before in my life: I am going to fine you $500 for making that stupid play. You may have cost us the game through your actions, but I'm not going to wait for the end of the game to find out."

That is the extreme example of a halftime talk that needed making. I had to make a point and could not let it pass.

I recall another player, a good player, who dropped two catchable passes before halftime, one of them for a touchdown. So when we came in I told him, "Now, you get paid primarily to catch the ball. So if you drop two balls thrown to you, your job is in jeopardy here. We cannot have 10 guys doing their jobs while you are dropping passes. I will not accept that on this team." It wasn't too long after that we released him.

We had another receiver who slipped and fell several times during a game. I told him the same thing the next day: "Look, you are getting paid to catch passes on any kind of field and under any kind of conditions. If you can't find a way to stay on your feet, you can't play on this team. There are no excuses." Excuses don't win football games.

He told me later that it was the turning point in his career, and that he felt he became a much better player. He learned from what happened and what he was told. When he retired, he wrote me a letter and thanked me for what I told him that day: there are no excuses.

Over the course of years, we also made exceptional plays just before the half. But I never once used a halftime talk to discuss the great plays. Praise came when we were all watching the game films; halftime is the time to address the things that don't go right. That said, I'm a firm believer in positive reinforcement. If a player makes a good play, it is important to make reference to it during the films because their fellow teammates likely didn't see it happen, having their own on-field assignments to attend to.

Practice, organization, and game preparation are important factors for any team, but I had a different philosophy on this than many other coaches. Football has evolved so much over the years. You have to be careful not to compare eras. When I played it was a different era than when I coached. And when I was done coaching, another era evolved. Now we are two or three other eras beyond that in terms of how the game is played. Rules also changed over time, and all of this affected how you planned.

For example, you might hear, "You have to be able to run the football. You can't win by passing the ball." Well, whoever coined that way back when didn't foresee the changes to the game. In my observation, teams that are unsuccessful often have a system in which they expect players to fit. The coaches and front office have learned a certain way of doing things and they believe in that way. Maybe they have had some success at it, and therefore the system has credibility for them.

My limited experience during my playing days sometimes showed me that we weren't running the right system for the personnel we had. During my senior season with the Gophers, we had a great team. We had some very good football players and were running the single-wing formation on offense. The single wing was on its way out, but our coach had won the national championship with it, and he was sticking with it.

The single wing is a knockdown power offense, but we had players who could do other things on the field. For example, in the single wing the quarterback is a blocking back, but we had Dick Lawrence, who was better suited for a different offense. We were a good football team back then, but we could have been absolutely dominant.

When I arrived in Minnesota, I used some of my experiences coaching in Canada and as a former player to develop a system around the players that I had. If we had a great running back, we wanted to get him the ball. If we had a great quarterback, we wanted to utilize his skills and expertise. If we had a great offensive line, then we would run the ball more. If we had a great defensive line like we had with Marshall, Eller, Page, and Larsen, we would hardly ever run a blitz.

Coaches can get hung up on what I call the gloried part of football—simply put, the X's and O's. You can go to clinics and listen to these guys talk about systems, guys who think they have all the answers. The problem is, you might not have the players to carry out the design. It's that simple. Having been a player who was fortunate enough to play several positions on offense and defense, I made numerous mental observations that later paid off for me as a coach.

Back playing for Winnipeg, we lost the Grey Cup by a touchdown one year. I had observed things just being a player in the game but I couldn't say much to change our coaches' game plan. The coaches and the quarterback were calling the plays and I was playing wide receiver. I could see that the guy assigned to me couldn't cover me in a week. With this kind of single coverage, if they had thrown the ball to me, I could have beaten him deep down the field, across the middle, anywhere. I'm not tooting my own horn; I just outmatched him.

At halftime I told our coach and quarterback, "Anytime you want to throw the ball to me I will be open. I guarantee it." But I still didn't get many looks at the ball. At the end of the game, we had a chance to win it. We were down by the goal line and ran two plays with no success…and I was wide open on each play.

My point here is it is very important to carefully analyze your team's strengths and weaknesses and identify who you need to get the ball to in order to succeed. When we had Ron Yary playing offensive tackle for us and it was third-and-1, everyone on our team, everyone on the opposing team, and every single person in the stands knew we were going to run the ball behind Ron Yary. I didn't care if everyone knew it. I'd say, "I don't care if they know it. Yary will knock that guy on his backside and we will get our yard."

So as far as all the X's and O's go, I'm not sure what all the analysts are even talking about. Football is a lot simpler than all of that, but I guess it makes for good discussion, good copy, that sort of thing. Football is not as complicated as people want to make it. If you decide that you are going to be a passing team but you don't have a good quarterback to throw the ball, even with all these fancy pass patterns in your head, you are going to fail. You have to have a guy that can deliver the ball, or you aren't going to look very good.

Early on we were a running team in Minnesota because we didn't have a great quarterback. When Tarkenton came back to the Vikings, things changed a lot.

Now, having said all this, it was the practices that emphasized our players' strengths. We were able to pinpoint where we were strong and where we needed work. But I was not a big believer in long practices. I didn't want the players out there without a purpose. We went out, got our work done, and came back to the locker room.

Essentially, there are two practices. There are the training-camp practices and then the regular-season practices. When I first came to Minnesota there were six preseason games on top of our 14 regular-season games. That's a lot of games.

I was never a believer in long training camps either. We were always one of the last teams to open camp. I told the players, "It's your job to report to training camp in good physical condition. If you don't report to training camp in shape, then that is a good indicator to me that something is missing with you."

We generally started camp at Mankato College about 10 days before the first preseason game. The fact is, no one likes training camp. So my message to the team was "Report in shape and we will go from there."

Many teams have their training-camp schedules determined weeks in advance. They know exactly what they are going to do every day. Some of them even have it timed to the minute. Everything is scripted.

I would never do that. If we had a good practice, we may cut it short. If we didn't get what we needed to get done, then we may extend practice—but it would be my decision. And I would never make that decision before we got on the practice field. If something wasn't meshing, I didn't have to look at film to decide if we needed to do it over or throw it out completely. Instead, we'd work until we got it right. But I always wanted to eliminate as much time as possible on the practice field. It worked well for us.

We never scrimmaged even though a lot of teams did during this era. Today, the players' union and the collective-bargaining agreement decide how much a team can practice and what kind of practices it is allowed. They even determine how many days players can wear pads. The fact is they have literally taken away much of the discretion in the coaching ranks. Then again, that's probably a good thing, because if you left it up to the coaches, some would likely practice year-round.

ONE OF THE REASONS I accepted the job and left Winnipeg was because in 1967 the Vikings had some very good players; that really tipped the scales for me. I had turned down the job in 1961 to be the franchise's first coach because I didn't want to build a team from scratch. It seemed like too high-risk a situation for me; I might well have been out of a job before the team meshed. But when Jim Finks called me, things were different.

In its first season, the team had the lower echelon of players to choose from in the expansion draft, and it took a while to build the team to respectability. When I began to take a close look at the roster, I saw they had some players. Bill Brown, now he was a player. Jim Marshall was a player. Grady Alderman was a player. There were 8 to 10 solid players; I could see there was a nucleus of very good talent in Minnesota. I believed the team had a chance to win. Before, I didn't think so.

In the beginning, we didn't have a great quarterback to go along with the good players, but I was working to build up the roster one player at a time. With the Vikings, we had what I like to call "special" players. They were not great, greater, and greatest, as some people like to say—they were special.

Take Bill Brown. As I looked at Bill Brown, I used to say, "This guy is a special player. He is 230 pounds, runs like a bowling ball, and is one of the best blockers out of the backfield I have ever seen. In addition to being an excellent ball carrier, he is an outstanding pass receiver." I mean, you could send Bill Brown 30 yards down the field and he would catch the ball for you. He was a special player. He wanted to play. He had enthusiasm—he would play every day if we would let him. I can't put it much better than to say he was a special player. I'd be willing to bet Bill probably thinks he could still play.

Jim Marshall was another. You can look at the film and it doesn't take long to realize that Jim was a special player. He was a great leader. He was competitive, very bright, and he wanted to win. I didn't get into a lot of philosophical back and forth with Jim. I would just tell him, "Jim, this is going to make us better if we do it," and he would say to me, "Okay, boss. We'll do it."

I had heard all the stories about Jim—his flamboyant lifestyle and late hours. Well, he never brought any of that off-the-field stuff on the field. He is a wonderful guy and was a special player for us for almost two decades, truly part of the backbone of the team. Jim and I are close to this day. He is as good a person and friend as anyone could ever want.

The other ingredient that Jim shared with many of our other special players was durability. He simply didn't get hurt. As a recruiter, when you talk about players, one of the top things that you look at is their durability. How many games have they missed? What type of injuries have they incurred? Are they reoccurring?

As a football player, the greatest strength that you can have is durability. If you are durable and can practice every day and play in every game—and get better as you go along—this is what separates the best from the rest. A player who spends a great deal of time in the training room and on the sideline does not bring very much value to his team. For us, when the game started, Jim Marshall was always on the field.

They key ingredient in durability is not what most people think. It has little to do with the time you spend conditioning. The key to durability is your parents. Heredity is the key. Still, players have to have a great outlook. You can refine good to great to some extent by your attitude. Work ethic is the key. If you look at all the great players, their work ethic and durability are the two virtues they share in common.

I do know one thing for sure about coaching. No matter how good you are, you will never be able to make a mediocre player great by practicing him harder. You can only sharpen a knife so much. A player must have the ability to go along with the durability. As coaches, we may be able to refine a player's ability, and teach him a thing or two along the way, but we cannot improve his durability. (As I mentioned before with Dave Osborn, he improved *himself* as a receiver by concentrating harder and working at it—my coaching had nothing to do with it.)

I played long enough to get a fairly good grip on how injuries affected a football team. I had seen them all: broken ankles, pulled muscles, torn ligaments, concussions. I usually could tell how long a player would be out with a certain injury. I had a good handle on the most common injuries and for the most part how long they took to heal. A player might receive a high ankle sprain. A doctor or the trainer would usually put a timetable on the injury. Usually an injury like it will take four to six weeks because the high ankle sprain is worse than an ankle sprain that is basically a turnover of the ankle. However, it is not quite that simple. A guy like Jim Marshall might get a high ankle sprain and play the following week. And another player might suffer the same injury as Jim and be out six weeks. In my mind, it is the player himself who dictates the timeline.

I like to use Jim Marshall as an example because he is an extreme case—just an invincible guy. He might break his leg and suit up on Sunday and play. He would get torn up and beat up and have a gigantic swollen ankle by the end of the game that he couldn't even walk on. By Wednesday, he would be out practicing again.

For me, the toughest injury to pinpoint was a pulled muscle. I never really experienced that, so I had a hard time figuring out a guy's recovery. That made things difficult for me. Even with all the doctors' and trainers' opinions, the bottom line was I was the guy who had the final say on whether a guy would play or not play. Can he function? Can he play? How bad is the injury? It was my decision, and quite often it was not an easy one. Particularly since most guys were competitive and wanted to play no matter what—even if it was potentially dangerous for them.

I felt pretty confident about tracking most injuries, except for those pesky pulled muscles. Groin pulls were really tough too. It depends so much on the player with a muscle pull. One guy will pull a muscle and play the next game while another will pull the same muscle and be out a month. It was mindboggling to me; there seemed to be no rhyme or reason to it.

Another issue with injuries is pain threshold. I'm not sure I totally understand it. Some people are very uncomfortable with pain while others seem not to be bothered at all. Some people think that every time you have a headache you have to take an aspirin. They have to find some way to alleviate the pain, whatever it might be. But others have the mentality, *Well it's there, but so what?* And that all comes down to a guy's makeup and attitude, nothing else.

A guy's pain threshold can have a huge bearing on his success as a football player. Some will worry about the pain, while others will give their attention to going to work in the morning. But in football, the reality is that every player has to function with some pain. It's a rough game and players get hurt. Pain simply comes with the profession.

Mick Tingelhoff was another of my special players who bent but never broke. A great player does that. They bend but they don't break. You might be looking at some film after a game and see their ankle get turned and then pop back to its place. And then they will limp around a little bit and keep playing as if nothing ever happened. You might not even know it until you see that film.

To the best of my recollection, Mick was one of those players who never had a serious injury. I do know for certain that he never missed any playing time due to injury. He had different contusions, bumps, and bruises, but he was always out there, without fail. If he had not been an All-Pro center, he sure could have been an All-Pro linebacker. He had that quality of competitiveness, along with the quickness and strength it takes to be an outstanding middle linebacker.

I have always felt that one of the biggest travesties in professional football is the fact that Mick Tingelhoff is not in the Pro Football Hall of Fame. When I see some of the others who have made it to the Hall before him, I shake my head. It is a true injustice. He was one of the best to ever play the center position, and he excelled at his job for 17 seasons!

Some who were very good players made it to Canton, but they primarily got in because they were on some great teams that won Super Bowls, in my opinion. Sure, they may have been good, but I will tell you, they were not the caliber of Mick Tingelhoff. He played longer than most and at a higher level.

If Mick played today people would know even better what a great player he was. He would have gone through free agency and would have likely played somewhere else for a lot more money. I was grateful to have him on our team, certainly. He was an outstanding player and an absolutely terrific guy.

When I came to the Vikings I knew I had to sell my program, my vision for the team, through the team leaders. I knew if the leaders bought into what I was doing, the rest of the team would follow. If I would say something contrary to what had been done in the past, I would always notice players that would look to the leaders to see what their reaction would be.

Jim Marshall was a leader, but he was also a great character. He brought an incredible enthusiasm to the game, and his buoyancy was amazing. I don't think Jim ever had a bad day in his life. Even with the physical toll football took on him, Jim never had a bad day.

I could see that in him right away, and during the very first week, I said to him, "Hey Jim, you are our captain." "Okay, boss," he told me, and that was that.

If I could sell Jim Marshall, and he was the team captain, I knew we were in pretty good shape; the rest of the team would follow. I would say something, they would look at Jim, and once they saw he agreed, we were good. He would be the first one out on the practice field. He would do anything you would ask him to do. And he would play harder and with more enthusiasm than anyone.

Mick was the opposite, at least personality-wise. He was quiet and reserved—but you didn't want to get into a fight with him because he could tear you apart. The players had great respect for him. Jim and Mick were two of our very best. There were others on the team who took on that leadership role, too—including Matt Blair, who was a terrific player for us for many years—but Jim and Mick were really influential.

During the first five years that I was with the Vikings, we had some good quarterbacks on the roster who stepped in to fill that leadership role. Joe Kapp came down from Canada and did pretty well. But we never had a great quarterback. Looking around the league and reflecting on past history, the one thing that stood out for me was the fact that the teams that won consistently always had a great quarterback.

In the Vikings' early years, before my arrival, the quarterback had been Fran Tarkenton. He went to the Giants right before I got there. One of the first things I told Jim Finks when I arrived was, "Jim, you got rid of the best player on the roster." I don't know all of the details of the trade that sent Tarkenton to the New York Giants, but I know it had something to do with a clash between Fran and Norm Van Brocklin.

During my first few years, in examining our quarterback deficiency, I would sometimes say and quite often think to myself, *If only we had Tarkenton.… Then we could move to an offensive team to go along with our great defense.*

I am not privy to what happened in New York. I don't know how it all went down, but somehow Fran became available. The instant I heard that the trade with New York was possible, I told Jim, "I don't know what it is going to cost us but if we want to go to the top of this business, we have to have a great quarterback, and Tarkenton can bring that to us. We can design our offense around him and it will make us strong on each side of the ball." And Jim made it happen.

It was a great day for the Minnesota Vikings when Fran Tarkenton came back to Minnesota. I felt really good about it. The fans were happy to have him back, and I knew we could expand upon what we were doing. It was going to be exciting.

Again, I had never met Fran but I knew what he was capable of doing. I saw what kind of a player he was, and the tremendous enthusiasm he had for the game was always on display. His longtime friend Grady Alderman had told me that Fran was extremely intelligent, about as smart a player as one could find anywhere. That was a big plus for me.

In addition, Fran, despite not being a big guy, was extremely durable. Other than breaking his leg late in his career, I don't remember him being sidelined by injuries. In every game he was out there, ready to go. He was a great fit for our team when he returned in 1972.

When Fran arrived on the scene for a second time with the Vikings, we were struggling. We had made the playoffs and the Super Bowl. Our defense was so strong, but without a top-notch quarterback, our offense was struggling. When Fran's name first came up with Jim Finks, I lit up right away. And when he finally got to Minnesota, the whole atmosphere changed.

He brought exuberance and intelligence, a strong work ethic, and a commanding leadership that we really needed. He put the dot behind what we were trying to do. He had great instinct for the game. If you take a look at the greatest quarterbacks, they all have or had outstanding instincts. Well, Tarkenton had them in spades. He knew what to do with the football—when to throw it, when to hang on to it. He knew at the precise moment what he needed to do, sensed pressure, read defenses. He could recognize what was happening at every stage of a play, and he could see the whole field. He really knew what to do.

When you have a player with that sharp of instincts combined with his intelligence, work ethic, enthusiasm, and athletic ability, you will have a special player—and Fran was just that.

Look at Tom Brady, Dan Marino, John Elway, Aaron Rodgers, Peyton Manning, all great quarterbacks with great instincts. I truly believe Fran is the leader in that department. When he retired, he held all of the most important records. He was the all-time leader in passes attempted, passes completed, yardage, touchdowns, rushing by quarterbacks, and wins by a starting quarterback.

He also played in an era that was tougher for passers. Pass blocking was more difficult back then and defensive players could hit receivers off the line, making it tougher for quarterbacks to find open receivers. Rule changes today have opened up the passing game for offenses, making it easier for quarterbacks to stretch the field.

I appreciated Fran so much when he was our quarterback, but in retrospect I appreciate him even more. It may not be fair to compare others to Fran, but I can honestly say he was the best. If you asked me today or 20 years ago or even 30 years ago who the best quarterback to play in the National Football League was, my answer would be Fran, unequivocally. He set the standard. He set the bar, and the rest of them had to reach for it.

There have been some who have surpassed his numbers, but the reality is Fran Tarkenton set the standard for others to aspire to. In my opinion, he is the best of all time.

With Fran back, I felt that the last puzzle piece had finally fallen into place. We were fully capable of making a good run. We also had the ability to develop our players, because they would be around for many years. Today, with free agency, a great or even good player may be gone in just a couple years. Coaches today never know who they are going to have on their roster for the long haul. I can't imagine how frustrating that might be.

Of course, free agency is great for the players today. They make so much more money than they ever did in the past. But it hurts the team in the long run, not knowing who is staying and who will be leaving. My background is in developing players, and I always planned for the long term. These days, coaches have to win right away and keep winning or they are dismissed. They don't even get a chance to develop the team long-term!

I can't even imagine what that would be like. During all my years coaching in Canada with Winnipeg, we focused on building a team and keeping our players for years—maybe as long as 10 years. When I arrived with the Vikings, it was the same. For example, Ron Yary didn't start a single game his first season. He'd say to me, "Coach, I would like to play more," and I told him, "You will." And I'd put him in games for some playing time, and he would just go crazy flattening someone. My philosophy was that you could build a player, bring him along, because we had the time to do it. And of course, Yary became a Hall of Famer.

Another key to building for the future is in the draft. There are no simple guarantees, especially at the quarterback position. We can look back and see a great number of high-draft-choice quarterbacks who never made it in the National Football League. Instead, we looked for other positions. In my opinion, the safest position at which to draft a player is the offensive line. You always know what you are going to get. If you take a highly rated offensive lineman, the odds are very high that they will be a successful player for a long time.

In most cases, after thorough evaluations, the top eight to 12 players rated in the draft generally turn out to be outstanding players, and beyond that, you really don't know.

We did know a few things about picking players who were coming out of college. There are players that do jump out at you, like Calvin Johnson with Detroit. He was one who you just knew was going to be exceptional based on his college play. But overall, the wide receiver position is quite difficult to evaluate. The transition from college to the professional ranks is a difficult adjustment for many.

You can never know the progression of players, especially at the skill positions. We do know that the bigger you are, the later you develop physically. You can go to a high school and see a kid at 180 pounds and know that he is at full maturity, whereas a 260-pounder in high school will be 280 in college and more than 300 pounds as a pro player. The big men develop later on and may play until they are 35 years old. Very few running backs play productively past the age of 30, though there are some big backs who stayed around for longer—guys like Franco Harris and Marcus Allen.

There is also a question mark surrounding defensive backs and wide receivers, because often they may have already developed. It's hard to know with them. The big man will always get better because he will mature later and get faster, bigger, and stronger. Some of the other positions are just harder to predict.

Today there is such a sophistication in the drafting of players. There is so much analysis, it is unbelievable. I always felt that I was adept at recognizing talent, but that came from my experience as a player. I knew what I was looking at. I knew the players' psyches. I felt like I knew the basics about an individual's abilities, so I could look at a player on a practice field, in person, or on film and determine whether they could play. But I wasn't sitting in my office crunching numbers. What I did was for the most part subjective; I had to follow my instincts.

In those days, all we had were scouting reports. We didn't have the tremendous advantage of looking at game tapes from all angles. My method in evaluating players was to look for the intangibles. It was easy to see the size of a player and clock how fast he could run, but those things weren't the keys. In my mind, it is what is in the heart of the player that matters.

In a sport like basketball, it's easier to recognize a "clutch" player, because an individual's actions are easier to isolate. Can the player make the key rebound? Can he hit the critical three-point shot? Can he make the game-winning basket? In football, we were looking for the same thing. We were looking for people who could make the great play at the precise moment we needed it.

I use the word "intangible" a lot. It is the unexplained part of why a player does what he does on the field. Why did Alan Page go the right way 99 percent of the time when he had an option to go a different direction on the football field? It is not something we could have taught him; it was just his instinct. The players just had it in them to do the right thing.

Why did Paul Krause know where the ball would end up? He couldn't tell you if you asked him; he just knew. He wasn't fast enough to overcome the flight of the ball, he just had a sense of where it would be. It is the reason why he still holds the record in the National Football League for total career interceptions, a record that may never be broken.

Of course, you can measure so many things in the game these days, from players' speed, their size, their technique, their catching ability, their throwing ability, to myriad on-field statistics. You could assemble a veritable phone book's worth of data on a guy. But to my mind it will always be the intangible things that make a great football player, what lies in their hearts. We had a lot of players with big hearts.

We drafted pretty well after I got to the Vikings and kept many of those players for a long time. They composed the foundation of some of our great teams. And so many of them were special players, guys who had all the qualities I would ever want in players, including the intangibles.

10 DEEP PURPLE

THE DECISION TO LEAVE Winnipeg and come to the Vikings was without question a major decision in my life. Everyone at one point or another comes to this type of crossroad. The scary part is that oftentimes these life-changing decisions do not turn out to be the right ones. But with the Vikings, I know unequivocally that I made the right call. With Minnesota, I was home.

Coaching might have seemed a glamorous profession to some, but we were by no means set. In those days, we didn't make anything near the salary of coaches today. We made decent money, but it wasn't enough to raise a large family and put some aside. My first contract with the Vikings was a three-year contract for $34,000 the first year, $36,000 the second year, and $38,000 the third year. And that was a $6,000 raise from what I was paid to coach in Winnipeg!

My relationship with Jim Finks was always good. Years before, when we had been on opposite sidelines, Winnipeg had beaten his Calgary team by some slim margins. He'd always say to me, "You are the luckiest S.O.B. in the world." Finally on the same side, he told me he was happy I'd brought my luck with me to Minnesota. It was a good situation for both of us. We operated well together, especially with player selection.

We had a great personnel department, including Jerry Reichow and Frank Gilliam. Both of them were tremendous sources of information.

With Jim, Jerry and Frank, I felt we had a strong connection and made sound decisions. We worked very well together.

Jim and I would talk over everything. We had a lot of discussions and always found a way to work things out to our mutual satisfaction. Jim would sometimes challenge a decision I wanted to make. He would play the devil's advocate, and often it illuminated discussions with our scouts.

Looking back, there was one major decision we made when I didn't use my veto power. Knowing what I know now, there is no question, I should have. We had the opportunity to draft Marcus Allen, and we passed on him. Who knows? If we had drafted Marcus Allen, I might still be coaching today.

At the time, the thought was that Allen was a great runner, but that he lacked some ability as a receiver and a pass blocker. In that case, I went against my instincts, which I very seldom ever do. And of course Allen became a Hall of Fame player, a great pass receiver and very durable. I guess it worked out overall for the best for both of us. And besides, I wouldn't want to be on the sideline still!

Our pick, Darrin Nelson, appeared to have versatility. And although he did not distinguish himself to the level that Allen did, he was still very worthy of the draft pick, a quality guy, and an outstanding player for us for many years. Another running back of that mold was Chuck Foreman, who was as good as any back in the league when he played with us.

I will say this about the personnel decisions we made: There was never a player we released who went on to play well with another team for any period of time. Now, we may have cut or released someone who hooked on and played a little while with someone, but there was never a player we let go who we looked back on and said, "We shouldn't have released him."

On the other side of the coin, we did pick up some players who turned out to be outstanding for us. Paul Krause is a great example. He was one of our best decisions, a true Hall of Famer in the defensive secondary for us. We got Ahmad Rashad from Seattle and he became an excellent receiver for us. Over the years, we found numerous players who helped us immensely.

I recall a young player who we drafted out of Ohio State. He was an outstanding runner who really ate up the yardage as a tough ball carrier. Entering the draft, he was thought to be a great candidate for professional football even though he had not caught many passes and had not been required to do much blocking. Unfortunately, we found that he was not prepared to do a lot of things that were expected of him in the pros. He was a big kid, and his attributes all centered around him running the football. He had been a high school star, and we thought he had a good upside as a fourth-round draft pick. Unfortunately, he had a very difficult time in the NFL. He could not pick up the blitz. He could not catch a pass or block very well at all. All he could do was carry the football—and he did a fair job of that. He just wasn't a good fit for us, or anyone in the league, for that matter. He had no dimension to his game other than running with the football.

His father came to training camp every day to watch his son play. When we played our first game, his son didn't get in at all. His father told me he understood and expected that we were saving him for the more important games later on. We weren't on the same page. When the kid didn't play the second game, his father said to me, "What's the matter? Why isn't my son getting in the game? He is going to be your savior."

I told him, "As soon as he learns to pick up the blitz, he will play. Until then, he is going to be on the bench. I won't put other players as risk because he can't find the right player to block. When he learns what to do, we will use him." But his father still didn't get it. All he saw was that tremendous running ability.

He never played a down for us—not one single play. When he left us, his dad told me, "This is the biggest mistake you have ever made. This kid is going to put you in your grave. He will become a star in this league and you will be sorry for the day you let him go." The kid never did have a career in the NFL.

I FOUND THAT FROM playing a lot of sports I was blessed with the innate ability to identify players who had instinctive qualities— players who could make that quick decision before they even knew they were making it. These kind of athletes know what their opponents are thinking before they even tip their hands.

Roy Winston was that kind of player. A linebacker with the Vikings for many years, he was small at 5'10"and about 230 pounds. He was not as fast as a lot of linebackers but all he did was make plays. He was a great player with incredible instincts. He could line up and in a fraction of a second react; that gave him a tremendous advantage over the other guy.

I keep bringing up Alan Page. He was perhaps the best instinctive player who ever played for the Vikings. If you asked Alan why he did something on the field, made a certain move, went a certain direction, he couldn't tell you—but he knew. And most of the time, he was right and made the play. Maybe the defensive call was for him to fill a gap on one side but there he was in another place, making the tackle. He was so quick and had superior physical attributes to go along with his great instincts.

Matt Blair was a leader and really dominant. I always felt that Matt never received the credit he deserved. He was really outstanding for us for many years. Matt would just swarm the field. He blocked many kicks for us over the years. He just knew where to put his hands, where to position himself. And he knew, to the exact second, when to leap. Instinct—he had it!

I think one of the reasons Matt never got the press recognition and attention that he deserved was he was not on some of our best teams. Had he been around during some of our greatest seasons, he would have received many more accolades. Instead, he was a super player on some of our average teams.

We had some others, such as Jeff Siemon, Fred McNeill, Wally Hilgenberg, and Scott Studwell, who were all exceptional linebackers. Scott was a low-round draft choice, thought to be too slow and small. Of course, he turned out to be a terrific player. So much for scouting. In the beginning, one of the keys for us was to find these kind of players and build our roster with them. We found some good ones. Our defense was stacked, pure and simple.

We had so many special players on the roster. Having said that, however, it is important to recognize that a team is a team and not a collection of individual players or superstars. The players who are team players are just as valuable as your most valuable player. After all, you can't play with three guys or five or nine. You have to play with 11 on each side of the ball, and each one has his own contributions to the game. You can start at the top of the roster in your evaluation process, but in reality you almost have to start at the bottom to get a true picture of what your team really is.

Players like Jeff Wright, who was an undersized strong safety, and Bobby Bryant—who was hurt a lot but when he was out there, there was nobody better in the defensive backfield—were enormous contributors. We had a lot of really strong team players who were happy to be a part of the team. I see this today with my son Mike, who is the head coach at Eden Prairie High School. He has a ton of kids who come out for football. The fact of the matter is that there is little chance that they will all play, but many of them just want to be on the team. This attitude carries on to colleges and into the professional ranks. There are players who will never be superstars. They may never start a game or may never even play, but they want to be on the team, and as a result, they contribute. In the pros, they obviously get paid, but substantially less than some of their counterparts. They like to compete; they like to be in the locker room, among their "band of brothers."

A good example of a team player on the Vikings was Jim Lindsey. He was a role player for us, and a very good one at that; he was happy to be on the team. He played behind Dave Osborn, Bill Brown, and Clinton Jones at running back. But there was not a player more proud to be a part of the Vikings. He simply loved to play. He would do anything we asked him to do. He could cover kicks, catch passes, run—just about anything. And Jim was not an integral part, he was a major part. He was the kind of player that you could call a soldier, like the Milt Sundes, the Wes Hamiltons, and the Jim Houghs. Those were guys who never got a lot of recognition, but they were, above all else, players. They were a part of the team, and that was enough for them. Those guys are as crucial to the team as the Fran Tarkentons, the Ahmad Rashads, and the Chuck Foremans.

One important thing I learned in developing a team is that it is crucial to be able to identify your players and refer to them by name. A person's name is important to them, and you will get more respect as a coach if you call a player by name. If you can use their family name, nickname, or other name that they go by, that's very important, too—and it shows respect. And respect for the players and coaches absolutely fortifies a football team.

It is also important to know when it is time to replace players on the roster. I think we did a good job in our preparation for that with the Vikings. When Fran eventually retired, we were able to go with Tommy Kramer, whom we had drafted beforehand. Tommy was a very talented quarterback in every respect. He was a tremendous competitor and had all the qualities and skills he needed to be a winner. We had been on the lookout for a quality quarterback and the draft provided us the opportunity to land Tommy, who indeed turned out to be a terrific signal caller.

Although Tarkenton played 18 years in the National Football League, we knew he couldn't play forever, and Kramer fit the bill when the time came. But while Tarkenton was there, it was a special time for the Vikings. Anyone who knows him knows that he brims over with enthusiasm. Between Jerry Burns as our offensive coordinator, Fran, and me, we had a million ideas about what to do with our offense—and we had to temper all of them, because tomorrow there might be a new, new idea.

Fran's experience and his input was very important to me. He was a smart player, and above all else he wanted to succeed. And along with that he had some favorite plays and some favorite players, which was

Cultivating a stoic coaching reputation, with the Minnesota Vikings.

Fran Tarkenton (No. 10), one of my special players.
PHOTO COURTESY OF GETTY IMAGES

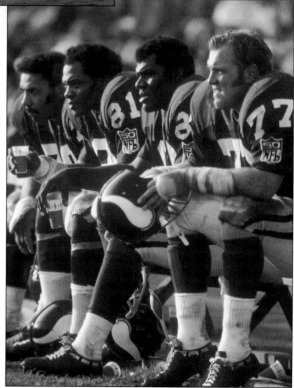

The Purple People Eaters in 1967.
PHOTO COURTESY OF GETTY IMAGES

Left: A mutual respect: with Hubert H. Humphrey in 1973.

Below: At the Metrodome with my sons, (from left) Bruce, Mike, and Danny.

Above: Running practice.
PHOTO COURTESY OF GETTY IMAGES

Below: Me and my wife, Pat, happy in retirement in 1984.

Top: With the Pro Football Hall of Fame Class of 1994, at the Pro Bowl.

Lower left: My Hall of Fame bust.

Lower right: Sid Hartmann has been a lifelong friend— one of the many reasons I asked him to introduce me at Canton.

Clockwise from upper left: Fishing for striped bass with former player (and now judge) Tim Irwin, hunting ducks with Jimmy Robinson, on the boat with then-Vikings player Wally Hilgenberg, and showing off the day's catch with Norb Berg.

Clockwise from upper left: Wildebeests in Africa, bobcats in Mexico, deer in Ontario, and fish in the Arctic Circle.

Top: *Ringing the bell on my property in Wisconsin.*

Right: *Me and my special new Pat in 2012.*

Below: *My wonderful extended family.*

common for quarterbacks. We certainly benefited from his familiarity with many of the players on the team. In addition, we got Bob Tucker from the Giants. Fran had had a lot of success with Bob when they played together in New York. Tucker was good, but he wasn't the blocker that Stu Voigt was, so we had to use each of them differently to complement their special skills. It worked out great for both of them.

The first year that Fran came back, we finished with a .500 record. But to say it was a bad season would not be a true accounting. You would have to go back to each game and give it a full analysis to determine the actuality of the season. For example, the last game of the year out in San Francisco accounted for a loss because one of our players failed to keep the clock running when he ran out of bounds. By stopping the clock, the 49ers were able to get the ball back and win the game. It is often those kinds of things you have to look at when you are evaluating a season. Sometimes one play can make the difference. I will certainly never forget that game.

It isn't very often that I would call out a player for his mistakes, but in this case I had to do it. After the game, we went into the locker room and I shut the door. I went on a little bit of a rant, calling out the particular play and how it cost us the game. I said to the team, "Look, the season is over and all of this is behind us, but when you all come back here next year you better be ready to play smart football. This will never happen to us again, or you will all be looking for work somewhere else." I added, "This football team will never finish with an eight-and-eight record ever again."

In the next few years we won consistently. We had a great defense, and with a great quarterback we had become solid on both sides of the ball. With Fran, we could run, throw, and open up on offense. We would rely on our defense, but we didn't need to lean on them so heavily. It really changed the dynamics of our football team. The whole scheme changed for us. We started running what is now known as the West Coast offense.

It's a fancy name that someone thought up, but I believe Jerry Burns coordinated that offense before anyone knew what it was. And with Fran, Osborn, Brown, Chuck Foreman, and our batch of outstanding receivers, we were tough to stop when we had the football. We dumped the ball out to Foreman and Brown and Stu Voigt. It brought a whole dimension we didn't have before. It was a true evolution for our team.

People have always used the adjective "scrambling" when talking about Fran Tarkenton as a quarterback. Well, the fact is, what he was really doing was buying time. He wanted to throw that ball! He was not tall for a quarterback and was not capable of looking over the top of rushing linemen who were 6'6" or taller. No one could. So instead, he bought time. He had to peek between them. He had to run, step outside, and move around to find a lane in which to throw the ball.

When I arrived in Minnesota in 1967, I was already a successful coach. But I also knew full well that success would not simply come to me if I followed a preconceived notion of how to do things. Running the same system I had in Winnipeg simply would not have worked. I wanted to strongly emphasize the great defense the Vikings had for so many seasons, and build the team up from there.

In the league today, teams that are the most successful are teams that have great defenses. What's more, these teams for the most part are led by coaches who are defensive specialists. (But for them, the blitz is a major part of their packages. We didn't have to do that because of our pass rush.)

Our Vikings teams back then, with our front four, put enough pressure on the opposing quarterback that we didn't have to use special packages and schemes to keep our opponents off-balance. It allowed us to lay back in our zones and control the passing game.

Another area of our football team that was really strong for us was special teams—although I never called it that. For me, it was always "the kicking teams." Whatever the name, they turned more games around than I could count. We worked hard at controlling that aspect of the game. We knew how important it could be in changing the momentum of a contest.

I'm not putting down coaches when I say there are a lot of them who feel they can win games with great defenses, and others who feel their bread and butter is the offense to win football games. Now, maybe they can and some are successful with those concepts, but I always felt a team could not succeed without a kicking game. We were prepared, and it often exposed weaknesses in our opponents' kicking teams. Pure and simple, we often won games because of them.

When I came to the Vikings, I brought everything I had learned from Canadian football back with me to the States. But the most important part of it is which players you choose to put on the field. It takes a special kind. When you have a player like we had in Joey Browner covering the kicks, it became much easier to coach. I knew Joey would either make the tackle or be in on it. He was just a super player, the best guy you could ever have on the kicking team. He was absolutely unstoppable. When you invest in putting your best players out there on the kicking teams, you are at a great advantage. Because some teams do not put their best players out there to cover kicks. They don't want to risk their so-called important guys getting injured. What can I say? That phase of the game was as important to me as any other.

I recall Joey once coming to me and complaining, "Coach, you have me out there on every single kicking team," and I quickly told him, "Joey, you are out there because you are the best." There was no one any better than him, so who was I going to put out there? I made him understand that my mentality was not the same as other coaches.

Bus Mertes, our backfield coach, would develop the lineup for our kicking teams. He and I would then meet and discuss all aspects of our plan, including who would be the key players on these teams and where their assignments would be on the field. It makes a big difference which guy comes in first, second, third, and so on. Chemistry is as important as anything. You have to find the players who understand the scheme and who can execute it. You can't have players running all over the field like a bunch of bumper cars. They have to fully understand their assignments and then carry them out to perfection if you are going to have any success.

I mentioned Jim Lindsey before. He was another key player on our kicking teams. He really loved it. He would get all fired up when we talked that aspect of our game. A lot of times, we did have players on the kicking team who were not our starters, but they had a special kind of talent that we could utilize. Maybe their specialty was covering kicks, blocking them, or holding up the wide receivers at the line after the kick.

Of course an integral part of the kicking teams was our kickers. Fred Cox was with us in Minnesota for a long time. He was a straight-on kicker and was also a valuable team member because he participated in a lot of other parts of our practices. He didn't just go out on the field and kick when his number came up.

When we prepared for our opponents in practice, Fred did a lot on the scout team. He was on the field at all times, assisting in our preparation for the upcoming game. He was naturally a good athlete. He could catch the ball, run with it, and helped out a lot during those key practices. One of the things that few people ever recognized about Fred and how we utilized him was with respect to how many times he would kick the ball on the ground. Fred was a soccer player in college, so he could kick the ball down the field and get it to bounce all over the place. I would guess that perhaps as many as a third of his kicks went that way—particularly if the field was wet, slippery, or it was snowing or raining.

It was certainly in our favor to have the ball bouncing around and presenting our opponents with the problem of who was going to pick the ball up. We were tremendously effective with it. We would have Joey Browner over on the side of the field where Fred would kick from, and he would be downfield like a shot, making the tackle. Fred was also very adept at kicking the ball into the corner of the field. He could regularly kick it within about 10 yards of the out-of-bounds stripe but rarely ever kicked it out of bounds.

No one ever talks about what we did with our kickoffs. Every time we kicked off, Fred would come over and we would talk it over. I know we really messed up our opponents with our strategy. They might have a return scheme planned that they had practiced, and Fred would bounce the ball down the field, screwing everything up for them.

Fred Cox was an integral part of our kicking game. He could kick the ball to any part of the field that we wanted. If I said to him, "All right, they got a single safety back there so we are going to kick the ball to the opposite side of the field and make that guy run all the way across the field to pick up the ball," he would do it flawlessly.

I can recall once when we played the 49ers, who were then defending Super Bowl champions. It was a close game, and we were down by four points near the end of the game. They had two players back to receive the kick and we knew one was more prone to fumbling than the other. Our plan was to kick to the guy who was more likely to drop the ball. Well, it worked. We kicked it right to him, he fumbled, and we won the game. It was with that observation that we won the game. Those kinds of little things are the keys to winning.

Another part of the game that never seems to get attention anymore is blocked kicks. A blocked kick is rare in today's game, but we blocked kicks all the time! Matt Blair blocked 22½ kicks for the Vikings! There are NFL teams that won't block that many kicks in the next two decades, and Matt blocked that many by himself. Alan Page was another great kick blocker, as were Karl Kassulke and Nate Allen. It took guys with tremendous instinct to be able to be in the right position at that precise second to block a kick. We worked on it a lot. And I mean a lot. We knew the significance and the importance of it, and more than ever how this part of the game can be a game changer, so it was a component of our practices.

We had a kid by the name of Dave Roller, who we got from Green Bay. He was a defensive lineman we got to fill in and we called him a "grubber." Well, he was our grubber, and his job was to get penetration, to run over their center. So we would send old "Roller Ball" in there to get their center.

Dave was a really squat guy, and he would get down in there. Then we would send someone in behind him to jump on his back to block the kick. Some of the rules today forbid some of the things we used to do, but in any event, there are always ways to make the kicking teams more effective. At the time, though, those moves were allowed. I suspect some of the rule changes were made because of what we pulled off against the Miami Dolphins. And it just so happened that, at the time, their coach, Don Shula, was on the competition committee and it was him that got the rule changed.

He changed the rule based on a humanitarian concept. He argued that no player should have to be subjected to another player cleating him in the back. It was inhumane! Of course, my thought was *What a bunch of bull. Shula just doesn't want us blocking his kicks!* But being on the competition committee, he was able to get the rule changed.

Blocking a kick takes incredible timing. If the punter catches a perfectly snapped ball and gets it in the air with only a short step, it is virtually impossible to block the kick. But if the ball is a little off, a little to the right or to the left or a little high or low, then you have a chance. It is the same with field goals and extra points: If the timing is at all off, there is a chance to block it. And you have to work as if you have that opportunity with every kick.

We had some good punters on the Vikings—Bobby Walden, Mike Eischeid, and Neil Clabo, among others. We had some very good, dependable punters and kickers for many years. Some, like Eischeid, were good athletes and could kick off as well as punt.

On the offensive side, we had a punishing running game that got even better when we were able to get Tarkenton and solidify the passing game with some outstanding receivers. Running the ball, we were extremely fortunate to have Bill Brown and Dave Osborn for many years. And then we got Chuck Foreman, who was really special at both running and receiving.

I recall playing Detroit early on. We would run Osborn to the right and Brown to the left and one would block for the other. It was incredible. We just dominated with the run the whole game. The two of them just punished the Detroit defense all afternoon. After the game, the Detroit head coach, Joe Schmidt, who had been a great linebacker for the Lions in his playing days, told me, "That Osborn and Brown were just killing us all day. Our linebackers are all beat up and we just hate playing against those two guys. Where did you ever find them?"

I talked briefly about having a plan. Most coaches have a plan. High school coaches have a plan. College coaches have a plan, and most certainly NFL coaches have a plan. I didn't have one. My only plan came from what the players showed me. I wanted to see what kind of players we had. For me, that meant being on the field. I could not develop a plan based on my philosophy from watching film. Obviously you could pick up from film which players were better than others at blocking and catching, but that wasn't what I was interested in. I wanted to see players in the flesh.

However, I will say this about coaching today: with all of the technology currently present, coaches can really see much more from film than we could back then. They can zoom in, slow it down to a fraction of a second, change angles. Today, a coach wouldn't know what to do without the video element of the job.

Today, it seems as if everything is timed to the minute by coaches. Blow the horn or whistle and everyone runs over here. Twelve minutes for this, 10 minutes for that, eight minutes for this. Everything is timed. We never did that. We would work on something for as long as it took to get it right.

WE HAD SOME GREAT teams and played in some terrific games. Unfortunately, as I think back, I can I recall the losses more than the wins. You kind of take the wins for granted, but the losses seem to find a way to linger.

The one thing I didn't do as a coach was go back. I always tried to look ahead, to look forward. If we played a game and lost, the next day we would look at the film, take the important lessons from it, and move on. After that brief review, we would put it away and never look at it again.

In a coach's life, you look at so much film that I never found it necessary to revisit games if it would not provide any advantage for us. I moved on. That was important.

We lost four times in the Super Bowl, and in all my years I never once looked at any of those games. They were the last game of the season, so there wasn't any adjustment to make. I just never saw the point of reliving the past. If you sit around and relive those kinds of bad experiences, they will destroy you. It is heartbreaking enough to lose the game in the first place; I never saw the point in going back.

People always say that our best team was the 1975 team, which lost to Dallas with the controversial call on the Drew Pearson touchdown at the end of the game. But that's easy to say because we never got the opportunity to prove that we were, in fact, the best Vikings team. We didn't advance to the Super Bowl that year. Though I do believe the thing that would have changed the outcome of the game was if we had made a first down on our last possession. We had made a long drive down the length of the field before that, which should have held up for the win. The plays that won the game for Dallas were the officials penalizing Nate Wright for pushing Pearson out of bounds near midfield when Pearson was already out of bounds, and then that controversial Hail Mary play. To my mind, the out-of-bounds call was worse than the non-call on the Pearson catch. Many thought the official should have called Pearson for pushing off on Nate Wright, but no one can dispute that Pearson did make a great play to win the game.

Over the years, I always had a contentious relationship with the officials. I called them all the "Philadelphia Mafia" because most of them were from Philadelphia and were involved in some horrible calls.

The losses were tough, especially in those big games, but nothing was as tough as having to cut a player. And it became even tougher when he had played a long time or if he had been a major contributor to the team. To arrive at that decision was one thing, but then to execute it was really difficult. It was especially tough when it was a guy like Bill Brown, who was a warrior for us for so many years.

We kept him on an extra year. I told him he wouldn't be playing much and made him captain, of the kicking team. I told him, "You are going to be the captain, Bill. You are going to cover kicks." Bill went from a star feature player to covering kicks—quite a drop. But it illuminated the true character of Bill Brown. All he said was, "Okay, Bud, if that's what you want me to do, I'll do it." That was Bill Brown, and he did his new job well. He was happy as could be.

Letting Dave Osborn go was very difficult also. He wound up landing in Green Bay and finished out the year there. But letting him go midseason was hard. I tried my best not to be emotional about it, because cutting players was just another part of my job. At the end of the day, personnel decisions cannot be emotional because they have to be practical. The good of the team has to come before all else.

Most players, especially those who have played for a number of years, become pretty perceptive. They can tell when the end is closing in on them, so quite often it does not come as a big surprise. They know when they have lost a step, are not quite as strong. It was always about the physical ability of a player to do his job. Not once in my career did I let someone go because I didn't like them.

I would like to think that I was always fair with the players. Obviously I liked some better than others, but that never entered into my decision-making process of whether to keep a player or let him go. I think we handled those tough decisions pretty well, and I would hope the players felt the same way. Looking back, I cannot think of a player who was really upset.

I always had good front-office support for any decisions I made. I had a great relationship with Jim Finks and, later, Mike Lynn.

Both of them did their jobs extremely well and worked very well with me. Jim left because, in his contract negotiations, he wanted a percentage of the team. When he couldn't get it, he quit and moved on to Chicago. With Finks gone, Max Winter became the guy in charge. But Max was not a day-to-day man. He needed to find someone to take over the day-to-day operations. I never knew how he found Mike Lynn. I think Mike might actually have put in an application for the job. All I know for sure is that we could not have been more fortunate in getting Mike. He came in and took on more and more responsibility.

Mike Lynn was as good a general manager as there was in the league, and he held the position for many years. He kept the integrity of the payroll intact. He would not pay the new players more than a veteran player, so the veterans never had any complaints in that respect. Today, that has all changed, but back then it was a very important aspect of keeping the payroll in balance.

I know he took a hard line with some players, and that ruffled some feathers from time to time. But he never interfered with my player decisions. Later on, he infamously did when he made the Herschel Walker trade, but he never usurped my authority. We got along fine. I just thought he was a great general manager—not just for us, but as our league representative.

I HAVE BEEN SO fortunate. Over the years with the Vikings, I had some terrific players. I was able to coach for a long time with a wonderful organization and with some of the best management in league history. But every good thing eventually runs its course. It was time to make a decision yet again.

Pat and I had a commitment we made to each other many years back. Our children were through school and on their own. We had accomplished what we had set out to do. It was time for me to make a difficult decision, but I knew it was the right thing to do. It was time to retire from coaching.

11
RETIREMENT AND RETURN

MY WHOLE LIFE HAD been in athletics. Most of my memories as a kid are of playing sports. There was always a pickup game, street ball, or another matchup. Competition and participation have always been right up my alley. I felt good being involved in something.

I spent my whole life in sports, and I never made a nickel doing anything else. I'm not smart enough to invest in anything, and I never did anything else with my money besides putting it in the bank, but we got by. I was able to support and take care of my large family. Most of my career decisions were based on family matters. I tried never to make decisions that were the best for me and me alone.

The most important thing in my life was to have a good home and provide stability. This was my wife's primary concern, too. We had both agreed early on that she would not work out of the home. We felt that it was very important that she be present in the home and there for the children. She was determined to be the best mother, wife, and homemaker possible—and she was. Pat was first-class all the way, an outstanding mother, wife, and homemaker.

Because of this, we were always a one-income household, and my coach's salary, not extravagant by any stretch, was all we had. And that was fine. We never lived lavishly. Indeed, we lived very modestly. We couldn't go out and buy the things that many people did. For many years after we were married, we only had one car.

One of the things that my wife really emphasized was our kids' education. I was never a very good student, but she was. She scrimped and saved and worked full-time to get through college. It was very tough on her, but she worked hard and she made it through. She came from a poor family, so education and hard work were the keystones in her advancement. It was paramount to Pat that she get a college education, and it meant a great deal to her for our children to do the same. "I want our kids to have the benefit of being college educated if they are capable and want that for themselves," she used to say to me. I agreed, and this became our primary goal while raising our six children.

We set some very specific goals for ourselves and for them. We wanted each of our children to be able to go to college and have their tuition paid for, free of any student loans that would put them into debt at the outset. It was very important for us to be able to provide that, and we made it happen.

By 1984, all six of our children had graduated from college. Some had even gone on for advanced degrees. We were able to pay for all of it. With that, our goal was met. So when my youngest son, Dan, graduated from St. John's, my responsibilities for the kids' education had been met. They were all finally on their own. Just like that, my thoughts now centered around another question: *Where do I go from here?*

Having spent some 36-plus years in sports, I felt as if there were other things in life for me to do. Coaching is an all-encompassing job. To do it right takes a lot of time. I may have spent less time than a lot of coaches in analyzing, planning, and watching film, perhaps, but the things I did took up the majority of my time. Sunday afternoon was just the tip of the iceberg; the myriad responsibilities might not have been visible on the sideline, but they were as encompassing as that iceberg below the surface.

You spend a great deal of your time mulling over all of the ingredients in preparing to put a winning football team on the field. It's not something you can simply turn off. I might think about kicking schemes after dinner, injuries in bed, and recruiting while driving to the stadium. It's truly more than a full-time job. What's more, it doesn't end once the season is over. It's truly a year-round job in every respect. It's little wonder that all those years I had spent doing it had taken their toll.

Don't get me wrong here—I have no complaints about any of it. It's what I signed up for and what I chose to do. I found out a long time ago that I can outwork anyone I compete against. I had more stamina and more focus than the majority of the coaches that I knew. Over the years, I encountered a lot of coaches who moved up the ladder and found themselves on a step that they could not handle. Once they got there, they simply could not manage the pressure or the workload.

The job had become so much a part of who they were that they could not do any of the other things they enjoyed. They had no time for their family, no time to golf, no time for anything but football. Some of them started to drink too much, or chase women too much. I was bound and determined not to let that happen to me.

I always felt that I could be successful by outworking people, but that didn't mean sitting in my office day and night. What I mean is that when I was coaching, the thing that was always in the back of my mind was, *What can we do to be better?* That question never, ever left me. It's not something I expressed outwardly, but it was an ever-present consideration; It never left me, no matter what I was doing. *How can we become a better football team? What can I do differently? What can the players do differently?*

To prioritize is crucial, because time is precious. You have to start at the top: *What is the most import thing that I have to do?* That is the question that you have to ask yourself—and then you work your way down to the least important.

Outworking people has nothing to do with the time you put in. In my mind, it's all about focusing one's attention on the things that need attention the most. There were a lot of coaches who were a lot smarter than me. There were coaches who understood the game better. Over the years, I have known plenty of football people who were far more into the intricacies of the game.

Some people have a different way of doing things, and I don't knock their methods. Obviously, many of them have had their own success. I would never want to leave the impression that what I did was the only way to do things. It just happens to be what worked effectively for me.

There are many stepping stones along the way to becoming a coach. You may go from an assistant in high school to the head coach to the college level as an assistant then head coach. Perhaps you're lucky enough to break into professional football. There is a certain level of attrition there; some coaches are not able to handle the increased stress. I have known coaches who have literally locked themselves in their offices and worked all night. I don't know what they did in there, but it obviously wore them thin. And even with all of that preparation, when it finally came time for them to make the final decisions on things, they often had trouble. Or they still could not grasp the concept. Or they had the wrong timing or the wrong information. Being decisive is not always easy. But in professional sports, tough decisions are made every day, and often they are the key to one's success.

Sports had grabbed my attention for a long time. But when our youngest son, Dan, graduated and left St. John's University in 1984, it was time to say good-bye. I said to myself, *Okay, my obligations are done. We had a great run.* And we did.

One of my claims to fame was that I had never been fired from any job I ever had. I had left all of them on my own accord. This was true as a player and a coach, and it was very important to me. I had no scars. I knew coaches who had been fired and they were devastated; their whole lives changed. That wasn't me. I had been on and coached winning football teams. I left with a good taste in my mouth.

But above all of it—the teams, the players, the coaches, the stadiums, the fans, and everything that went with the type of career that I had—the most important elements to all of it had always been my home, my wife, and my children. They have been and always will be my biggest successes.

Knowing they were all through school and could stand on their own two feet, there were other things that I wanted to pursue. In the past, I had tried to shoehorn some of these things into everything else. It was okay, but it wasn't enough. The thing that often got short shrift was hunting and fishing. I might take a day off to go fishing, for example. And I would think to myself, *Wow, it would be nice to do this more often than just a day once in a while.* But it would be a passing thought, because I was not willing to sacrifice what I had signed on for at the time as a player and then a coach. I took a little time in June to get into the woods or on the lakes occasionally, but it was never quite enough.

But even when I was off work, I never really got away from the job. I remember once sitting in a tavern in northern Wisconsin, making trades. We didn't have a phone in the cabin, so there I was, at the bar in town, making trades. We traded our offensive tackle Steve Riley to New Orleans while, in the background, country music blared. It was a big deal at the time, and I did what I needed to do to get it done. Steve is a wonderful guy who I still hear from from time to time.

We had a decent season in 1983, and I thought we had the potential to be pretty good in the future. But I was resolved that the future would not include me. I have been asked if playing in the dome had anything to do with my retirement. Let me say resolutely that it did not. It was never a factor. It was simply the right time for me to move on.

So I went to Mike Lynn and discussed my plans with him. Of course, Mike had to think about the team and what the future would be if I left, and all that goes along with it. He spent a good couple of days trying to talk me out of retiring. When that didn't work, he called Max Winter, who told him, "Give him whatever he wants to stay—more than the highest-paid coach in the NFL."

It never was about the money for me. At that point in my career, I was led to believe I was the highest paid coach in the National Football League. (Sure, at that time, what I was making was not a lot of money, but it was still comfortable.) I told Mike that it was not about the money; it was the lifestyle. I wanted and needed a change.

Mike wasn't convinced. He suggested that we fly to Hawaii to talk to Max in person. Before we went, I went to Sid Hartman and told him, "Sid, you are my very best friend, and I have something to tell you. For whatever this story is worth, I want you to know first." I told him, "There is a big story that is breaking and I want you to know about it, but you have to get on an airplane and come with us to California, where we are going to stop on the way to Hawaii." Sid got on the plane with us, and on the way I told him what I was going to do. The thing is, Sid does not like to fly—least of all across the open ocean. I told him that he could not break the story until I talked to Max first, and Sid respected my wishes and held on to the story. He didn't go with us from California and told me, "Bud, just tell me when. I won't do one thing with the story until you give me the go-ahead."

When we got to Hawaii, Max tried to talk me out of leaving himself. "Is there anything we can do—money-wise, position-wise, title-wise? Anything?"

I told Max, "Mike and I have spent a great deal of time talking about it, and I think he has come to grips with the fact that I am going to leave." Once I knew Max also fully understood, I called Sid and he broke the story that I was going to retire as head coach of the Minnesota Vikings.

Other than my family and Sid, I hadn't shared a whisper of this with anyone else, which meant that from Hawaii I had to make some of the toughest phone calls I have ever had to make. I had to call Jerry Burns, John Michels, Bob Hollway, and the other staff and let them know I was leaving that after 17 years as head coach, I was retiring.

Once all of this was settled, Mike looked toward filling the head coaching position. I told him that he had people on the staff who I felt were very capable of taking over the team. My first thought was Jerry Burns, who had been with me a long time as our offensive coordinator. Les Steckel was also a possible candidate in my mind. He was a very bright assistant who would do anything he was asked to do. I was fortunate to have hired some very young, up-and-coming coaches in Steckel, Mark Trestman, Pete Carroll, and Floyd Reese. These were all bright and very good young coaches, eager to please and do the best possible job. As a result of their capabilities, they each took on a lot of team responsibilities.

Mike did ask me what I thought about the next coach. Without hesitation, I again mentioned Jerry and his long tenure with me and the league. I felt there would be a lot of continuity if he was named the new coach. "What about Steckel?" he asked me. I told Mike that I thought he would be fine. Les had done a good job as an assistant and was obviously preparing himself to someday become a head coach. I knew they were connected somehow.

He asked me directly, "Do you think Les Steckel can do the job?" I said, "Well, from what he has done around here, it is obvious that he wants to be a head coach. But if you asked me about Mark Trestman, Pete Carroll, or Floyd Reese, I would say the same thing. They are all good coaches in the same category."

Steckel seemed to be in contact with Mike Lynn more than some of the others, and therefore I always felt that he was rather close to Mike. I'm sure this had a great deal to do with Mike's decision-making. Les had no idea that I was going to retire, so his connection to Mike Lynn could never be ascribed to an ulterior motive. It was just his enthusiastic coaching approach that seemed to resonate with Mike.

But there was another factor in this that came to light: the connection that Les had with Tommy Kramer, our quarterback. Tommy had some off-the-field problems that Les had helped him work out. As a result, they had developed a good relationship. I'm sure this played into Mike's decision as well. In addition, Kramer and Steckel often worked together closely on the game plans.

Obviously, I felt the decision was Mike's call. I was leaving and therefore ending my involvement with the team's operations. Mike never asked me directly who I would pick, but he did seek my input. In the end, he wanted to be the one responsible for the decision. He wanted to be the person in charge, the power behind the big decisions. And surely, this was one of them. It would not be a committee decision; it was Mike's call and he was going to make it. Eventually I knew what he was going to do and that it was going to hurt Jerry a lot. I really felt for him.

I did tell Mike one thing once I knew what direction he was going. I told him, "If you are going to appoint Steckel to succeed me then you have to retain Burnsie. You have to retain the continuity. You have a good thing in place here, and it is important to keep it intact." I said the same thing about John Michels.

I always felt that Mike picked Les for the head coaching job because of their connection. It shifted the balance of power to Mike and gave him more control, which he did not have when I was the head coach. If Mike came to me and wanted something that I didn't agree with, all I had to say was no, and that would be the end of it. With Steckel, that would not be the case. I'm sure that entered into it when it came time for the decision.

Mike didn't make the call to hire Steckel while we were in Hawaii. He waited until we returned. It was afterward that Sid broke my retirement story. I don't know how it was all engineered, but once it came out, it was pretty big news.

Fortunately, they were able to keep Jerry and John Michels on staff because, as we now know, Steckel imploded. He seemed to forget everything he had learned and went about changing everything. All of a sudden, as the players have described it, he acted as if he were running a boot camp instead of a football team. He had a plan all right, but it didn't work.

Fortunately Jerry Burns was still around to take over down the road. And it wasn't very long before Jerry led the Vikings to just a play short of going to the Super Bowl. And I believe his team probably would have beaten Denver that year and won the Super Bowl.

In the end, Jerry did an excellent job once he was named head coach. The one thing that disrupted his years was the trade Mike Lynn made with Dallas for Herschel Walker. Herschel was a great guy and a good football player, but not worth all that the Vikings gave up. It hurt the organization deeply, and it became Mike's legacy.

I had no involvement in the team after I retired and Steckel took over. However, I still had an office at Winter Park because my contract called for it for 10 years after my final season as coach. My contract stipulated that some of my salary was deferred, so I would be paid for some years going forward. I always felt that I needed to have an office, and the Vikings have been very good to me in that respect ever since I retired.

I mean, what was I going to do at home? I didn't have any other business. I wasn't going to run an investment brokerage firm or anything like that. I knew everyone in the Vikings organization, so it was a good fit for me. I have had access to space, a secretary, a phone, and basically everything else I needed. It was a good place for me to go and handle some of my personal business. But I made sure that I was never interviewed about anything to do with the football team. I had no interest in doing a radio show, a television show, or writing a column—anything like that. Don't get me wrong, there is nothing wrong with doing those things, but they are not for me. I didn't want to be in a position where I analyzed how the Vikings should operate. I really wanted to put all that behind me.

When the Steckel era collapsed, it was tough on the team, the organization, the fans, and certainly me. After all, I still cared deeply about the team. I hated to see it happen. No one came to me during the season to talk about what was happening, and I wouldn't have expected them to. I never once talked about it with Steckel. Or Mike. And I'm glad we didn't. I was not a consultant or a coach; I was retired.

I was off enjoying my retirement, and it agreed with me. It was the first time that I had the summer and fall away from football in many decades. I felt bad about what was happening with the Vikings, but there was nothing I could do about it. As the season progressed and things got worse and worse, Mike came to me and asked if I would consider coming back. I said, "Mike, you have a coach. I'm not going to sit here and cut somebody's tires."

Mike looked at me and said, "Does that mean you would consider it if we *didn't* have a coach? Can we talk about it?" I said, "Mike, don't put me in that position."

Eventually Steckel was fired and Mike came back to me again, this time getting Max Winter into the mix. "Come back for Max," was the rallying cry. Mike was pulling the strings behind the scenes, but they wanted me to think it was Max asking me, out of our personal friendship, to return as head coach of the Minnesota Vikings. Max and I had worked together on and off for many years, going all the way back to my days as a player for the Minneapolis Lakers.

Returning to coaching again was not an easy decision to make. I had been resolute when I made the decision earlier to retire, had really enjoyed my year off. But I was deeply troubled by what had happened to the team in just one season.

I told Mike Lynn, "If I come back, when I decide to leave again, this time Jerry Burns succeeds me as the head coach." I wanted that guarantee. I was told, "That's fine. If you take the job, when you leave Jerry will be the coach."

The Vikings wanted me to return, and I did. I was given a two-year contract (although Max said to me, and publically said it too, that I had a "lifetime contract." But the reality was, it was for two years. I was honored by the opportunity and pleased that Jerry would be around to take over when and if I left in the not-too-distant future. That made me feel secure about my decision and the team's future.

I was never the flamboyant type of coach. I didn't go out and seek a lot of attention. I suppose in some respects that made me different. I was going to return but didn't know for how long. I have been told often that it was perhaps my personality and mystique that kept me popular through the years. Who knows? Maybe it was the distance that I kept that made me unique.

There is a reason for the way I presented myself that I have not talked much about in the past. I don't go out and expose myself to a lot of things or give my opinion on very many issues. Even at press conferences, I shared very little, and I know that was sometimes frustrating for the reporters always looking for that controversial quote or that unusual behavior.

I have always believed that the more you talk, the more chances there are to offend someone. And if you talk a lot and give your opinions a lot, you will soon offend enough people that you will be standing alone—and likely out of coaching. As far as I could tell, there was no need for it.

I recall traveling to the stadium from the airport for one of our road games many years back. Along the way, I kept seeing signs throughout town with the opposing team's head coach prominently displayed on the signs and billboards. The coach thinks this. The coach supports that. The coach uses this product, drives this car, and on and on. It was amusing to see, and I couldn't help thinking to myself, *He's going to be gone soon.* You can't put yourself out there that much without ruffling some feathers. That guy did, and he was gone not long after. Of course, his losing football team didn't ingratiate him much either, but you see my point: This guy was an authority on everything and eventually talked himself right out of his job. He drove this car, upsetting the other car dealers. He wore this jewelry, upsetting other retailers. It was the perfect example of why you keep your head down and your mouth shut.

As a coach, I felt it was important for me to answer the questions I was asked but to never, ever promote myself. I am not and have never been a self-promoter. I wanted the actions on the field to speak for the team, not me. It was never about me. But because of this, I think I gained a mystique for being cagy, mysterious, or unknowable.

I had a knack for never quite answering the questions from reporters or giving them much of a story. "Coach, why did you do this or why did you do that?" they'd ask. "Well, it seemed like the thing to do," I likely said. There is not much of a story line there. After all, how do you write about "It seemed like the thing to do"? I didn't elaborate, and the answer doesn't draw too many follow-up questions. Maybe that was wrong, but at the time it sure seemed like the thing to do.

I am a strong believer that the less you say the better. And the less critiques you make, the better as well. If you talk to some of my former players, you will find that they appreciated the fact that I never dressed down players with the media. I always thought that this approach gave me credibility with the team. Privately, is one thing—and I even did that very seldom—but publically, I felt that was the wrong way to do things.

Some players also appreciated the fact that I did not swear at them or around them. It just wasn't my style. Some coaches do that. Again, I'd never presume to tell coaches how to coach, but getting angry and agitated was never me.

RETURNING TO THE VIKINGS in 1985 was not too difficult because I had only been gone for one season. I still knew most of the players on the team, and I hadn't gotten so out of my routine that I'd forgotten it all. I returned hopeful that I could get the team back on the right track. I felt like we had a pretty good nucleus of players, so I was encouraged. Both Mike Lynn and Max Winter had said the same thing about getting the team back on the right track. Pat was with me on it, too. She was always supportive of whatever I decided when it came to my work.

Now, if we were going to buy a new house or something like that, then she would have plenty to say. But when it came to my jobs, she was my ultimate supporter. She trusted and understood that I had our entire family in my heart when making such decisions. Pat and I had a great relationship. It was never her and me, it was always "we" with us. We always talked in those terms. She really was the best.

So with her blessing and my resolve, getting back to the coaching role again was actually quite easy for me. As to how long I would coach, I really didn't know. My philosophy on decisions has always been not to make one until you have to. This was that kind of situation for sure. There was no need to wonder about what the future would be. The two-year contract was just an arbitrary time period.

As I said, we had a good nucleus of players, and they carried us pretty far. Jan Stenerud was our kicker and he missed three field goals in different games that would have put us in the playoffs that season. That's how close we were. After the last game, he came to me and cried and apologized for missing the field goals. He retired after that season. Jan was a great guy and one of the best kickers ever to play in the National Football League. Along with George Blanda and Lou Groza who were both players too, Jan is the only true kicker in the Pro Football Hall of Fame.

Even though we didn't advance to the playoffs, it was quite a turnaround from the previous season. The team was respectable again. As I looked ahead to 1986, I could see a very bright future for the team. I also knew that Jerry Burns was able and ready to take over as coach. It was the right time to leave, again. And this time I knew the team would be in good hands. The ship had been righted; I was not turning over a sinking ship. Burns was ready to captain it. And of course Jerry did a great job during the next five years as the Vikings head coach.

I echoed back to my previous desire, thinking, *I have done this all my life and now I want to do some other things. I have some mountains to climb, some streams to wade, some fields to cross.* It was the right time and the final time. Or was it?

12 MY HOME AWAY FROM HOME

EVEN THOUGH I HAD longed for retirement, when it finally came, I didn't think a lot about it, I just got to it. I had somewhat of a plan and a little bit of money to do it with. I have said that "You don't retire *from* something, you retire to something. If you only retire from something, then you are lost." And you find a lot of people in retirement who are lost.

I know people who retire and they don't know what to do. They don't have a grand plan, so to speak, to fulfill in their remaining years. I think that definitely takes its toll. When I retired, I retired to things that I had already set in place. I had a piece of property in Wisconsin and I had built a home on it—or cabin, as some might call it. To me, a cabin is a shelter with no plumbing or electricity. So, the word "cabin" is out. Ours is a summer home with television, laundry, indoor plumbing, and all the features of a year-round home that I did not have growing up.

So again, when I retired from football I got to head straight to Wisconsin. I had the house and the nice lake to occupy my time. The kids had been introduced to our lake home growing up, and it really was a great place for us to go in the summer or to escape during other times in the year.

They saw it grow from its original hole in the ground to what it is today. Our place is nothing fancy, but it accommodates the members of the family comfortably.

Over the years, I had a lot of friends who built lake homes. For many years I was unable to do that. I'd owned the land for a long time, but I spent 14 years far away from it, in Winnipeg. In retrospect, that might have been a good thing. It gave me an opportunity to see what some of my friends had done with their "cabins," so I had a good read on what I should and should not do. For example, I learned the importance of having a basement for central heating purposes, and a fireplace. Those were things that I could implement right away instead of adding on later.

As I mentioned earlier, I purchased the land way back in 1946. We didn't build our place until 1969, when I was back in Minnesota as coach of the Vikings. During the year, we all had a good portion of the month of June off, so our family spent a lot of time at our lake home. Later on as the kids got older they spent most of the summers there.

It was kind of unusual how we got our place built. With a large family like I had, most of the money got exhausted. That meant we scrounged to get things done and acquire the necessary things for our new house. Things such as a canoe, a boat, and a furnace didn't come about easy for us. But we had to find a way. And we usually did.

I knew a guy in Osceola, Wisconsin, who did some building, but it was a long way from Osceola to our place. Even so, he said he would like to build our lake home with his brother, so we had to figure out a way to make it work. He couldn't afford to go back and forth every day, and they had their families in Osceola.

I made a proposal to them. On our lake, nearby, there was a resort. They had a few cabins there, I paid for the brothers to rent a couple for the summer. So they brought their families up to our lake and built our place for us. It was a good deal for everyone; the families got a summer vacation, and the brothers got some work. They were able to build our place while living close by.

Part of the construction went on while I was at training camp with the Vikings, so I wasn't able to consult with them on a daily basis. I had laid out a general plan for them—it would need to sleep so many people, have a furnace in the basement and a fireplace, and so on. I told them to take care of the rest. And that's just the way it happened.

They built it and did a great job. I was extremely pleased with the work they did and with the final results, something we have enjoyed for many years.

When I purchased the land back in 1946, the land values were obviously not what they are today. The average income back then was maybe only around $2,000 a year. Even though the war was over, people still did not have a lot of money. The property at the time was less than a dollar a foot on the lakeshore.

When I got out of the service, I lived in a tent on the property while waiting for football practice to begin at the University of Minnesota. It was a long time before I had the time and the money to build anything on the property. Every nickel that went into that house was earned from sports. I'm no investor, but that property now represents quite a bit of value because I have had it for a long time.

Before that land, I never owned anything. When I look at the land, I like to say I own it, even though I never do anything with it other than live on it and enjoy it. It is very special to me that I own it because I never owned anything. Of course, the real value is in how I feel about it. If you are raised with nothing, owning something is important. When I was growing up, the only thing of any value that I owned was that jackknife. It was my prized possession, and I took it with me everywhere.

I bought the original 1,500 feet of lakeshore and the 60 acres. I thought for sure that was all I would ever own. Later, I inquired about some adjoining property, but the owners had no interest in selling. There were four of them, and they could not agree on what they wanted to do with it. When one of them died, two of the other three decided they wanted to sell—but they didn't come to me about it.

One day I was looking down the shoreline and I noticed there was a guy with a transit on the land, looking over the property. He was a surveyor from Hayward, Wisconsin. I asked him what he was doing. He said, "Well, we are going to survey this, buy it, make lots, and then sell them. I asked him how much he was going to sell the lots for. He told me, "I'm going to sell everything for $110,000 and we can make a profit on that."

I said to him, "What if I paid you $90,000 for the land and you don't have to do anything? You don't have to make a road, you don't have to put in power, survey it, sell it, and do the commissions. What do you think?" He thought about it and said, "You know, that might work out."

This was in the early 1970s, and I certainly didn't have that kind of cash just laying around. But I knew I had to go and borrow some more money so I could somehow get that land. We shook hands on the deal, but I had to find the money. My kids were starting to go to college, and football coaching was a good living, but believe me, we did not get rich on our salaries in those days. I was able to get a loan for the money, and eventually paid it all back. With the new purchase, I owned another 120 acres and 800 feet of lakeshore. But my land purchasing wasn't over yet.

There was this little lake nearby, about 15 miles from our lake place. I was interested in acquiring it. By this time, I had pretty good credit, because I always paid back my loans. So again, I borrowed the money and paid it all back. I found out that banks are very anxious to lend you the money when you pay it back. So I bought the lake and cleaned it all up and eventually sold it. It is still all privately owned and a really nice setting.

There was another lake nearby. This one was owned by a man who had bought it after the war and then raised his family there. He was a nice gentleman with a very nice family. The kids eventually grew up and moved away, and he put the land up for sale. I guess he had a hard time paying his bills and had to put the property up for sale, and the lake along with it. Well, we couldn't agree on a price for the property. We went around and around in negotiating, but the bottom line was he was asking too much. I didn't have the money to buy it, but I knew if we could agree on the right price, I would find a way to get it.

We talked for probably a year or more, but to no avail. Then one day he said to me, "Bud, my kids are gone now and I need the money, so we are going to work this out." I reminded him that we'd been talking about it for months on end and had come no closer to a deal. "No, no, no," he protested. "We will work it out. My daughter is having a baby out of town, and when I come back here on Monday we can work out that price and make the deal." I told him if we could work it out, I would be all for it.

Well, he left town to be with his daughter and dropped dead. It was tragic. As for the property, it went into his estate. I was still interested in the property, but it was then his three kids who owned it. They didn't have any money either. I found out later that their deceased father owed almost the purchase price for the property to the bank in Hayward. So the kids then either had to come up with the money or sell the property. If they didn't, the property would go into receivership and the bank would own the property.

The kids wanted to keep the property, but given the situation, they had no choice but to sell. I had the property appraised, made an offer a little higher than the appraisal, and I owned it. With this new purchase, I owned about 400 total acres. When I say it, it is kind of impressive. Maybe if it was in corn or soybeans, it would be worth a lot of money! But it's just jack pine and scrub oak. Aesthetically, sure it is really beautiful, but I suppose practically it is not worth a lot, other than the timber on the property. I wish I could convince the tax assessors of that, because they think it is worth a lot of money.

The value to me is immeasurable in monetary amounts. It is our home and our happiness.

In the end, I truly did retire to something. I have a summer home in Wisconsin and a winter home in the Twin Cities. I maintain both of them, and just keeping up two homes is a project in itself. And as you get older, it gets tougher—and that's what I do, and it does keep me fully engaged and quite busy. I get up every day with things to do and things to look after.

I am finally able to do all the things that I never could do when I was working my full-time job seven days a week, six months a year, and 26 weekends in a row (leaving aside all of the off-season work that comes with being a football coach). I do all the things now that I thought about when working that I couldn't do because there was no time to do them.

Fortunately, the lifesaver for me with all my working was my family. I took care of them, and in turn they took care of me. It made it all worthwhile. Having a wife who could handle all of it enabled me to do my job and provide for the family.

Now that I was finally free from work, I could also ask myself what it was I liked to do. Well, hunting and fishing was high on my list. Now, I could go to Canada and fish for four or five days. I could go hunting in Iowa for a week. I could go to Texas and other places when I wanted to go. I never had the opportunity to travel because I was always working. Sure, I would have a day here and there to go off and hunt or fish some, but I could never take the time that I treasured to really do it right.

Sometimes I would sneak away for a half a day here and there to do some fishing in the early morning—that kind of thing. But never for any length of time. Three or four or five days was never an option. Finally, it became part of my life.

But in retirement, I was still a man who remained busy. And I mean really busy. I like to tell people who are working, "If you think you are busy now, retire." I never once had a time since I have been retired where I have not been busy. In fact, early on especially, I found that most of the time, I overbooked. My schedule was jam-packed. I had so many things backed up in my date book and my mind that I figured I would have to live to 140 to accomplish everything that I had planned to do.

But it worked because I lived by the concept of never looking back. Do what you have to do and move on. Even when I was playing and coaching, I never looked back, always ahead. We had some thrilling games that I have never replayed or looked at again. I never watched any of them. I never saw the point. I suppose it might help at times to convince you that you are not a coaching genius, because there is so much luck that plays a role in wins, but I never saw the purpose in looking back.

I could have stayed and made a lot of money but I didn't. So that's what I turned down to catch sunfish. I was offered a three-year contract higher than what any other coach in the league was making, and the money was guaranteed. And there were some pretty good and high-paid coaches at that time, including Tom Landry, Don Shula, and Chuck Noll. I had also been offered coaching jobs by other teams over the years. People often ask me if I miss coaching. My answer is always, "Only every time I go to the bank."

Seriously, though, I had a great wife and six wonderful children. Sometimes I have to sit down and think about how really blessed I was and am to this day. The family is so important to me, and I am so grateful that they have all stayed close by. All of the kids and all of my grandkids live within about 20 minutes of my house. I attribute this to them wanting to be close to their mother, my wonderful wife, Pat, not me! But I'm grateful just the same.

Our lake place is not just our home, but a gathering place for the extended family away from home in the Twin Cities. It keeps us close. There we can all enjoy the land and the lakes, and it affords us the opportunity to hunt, fish, and just get away from it all. It's a great place to be in the summer months. I enjoy it, the kids enjoy it, and the grandkids and extended family enjoy it. They come in shifts. We may have a few or as many as 20 or more at the same time.

It is a great place with a small-town atmosphere, lots of acreage, woods, a couple of nice lakes, and good fishing. I would be remiss if I didn't mention one more thing. There is an object on the property that stands right out front between our home and the lake. It is a huge iron bell mounted and available to view—or ring, if the need arises. And there is quite a story behind it.

The town of Gordon, Wisconsin, is located near the St. Croix River, maybe about eight miles from the headwaters. It is in the confluence of the Eau Clair River, which runs from the east at Gordon and forms the St. Croix River. The stretch of waters used to be a trading avenue. Merchants would come from the north down the Brule River and portage to the St. Croix and go to St. Paul, or they would come from the Eau Clair River from the east and go down the St. Croix. Many decades ago, in the lumber days, the white pine was harvested in this area and brought down the St. Croix into Stillwater.

As a result, Gordon is an old town that never grew into a big town. I always thought it could have or should have, but it didn't. I suppose in those days some would have called it a big town, but today it would be considered quite small. Gordon was mostly made up of an old one-room schoolhouse surrounded by houses, where most of the people lived. Most did poorly. They tried to raise sheep and grow potatoes but the majority almost starved to death trying. Back then the population was larger than it currently is today. The tourist industry and summer homes have bolstered the population somewhat in recent years, but when I was growing up nearby it was struggling.

Now, back to the one-room schoolhouse. The school was similar to those that dotted the countryside all over the Midwest. After the war, most of these types of structures had closed and the schools had become consolidated. When this school was closed, the building was used as a meeting place during the winters. It was a viable structure used for town meetings, the local garden club, book club, and conservation club, among others. On the top of the building was a school bell.

When I bought my property over on Simms Lake, I drove by that schoolhouse all the time. And I kept looking at that bell. I'd known about it for years, but I only became interested in it after I owned land in the area. I would think to myself what a nice bell it was. And the more I looked at it the more I thought, *Well, that bell really isn't doing anybody any good because it's not a school anymore.*

I shared my interest in the bell with a friend of mine. He didn't have the same interest in it that I did but he listened when I said to him, "We should really get that bell before it disappears. I mean, *someone* is going to get it."

So one night he borrowed his dad's car and we went out. I suggested that night might be the night we finally got ourselves that bell. He agreed, and we got a crowbar and proceeded to the schoolhouse. I had climbed up on the building before, so I was pretty sure that with a crowbar we could get that bell off of the roof.

We waited until dark. We got a rope around the bell and got it off of its mounting and onto a sloping roof. Well, that bell likely weighed 400 pounds or more, and we found out quickly I was not going to hold it. When we went to lower it, the bell slid down the roof and landed on the ground. Fortunately, it landed safely in sand.

My friend and I were able to slide it up some boards and loaded it into the trunk of the car. The vehicle was a Terraplane, kind of like an old Studebaker, and we brought the bell out to my property on Simms Lake in it. We had accomplished our mission and we were just as proud as could be. At the time, we were living in a tent on the property. We sat the bell down on our property proudly; we really thought we had something special.

A couple days later, my friend and I were back in town at the local tavern. Some women who had gathered in the corner were talking. All of a sudden, their voices raised: "Someone has stolen the school bell!" They were going to find out who did it, and when they did they were going to string them up by their thumbs.

Well, out the door we went, back to my property and buried the bell. We dug a hole and put it about three feet into the ground. It took a couple of years before the bell talk cooled down.

Many years later—21, to be exact—when I returned to the US from coaching in Winnipeg, my thoughts returned to the bell. I had hoped it would still be where we had buried it after all those years that had passed. Sure enough, it was right where we had put it—and in good shape besides. We took it out, cleaned it up, and it looked great.

I figured I was safe to dust off that old bell. After all, hadn't the statute of limitations on the pilfering of the old bell passed by that time? I thought so. So I had the bell mounted. And on special occasions, even to this day, we ring the bell. When it's rung, you can hear it all over the lake, but not many people know the history of how it got there—until now.

A couple years later, after I had built our lake home, I was talking to a longtime friend of mine who had lived and worked in the area for many years, Dunk Wilkinson. He and his wife had a souvenir shop along the highway. He was parked along the road across from the old schoolhouse, and I stopped to talk with him.

I asked him what he was doing out there. He told me that he and his wife were interested in some property nearby and that they were thinking about purchasing some timber rights on the land. Anyway, we got to talking away and he said to me, "Bud, I have to tell you a story. You see that old schoolhouse across the road there? Well, there used to be a bell up there on that schoolhouse. I always wanted that bell to bring down to our gift shop along the highway. I was trying to negotiate with the town board to get the bell, but the garden club, the book club, and the rest of the groups that met there didn't want that bell removed. Well, I decided that possession being 90 percent of the law, I was going to have that bell."

I just listened quietly as he went on with the story. "Well, one night we sat in the town tavern until about 1:00 in the morning, and my friend and I decided that that night was the night that we were going to get the bell. So we got our tools all lined up, had a trailer to put the bell on, and we headed to the schoolhouse. I climbed up to the top of the building and the damn bell was gone! I know it was there at 5:00 that same day because I had gone over to the schoolhouse and checked it out. And now it was gone! That bell had disappeared between 5:00 PM and 1:00 AM, and I never heard about it again."

He looked at me and said, "For the past 21 years I have been driving by that old schoolhouse wondering what happened to that bell."

I looked at him soberly and said, "Dunk, I'm going to tell you something in strict confidence. I know where the bell is." I barely finished the sentence before he cut in, "Where is it?" I told him I had it. I said, "We got the bell that night and buried it for 21 years. I have it out on my property, all mounted and everything."

Well, Dunk was a nice guy with a good sense of humor, and I never saw him laugh so hard. "Now I am able to go to my grave knowing what happened to that bell," he told me. "There is not one time that I have driven by here and not looked up to the top of that old schoolhouse and wondered what happened to that bell. I can go to my grave happy."

WHEN I WAS A coach, I always prioritized things in order of their importance. The same was true for me in retirement. The most important things are first. It's always been my family, my job, then hunting.

Too many people in life work on the little things first and then find they never have time to get to the important things. The most important things in your life have to be taken care of first, even though the things lower on the list may be more enjoyable to do. And when you have your priorities mixed up, your time, effort, and money will be spent in the wrong places.

Our place on Simms Lake puts it all together. It was one of the things I was able to retire to that made it easy for me not to look back to what I was retiring from. It has given me the opportunity to enjoy my family more than ever. And as far as that big old school bell goes, well, that's just the icing on the cake.

13 THE GREAT OUTDOORS

WHEN I RETIRED FROM coaching football I made the statement, "There are some mountains I want to climb, some streams I want to wade, and some fields I want to cross." These days, the mountains are tough; I can't climb them anymore. Actually, I didn't mean any of it literally—I simply meant that there were some things I wanted to do that I had not had the opportunity to do in the past. My job and my family responsibilities had taken up all my time.

I have always had a lifelong interest in nature—the lakes, the woods, the streams…all of it. I'm not sure where all that comes from; my two brothers never shared that interest with me. They had perhaps a passing interest in hunting and fishing, but it was nowhere near mine. Considering we were raised in the same household, it's odd.

For as long as I can remember, the outdoors has been a great passion of mine. As a young boy I remember wondering such things as why an ant builds an anthill. Or why a certain worm would crawl up a tree and then become a moth or a butterfly. I became fascinated by things like that at a very young age. I didn't get this from my parents either. The simplest way that I can put it is that I was born with it. I have always wanted to know everything I could possibly know about nature.

Passion is everything. You know the old adage, "You can take a horse to water but you can't make him drink"? Well, the same thing happens with people. Just because I take piano lessons does not mean I am going to become a pianist. I had two daughters who took piano lessons and neither one became a pianist. Just because you introduce people to something does not mean they are going to pursue it. You have to have a passion for it.

All my life I have seen such examples of people following their passion. For example, during the war, the military wanted personnel who would make the best fighter pilots, so they looked for the guys who drove the motorcycles, the fast cars—the daredevil types. They were the ones who became the best fighter pilots because they had the aptitude for it (and the good eyesight, of course). They were born with it, whatever that "it" was. It was something inside them.

I am a great believer that people are born with certain traits and abilities that make them focus in on certain things. For that reason, I think it is important for parents to expose their kids to a lot of different things. Eventually they will hit on something that the kids are good at and enjoy.

I was lucky to know it from my earliest days. I just wanted to be outdoors all the time. In Superior, Wisconsin, the winters are dreary, cold, and snowy. The wind comes off the lake and it can be really miserable outdoors. But it never bothered me. I loved to be outside no matter the weather. In fact, oftentimes the worse the outdoor conditions were, the more I wanted to be out in it.

Snowstorms were my favorite. I would put on my buckle overshoes, a scarf around my neck, and walk outside and into the storm. I would go around a corner and get out of the wind and think to myself how good it felt to be out of the wind. Or I would find a cave or a tunnel in a snow bank and think, *Boy this is really good. I am nice and warm.* It could be blowing and snowing and there I was, out in the chill and weathering the storm. Being out in it always appealed much more to me than being warm and dry and playing a jigsaw puzzle indoors.

I never could plant myself inside to do some type of mundane activity. Some people really love that stuff, though—the jigsaw puzzles, maybe a little reading or wood carving. Not me. Any opportunity I had to be out, I would be out.

As I grew up, I took time to study nature and all its facets. Whether it was bugs or field mice, I wanted to know more about them. If a robin flew to its nest, I wanted to know more about what it was doing. There is an observational component to all of this. If a bird flies over, I will see the bird and I will try to identify it. If a bird sings, I will listen closely and try to pinpoint whose call it is. I am interested in how a robin pulls a worm out of the ground and how a hawk catches a mouse.

When I would walk to school as a kid, I was always looking for something unusual or of interest. It was almost a game for me. I couldn't wait until certain times of the year when I could go out and pick blueberries, raspberries, and strawberries. I used to pick a cup full and bring them home, and my mother would fix them all up for me to eat. Nature's yearly cycles were an endless fascination.

Part of being a watcher of nature is good eyesight, I think. My son Pete, who was interested in a lot of things as a kid, could not see very well. When he was really young and we were all in the car together we would play a game with the kids like, "Okay, who can see the first white horse?" or "Who can see the first black and white cow?" Well, Pete didn't do very well at those games because he had bad eyesight. Once we figured all that out and he got corrective lenses, he was just fine—and his life became more fulfilling. Today, he has a great interest in the outdoors. He loves to fish and hunt and has a hobby farm.

All my life, I have been able to see very well. I had 20/10 vision so I could really observe the outdoors. I would count the number of crows sitting in the field and enjoy the things I might not have been able to get close to just by seeing them. When I got older and was able to actually go further afield—which included taking hunting and fishing trips away from home—my interest in everything expanded.

Of all of my interests in the outdoors, hunting ranks near the top. But because football is in the fall, it interfered with my ability to take advantage of the hunting seasons. (Young animals are born in the spring and you hunt them in the fall.)

The best fishing is in the summer, so I had the opportunity to do some before football camps started in the late summer. But football was an all-encompassing sport, especially when I was in college and the professional ranks. It was extremely time-consuming, and I missed a lot of opportunities as a result.

Once, there was a newspaper article written in which I mentioned missing hunting and fishing due to my schedule. Because of this article, I met Buzz Kaplan, who turned out to be one of the great friends in my life.

Buzz, who owned the Owatonna Tool Company, had read the article and called me. He told me, "If you want to go fishing or hunting, I'll take you. I have access to a plane and we can go wherever you want to go, whenever you want." It was the beginning of a tremendous friendship. We went on many adventures, on occasion to places where no one had ever been before. We once slept in a tent together for 10 days, and always got along. I will never be able to say enough about our wonderful relationship.

Buzz always thought of others first. Whenever I would call him and ask him about going somewhere, he was always ready to leave. The first thing out of his mouth was always "When?" We went on some wonderful adventures together. We hunted in Minnesota, the surrounding states, and even went as far as the Arctic Ocean.

Buzz was so easy to be around, even on long trips. Sometimes we would be hunting or fishing for as long as 10 days and Buzz never complained. He was always fun to be around, and was an extremely interesting conversationalist.

One time when we planned to go hunting together and Buzz had a heart attack. While he was in the hospital, he still wanted me to have opportunity to go hunting. He was just that sort of guy, putting others' needs before his own. Over the years, we had some pretty interesting—and sometimes rather harrowing—experiences as we hunted and fished together. He was a wonderful friend and a good person. Buzz died in a plane crash several years ago, and I still miss him terribly.

EVEN BACK IN HIGH school, before sports dominated my time, my schedule still allowed little time for fishing and hunting. What scant free time I did have went straight to those pursuits, so the casualty ended up being dating.

At the time, I never knew a girl or had a girl who was interested in what I was interested in. They wanted to go to the local drugstore and sit at the soda fountain to have a chocolate soda and talk and gossip and giggle—or whatever else they seemingly did. That simply didn't appeal to me. On Friday nights I was busy playing football or basketball, and then Saturday and Sunday I was gone. I might be out in the woods or near the water. Wherever I could be to get out into nature. The biggest source of frustration for me was that, without a car, there was only so far I could explore.

With the winters we had, I didn't always have the opportunity to get out and hunt as much as I would have liked. Usually, it was that I couldn't find anyone to go with, but sometimes it was transportation. Sometimes my dad would drive me several miles out of town, leaving me to spend the day out in the woods, and then pick me up in the late afternoon.

Unfortunately, I couldn't spend every minute hunting. I might have if I could have gotten away with it. But I still had to go to school. I still had to practice and go to sports activities. I had a family, a good home, and I enjoyed that part of my life, too. I spent a little time at a local pool hall in my free time, too. But when I got older, my aim was finding a way to make a couple of bucks. This took precedent over hunting and fishing and really cut into my time to do much else.

I tried to find ways to do what hunting I could, but fall was always crowded. And hunting back then was only in the fall. Grouse hunting was in September, ducks in October, deer in November. We would also find time to shoot rabbits and squirrels a lot. Between December and April in Superior, that was really the dead of winter, and you couldn't do much. Maybe we would get out once in a while to hunt rabbits, but for the most part, hunting was nonexistent.

I had a couple of friends that went with me often, as well as a cousin my age who I went with occasionally. But just as often, I went alone.

As a family, we never had a lot of food. During the war, there was food rationing, so meat was scarce on the table. So if we were able to shoot a deer, we would eat the whole deer. Ducks made a nice meal, too, as did grouse or even squirrels and rabbits. In fact, both rabbits and squirrels make good eating if you know how to cook and prepare them. You can't just throw a squirrel in a pot and expect that it will taste good. You have to know a little about how to clean them, skin them, and keep the meat clean. But under a skilled hand, they are very good to eat.

By the time I went to college, I found some friends who were enthusiastic about hunting. We didn't practice on Sunday, so Saturday afternoon after our game we would take off and go hunting. A lot of times we went duck hunting in Morris, Minnesota. One of the guys had a place in Pipestone, so we'd go hunt pheasants there. Because of fall practice and games, I surely spent more times thinking about hunting than I did actually getting out and doing any. There was no question my time was very limited. As I got older, though, things changed.

For one thing, I had a car. There was also so much more information out there on where to hunt, buy equipment, and more. When I was playing for the Philadelphia Eagles, I had some connections and would travel to New Jersey and hunt ducks on my day off. Or I might go over to Valley Forge, Pennsylvania, to hunt pheasants. But the longest I could get away was just a day—and sometimes only half a day.

When I went up to play in Winnipeg, all that changed. In fact, Pat was convinced that the only reason we went to Canada was because the hunting was going to be considerably better! Of course, the money was better, too, but Pat was certain. She was half-right.

There were a few times when I took Pat hunting with me. One of the times was not so pleasant, and she can tell the story much better than I can. And believe me, over the years I heard her tell it many times. When we got married, we didn't have a dime to spend so we didn't have any honeymoon. I can recall telling her that after playing with the Minneapolis Lakers, we would finally have a little money.

Pat was working at Margaret Playground on the east side of St. Paul, so she made a little bit, but not enough for us to travel anywhere. About a month after our wedding, I was in Mankato with the Lakers, playing our last preseason game. We were going to have a couple of days off before the start of the regular season so I said to Pat, "I have two days off. Why don't we go hunting for our honeymoon?"

The main point was we were going to be together and we had someplace to go. The hunting part was kind of a throw-in. I had a friend in Graceville, Minnesota, south of Ortonville and near the South Dakota border. I had heard the hunting out there was pretty good. Dave Skrien who was from Morris, Minnesota, had a friend who owned some land where we could hunt.

John Kundla gave me permission to leave from Mankato with Pat rather than riding back to the Twin Cities on the team bus. So we left on about a three-hour trip to Graceville, arriving after midnight. We had called ahead for a hotel room and got the last room available. It was the opening day of duck season.

Our room was next to the kitchen, and in our room was a vent that adjoined the kitchen. Of course we hadn't noticed that until about 4:00 in the morning, when we were awakened by the banging of pots and pans. Her rendition of that night is much better than mine, but it seemed to both of us as if our room was right in the middle of that kitchen. We had little sleep that night, to say the least.

After a tough night, we got up early and went out to the property. I didn't have a boat, a canoe, a duck boat, decoys, or anything. Our plan was to hunt on this strip of land between two bodies of water. On the strip were some pits we could climb into and then we'd shoot the ducks as they flew over from one body of water to the other. It was a pretty good spot to hunt. We were in a duck pass and they would fly right over us.

Well, when we got there, it was raining. It was not a hard rain, but while good for ducks, it was not good for a honeymoon. We got down in the pit with our dog, Cap. Pat had bought Cap for me the year before and he was a great dog and companion. Early on, a few ducks came by and I shot a couple. It was great.

Pat wasn't shooting herself; she was just along with me. We were there for a couple of hours and I guess we got three or four ducks and I was really in my element. I was really enjoying myself. And then I heard a goose about 200 yards down the slew. I could hear it honking. I told Pat that I was going to go down to where I heard the honking and see if I could get that goose.

Back then to get a goose was not like it is today. If you shot a goose in those days, you took a picture of it. It was at top of the list of accomplishments for a hunter. So I snuck down the slew toward the honking, flushed it out and got it. By then I was really having a great day!

But while I was gone—maybe a half hour to 45 minutes—Pat was in the pit with our dog. On her honeymoon. In the rain. The pit was in sort of a pasture, and pretty soon some cows came by. Now if you have ever been in a pasture with cows, you will know that they are very curious. If they see something strange, they will walk over to see what it is. They really don't have a fear of anything. Well, a cow is an imposing figure when you are down in a pit and it saunters over. To have one looking down at you can be pretty intimidating.

The dog—who had no experience with cows that I'm aware of—was of no help. I guess he let out a few woofs, but that was about it. Meanwhile, more cows began to approach the pit. Pat decided to get out of there, so she crawled out of the pit and started walking to the car...and the cows followed.

Pat started walking a little faster, then a little faster after that—but the cows were doing a good job keeping up with her. She made her way to a barbed wire fence—she was either going to have to get over or through. Again, the dog provided no help. He was more concerned with what the cows were doing than to worry about Pat. Which is when she got caught in the fence.

The cows were now a foot away. Hurrying to get over the fence she had torn her pants. Finally she made it over the fence, helped the dog get through, and got back to the car. But the doors were locked! So she had to stand by the car. With the dog. In the rain. With her torn pants. And on her honeymoon. Meanwhile, she knew that I had no idea where she was.

When I got back to the pit with my prize goose, I found it empty but for the ducks I'd gotten earlier. Eventually I found Pat back by the car. She was not a happy camper, to say the least. Fortunately for me because of her temperament she was a good sport about it all. But suffice it to say it was not the most enjoyable honeymoon anyone ever had. Then again, I had three ducks and a goose to show for it.

It was still raining when I found her, so we went back to the hotel to clean up. We decided that we were not going to spend another night in that hotel room. Pat had had enough of duck hunting, so we headed back to Minneapolis.

I have had so many outdoor experiences over the course of my life that there is simply not enough paper or pages large enough to get all of my experiences in print. I have been so many places. Usually I do not go to commercial camps, but instead I go to places where I have been or know someone who knows somebody where I can use their land to hunt.

I have gone through outfitters to farther-flung places—Africa and South America, for example—but most of the time I like to make the arrangements myself and travel with one or a very few companions.

I like to make my own calls. *Do I want to hunt here or hunt there? Do I want to sit up in a tree or walk over there? Do I want to walk into the river or fish from shore?* It's always more enjoyable without someone telling me where to stand or go.

Hunting, like many things, has evolved over the years. I was recently at a game fair and was talking to some hunters about deer hunting. I told them that deer hunting was the wrong term: it should be called "deer shooting." When I was young, deer hunting was walking through the woods, finding the deer tracks, identifying the deer trail, and figuring out where the deer would come to feed. It was studying the animal and its habits so I could track it down. I tried to think like a deer—and maybe intercept them and maybe have a chance to shoot one. To me, that was hunting.

Today, I call it deer shooting because most people are up in a deer stand just waiting for a deer to walk by so they can shoot it. That, to me, is not hunting; it's target practice. They sit in a stand or a little structure with a seat and wait it out. All you do is sit there with a gun and wait. I'm not knocking it, necessarily, because I do it too—but it is far different than it was in the past. Hunting, to me, involves more thinking, more time out in the elements, and more enjoyment of the environment.

The other thing is a lot of people always do their hunting in the same places. Some people have 40 acres up north in the woods and go there every year, sit up in a tree in the same place, and "hunt." Well, that's okay, but after I have done it once or twice, I like to do it a little differently—get a different view of the land. Since the beginning, I have always wanted to expand my horizons by going to different places.

This is true no matter what I'm hunting. There is a time in our lives when it may be important to say, "How many did you get?" And you can say, "Well, I got three ducks or 10 fish or I got my deer." I suppose I have lived through that stage in my life and am beyond that now.

I just enjoy the experience of going out in the field or being on the lake. It may be in Montana or in Iowa or Nebraska. It may be in Minnesota, Wisconsin, Texas, or Mexico. Going different places gives me a chance to see how other people hunt. I like to see the game in their natural environment. It is vastly different hunting in the woods of northern Minnesota than the Texas plains or the Kansas flint hills.

As I said, an appreciation for the outdoors is either born in you or not. You can't convince people to enjoy fishing or hunting. Sometimes fathers try to do this with their kids with unpleasant results. There is generally the right time and the right place to first make the introduction to young people. I used to go hunting from time to time with some of our players. Once Roy Winston asked me about his son. He said to me, "You know, my son wants a gun. When is the best time to get him one?"

And I said to him, "What kind of a gun would you get your 10-year-old son? Has he asked for a gun?"

"Well, no, not yet, but I want to, you know, be ready when he wants one," he said. I told him, "Roy, he sees you hunt. He knows what is going on. Wait until he asks for a gun."

Roy said, "Oh, I see. Wait until he asks for the gun and then get it."

I said, "No, then you wait a year before you get him a gun."

First of all, I feel it is important to determine the interest level that a young person has in hunting. If there is interest, you teach him or her how to hold a gun, how to shoot a gun—all of the important and necessary aspects of gun safety. You can shoot at targets and get the young person familiar with how to use and handle a gun.

At that age, it simply does not hurt to wait a year to really heighten the interest level. By the next year, if the interest is true, a child will be very eager to get that gun. There is no "magic number," no age that is right for every kid. It will be obvious when the time is right. In my mind, it is absolutely crucial to expose young people to guns in order to gauge their level of interest, but never, ever to force guns or hunting on them.

In my family I have four boys and they have all been exposed to hunting. When I was coaching the Vikings, I used to hunt on some personally leased land of Norb Berg, which was owned by Control Data. I used to get up early every morning and go hunting on this land near the Minnesota River bottoms. Sometimes Norb would be there with me, and we really got to know each other well over time. I always like to say that Norb "saved my life." Football has been a vocation for me, no doubt about that, but hunting was another one—and Norb saved it for me. With its deer and pheasants, ducks and geese, that land was a real haven for me to visit in the mornings.

And Norb himself was a wonderful sounding board. I used to run things by him to get his opinion. He was someone who I could always count on for good advice. He was a really analytical thinker and would offer his comments and opinions on a variety of matters. I trusted him implicitly. Ultimately, I can't describe him any other way than to say he was a good person—and to say that someone is a good person means a lot in my book. He is a wonderful friend and has been for a long time.

Back then, I would get to the land at about 6:00 in the morning and hunt there for about an hour and a half before jumping into my car and heading for the office. I would do this almost every day in the fall. Oftentimes I would bring one of my boys down there with me. On some occasions, I would even take them out of school for a couple of hours to expose them to hunting.

During the regular season, I would take them to practice on Saturday, and then after practice we would go hunting. I had scheduled early practices for the team to accommodate this. Some of the players didn't like it. "Why do we have to have an early practice on Saturday morning?" I would be asked. I would usually have a pretty good answer for the question: "Well, tomorrow you have to get up about the same time to be ready for the game at noon. So this is getting your timetable and your body in sync." Then they would look at me and say, "No, this is so you can go hunting on Saturday afternoon." I guess they had it figured because I had my boys with me at practice, my dogs in the car, and my hunting equipment, too.

Happily, all four of my boys enjoyed hunting, and they have all been with me at various places and at many times. My son Bruce is no exception, but one day he came to me and told me that he would rather play golf. Of course I understood. He had been exposed, enjoyed it, but one day found his passion for golf. We have enough hunters in the family, my sons-in-law included. My daughters have also been exposed, but they have never had quite the same enthusiasm as my boys.

Over the years, I have cultivated a keen interest in various outdoor causes. One, which I took on for more than 10 years and helped to raise more than $1 million for, was the issue of netting fish on Lake Mille Lacs. This was a broad-range issue that I became involved with because I was strongly against gill nets being used by the Native Americans to catch walleyes and other game fish. Not only do gill nets give fishermen an unfair advantage that no one else in this country is allowed to employ, but they vastly deplete the fish population for others.

It is a long story—probably a book in itself someday—but it basically involved a treaty dating back to the 1800s that granted them certain fishing rights on the lake. The matter went to the local courts and eventually became a tremendous political issue. I think most of us are aware that politicians want to stay away from anything that is controversial. It became a very emotional issue, so the politicians shied away, and even the DNR, which has its own politics, was not of much help, nor was the governor.

The issue made its way to the courts, and it was ruled that the treaty was legal. It was appealed and eventually ended with a decision by the United States Supreme Court. And of course, along the way, the process required a lot of money in attorney's fees for court appearances and filings.

The chief justice of the Supreme Court at the time was William Rehnquist. He agreed to look at the case and have a hearing on the matter. It was our feeling at the time that we had a good chance because there were five of the nine justices that were conservatives. Eventually a verdict came down: 5–4 in favor of upholding the treaty. One of the justices, Sandra Day O'Connor, switched her vote; we were convinced she was in support of the cause. The outcome was devastating.

The justices wrote their opinion, and Chief Justice Rehnquist gave a dissenting opinion along with Justice Thomas. The interesting part of their dissent was they really took on the justices who voted against us. They railed against the opposition's votes on an almost personal basis—to the point of literally questioning their reading abilities. That was a surprise to me.

We lost. There were no more appeals. We had spent a lot of time and effort for a cause that we believed very strongly in, only to lose in the end. To this day, it is still a huge issue on Lake Mille Lacs.

There are so many outdoor groups doing great work for the environment—Trout Unlimited, Ducks Unlimited, Deer Hunters Association, Delta Water Fowl, among many more. Some of them provide more wetland activities, provide more hunting opportunities, plant more fish. All of them are very worthwhile causes. There are two in particular with which I have been closely involved while living here in Minnesota. Both of them are close to my heart.

Most hunters—and in fact, most anyone who has spent any time outdoors—has probably heard of TIP (Turn In Poachers). If you see somebody who is violating a hunting or fishing law, there is a phone number that you can call at the Division of Natural Resources, and they will send someone out to investigate your call to correct the situation. Maybe someone has caught more than his limit of fish or is hunting out of season. TIP provides safeguards for our hunting and fishing laws, which are extremely important in the management of our outdoor resources and very important to the Department of Natural Resources, which oversees them.

For many years we did not have anything like this in Minnesota. One day I got a call from a retired army colonel and a big Vikings fan who lived in New Mexico. He had heard me say in an interview that I missed the hunting seasons because of my responsibilities as coach of the Vikings. Once my football responsibilities ended, often in January after the playoffs, the hunting seasons had ended. He told me that if I was interested, they had a season down there in the winter during which they could hunt Barbary sheep, an imported species. And they had enough of them down there where they actually had a hunting season for them. He had a big ranch and invited me down to hunt on his land as his guest.

Now, this was right up my alley, so I jumped on it. As soon as the football season was over, I went down to see him. He wasn't a hunter himself, but he hooked me up with a local game warden to go out and hunt. In the course of our hunting and conversation, the warden told me about the problem they were having with elk getting poached out of season. So they advertised and offered a reward for anyone who turned in someone who was hunting illegally. He told me that this simple program stopped their problem immediately. This got my wheels spinning.

When I got back to Minnesota I called Joe Alexander, the DNR commissioner, and told him what they were doing down in New Mexico. He told me that he had heard of the program, but they didn't have any money to pay the reward. I suggested that we find a way to raise the money and he agreed to institute the program.

And how do you raise the money? Well, you have banquets. I can't tell you how many banquets we put together to raise the money for the program. There were auctions, silent auctions, live auctions.... We got donations from local sporting good stores and were able to raise a fair amount of cash to get the program off the ground.

I do not want to take the credit for the program, but I am proud of the fact that I was one of its originators. Today, it is the most effective tool the DNR has in place to control violators of our game laws.

Once we got it going effectively in Minnesota, many states followed. Today, each state is involved in one form or another.

Another organization that I have long been involved with is Pheasants Forever, a program that provides and preserves natural habitat for pheasants. I helped found the group and it has grown nationwide. It is a cause that I believe in deeply, and the organization has done great work over the years.

As I look at the measure of my life, I know for certain it has been more than just sports. The outdoors has always been a key component in my life, and I like to think that I have dedicated a good amount of my time and efforts not only to enjoying and appreciating nature, but helping to preserve it for future generations.

MY SPECIAL ANIMALS

OVER THE COURSE OF my life, I have had some great dogs who were wonderful companions—truly "man's best friend" to me through the years.

Growing up, it seemed as if we always had a stray dog. Back then, there were no fences or leash laws, so we never had dogs for long periods of time. There was Duty. Boots. Skippy. And many other animals, too. I used to catch field mice, garter snakes, and other animals. If I found a baby bird on the ground, I would take it in and raise it until it could fly. I have always been interested in that kind of thing.

I had a pet squirrel at the University of Minnesota that stayed in my room—Sid knows about that one. I would open the window in the morning and it would go out and come back in. I found it as a baby, fed it, and took care of it. It would curl up and go to sleep and I would put it in my dresser drawer. We got pretty attached.

I raised it all spring while I was living at the fraternity house. During the day, it would sometimes scare the cleaning lady half to death. She would come in and it would jump right on her. Suffice it to say, she was not happy about my pet.

When summer came, I brought the squirrel home. It traveled in the glove compartment of my car and I brought it right into the kitchen of our house. My dad was not very fond of my new friend. It stayed on a screened-in back porch. Once went after it with a broom, which resulted in him getting his finger bitten. That was the end of my companion's kitchen pass.

We had more hospitable surroundings on my lake property, where we slept in a tent. There was an open flap on the front of the tent and one morning, just as the sun was coming up, I heard this loud swooping noise coming from outside the tent. I looked out and saw an eagle descend and grab my squirrel. It was a painful ending to a great relationship.

Having enjoyed pets all my life, I couldn't wait to be in a position to one day have my own dog. Pat knew this. We had talked about having a family someday—and of course our family would have a dog, too. Then lo and behold, one day right around Christmastime, while we were still in college, she bought me a dog. Cap was a great dog, a beautiful yellow lab and a marvelous friend. He was also a terrific hunting dog.

One morning I looked out in the front yard and saw him writhing around on the ground. Someone had poisoned him. He had been thrown a hot dog by someone, and there was strychnine in the hot dog. I picked him up, rushed him to the car, and brought him to the vet. By the time I got there, he was gone. He was only five years old.

This kind of sudden death is unusual but the fact is, tragedy awaits all pet owners. The most difficult thing about having pets is knowing there will be a tragic ending because you will outlive your pet 99 percent of the time. And the ending will not be pleasant, no matter what. It is all the more difficult being unable to telegraph when that end will come.

The other reality about dogs is that one of two things will occur: You will either train the dog or the dog will train you. You have a choice in the matter. A family that has an incorrigible dog is the same as having an incorrigible kid. You give in, and you either get very lucky or you have trouble ahead. With dogs, if you are not the one doing the training, it generally does not work out very well; hiring someone out defeats the purpose. I'll also allow that there is such a thing as an untrainable dog—I have had a few over the decades. My opinion is that you just can't keep them.

Dogs come in all kinds of various types but they also come in all kinds of degrees of intelligence. And just as I was a better football coach when I had smart players, I am a better dog trainer when I have a smart dog. You can't teach a dumb dog new tricks any more than you can teach a football player who isn't very smart to be a great football player.

Dating back to about 1950, our family has had numerous dogs. Cork was the oldest, living to the ripe old age of 15. The last dog I put down was Annie, who made it to 13 years. I cried like a baby for the better part of three days. It was really tough. Grieving is natural and you eventually get over it, but you cannot be a pet owner without facing this part of it.

How do you know when it is time to end a pet's life? If you are observant it is usually not too difficult. Dogs have no way to communicate with you where they hurt. You have to figure it out. Paying attention to their moods and their behavior, you can sense the differences. You will be able to see them gradually (or suddenly) start to change. Perhaps the dog is losing weight. Or his disposition changes somewhat. The bottom line is, if you have to decide whether or not to put the dog to sleep, then the decision has been made for you. The time has come, as sad and as difficult as it may be.

I am a strong believer that parents should not get a dog for their kids. I think you get a dog or animal for yourself, and your kids grow up around it. A dog is not a child's responsibility. It can be a good tool for teaching responsibility, but a dog needs an adult to nurture it.

There are so many dog breeds that you can get, and most of them are very good. I strongly recommend going to a reputable dog breeder who breeds smart dogs. As I said earlier, dogs span a whole range of intelligence levels—and not every dog in a litter is smart.

I will give you a good example. I did a favor for Dennis Anderson, the outdoors writer for the Twin Cities. In appreciation, he wanted give me one of his new litter of puppies. In fact, he said I could have the pick of his litter; I just had to come out and pick the one I wanted. For one reason or another, I didn't get out there right away. I went fishing and was busy doing other things. Well, he called and told me to rush out there, because there were only five left. Then pretty soon he called again, saying there were only two left. Soon enough, there was only one left, and that's how I wound up with Maggie.

Maggie was the only puppy not picked, the odd dog out. Her head was too narrow. Her legs were too short. Her body was too long and her tail was crooked. It was obvious why no one picked her. But it turned out she was the smartest dog of the whole litter. She was a wonderful dog.

In the beginning, it is very difficult to judge how intelligent a dog is going to be. It's not until about six months that you will really to be able to tell. Then you are able to see the deficiencies. When the puppy is at six to eight weeks, you might just as well close your eyes and pick one out at random. There's simply no way to tell at that age.

Once the litter is broken up, the bonding starts with a person rather than the other puppies. Keeping this in mind, it may be a lot better to get the puppy at a younger age. Once the bonding starts within the litter, the dog-human bond is more difficult to solidify.

As much as you study the process of how to do it, for the most part I think you have to be lucky. Dogs are built differently. They are all different sizes, look different, and are different colors. You have to watch puppies carefully and see how they react to people to strange surroundings, strange noises, and strange smells, and in their new home. Some dogs are happy all the time. For a hunting dog, one easy test is that you need to have a dog that is not gun shy. You can introduce a dog gradually to this kind of thing. You can bang pans together and find other ways to gently introduce them to loud and abrupt noise. If they react in the beginning, it's okay; they can outgrow that kind of a reaction. But if you are not careful, a dog can become traumatized by someone shooting off a gun next to it. In some cases they may never forget it.

Every dog is special in its own way. Annie, like many of my others, was really special. I like to have a dog that is well behaved. I want to be able to take the dog anywhere and not worry about it getting into trouble. I don't want the dog walking into a kitchen and pulling a chicken off the table or going outside and chewing up a hose. I want the dog to be able to go on an airplane, in a hotel, and (if allowed, of course) to go to someone else's house and behave properly.

Some dogs simply don't behave properly. As an owner and a trainer, you have to be careful and not put dogs in a position to do some of those things while they are learning. Most dogs are good dogs with few faults. It is up to the owner to be sure the dogs are not in a position to have those faults surface.

It has to be difficult to be a dog. I certainly wouldn't want to be one. They have a tough life. They have to adjust to your lifestyle and schedule, and as a result they never know what is coming up next. After all, you can't tell your dog, "Well, tomorrow morning we are going to go hunting," or "Tomorrow morning we are going to take you to the vet." They don't know where they are going when they get in the car. And to make matters worse for them, when you get there, they have to be able to accept where they are, what you are doing, and go from there.

This is why I think dogs are so observant. They can anticipate your behavior based on what you do. When they see me get my boots on or get my gun down, they know it's time to go hunting.

When my Annie passed a couple years ago, it was really tough on me. It also meant that I didn't have a dog to take hunting. I had never gone hunting without a dog before. As far as I was concerned, that was as useless as going hunting and leaving my gun at home. So I started asking around about dogs. By this time, I had raised enough puppies, so I made the decision that I needed to have an older dog with some experience and some training. But I wanted to judge the dog before I took him for keeps.

I got a lot of referrals and went out and looked at six different dogs and traveled through Minnesota, Wisconsin, and even Iowa to see them. Then I got a call from a friend who knew where there might be a good dog for me. It was from a place up in Sauk Rapids. The man had five kids and three dogs. He was a Little League coach and an insurance salesman, and overall a busy man. He liked to hunt, but with a family he didn't get to do it much.

I went to his place and looked at the dog, named Boom. I could tell immediately that he was a happy, friendly dog. I was sold. I can take him anywhere and he will behave exceptionally well. He loves attention and I give him so much, to the point that he thinks he is a person. He goes with me everywhere and is very intelligent.

Boom saw me go after a gopher in my yard at the lake one day. All it took was that one time, seeing me chase that gopher with a stick, for Boom to get the message. He now thinks he is a gopher hunter; every time he is out, he will go looking for that gopher. He checks those gopher holes every day.

THE BEST THING ABOUT a dog is his wonderful companionship. They have unbounded love for you. Their whole life they depend on you. I consider it a real responsibility to have pets because of the loyalty and love that they bring for you every day. A person can be the worst person in the world. He can do the most dastardly things, but his dog will always love him. Dogs have no judgment; they just love.

What I want in a dog is a happy dog. My dog, Boom, is a happy dog—you can tell right away. If he can be close to me the rest of his life, well, then he is happy. He has to wait until I let him out, wait until I let him in, wait until I make my next move—but as long as he is next to me, you can just tell he's happy.

Over the years with my family we always had room for dogs. In addition, we have always made room for other pets. By the time we moved from Canada back to Bloomington, Minnesota, we had more room for animals. I built some pens in our backyard and we had pigeons, pheasants, ducks, and wild turkeys. We also had several pet ravens. Surprisingly, they are the smartest of all the critters we have ever had. Truly, the ravens are the brightest by a mile. We've had pet crows, pet owls, pet seagulls. We had foxes and skunks. All of them I found in the wild.

Once, I helped someone in Bloomington cut down an old tree and out jumped a baby raccoon. I took that baby home and raised him. We named him Rocco. Raccoons grow really fast. They are very playful, easy to train, and really fun to be around. They are also extremely curious. Rocco was kept in a cage, but we sometimes took him into the house. We would let him run around and he was very playful.

Ultimately he got big—really big. By spring he was about 30 pounds, which is very large for a raccoon. He was able to understand my voice and anticipate what I wanted some of the time. When he was in the house and it was time to go out, he didn't want to go. I used to have to grab him by the back of his neck and lift him up to take him out. He would twist and fight me the whole way.

Finally the time came when we knew Rocco had outgrown house life. So we brought him up to the lake and released him into the woods. I put a red collar on him with a bell. I told him, "Well, Rocco, this is it. Now you are on your own." I didn't see or hear a thing about Rocco for some time. Then later on that summer I was in the bar in Gordon, talking to a friend of mine. He said, "I have to tell you something. I was fishing in this stream and I heard this rustling in the grass. At first I thought it was a bear but then I saw this big raccoon. When he saw me, he jumped in the creek and came right at me. I didn't know what to do. I was looking for a tree to go up, but I had my fly rod and equipment with me. Before I knew it, that raccoon came right up to me and put his paws up, as if to say hello. It was incredible. At first I was scared to death but then I looked and he had a red ribbon around his neck."

My friend said he almost had a heart attack! He told me, "I thought I had a rabid raccoon and didn't know how I would defend myself. So then I went back to fishing and this raccoon stayed with me the whole time." That was Rocco.

We also had some great horned owls in the backyard that whooped every night. I usually fed most of our animals or birds some kind of grain or corn. We had most of them in a pen, but the squirrels would get in and eat the feed, too. So I would have to go out in my backyard and shoot the squirrels. I had a pellet gun and would shoot them and leave them on top of the pen. At night, the owl would come down and eat the squirrels. That was the best-fed owl that likely ever existed. He loved those squirrels.

When I was coaching the Vikings, we had some great employees at Winter Park and we always had a lot of fun together. I would at times play practical jokes on them. At one time I had some fighting cocks—great big roosters, the kind that are used for cockfighting. I had one at home, about three feet high. I brought him to work on April Fool's Day and put him in the women's washroom. These roosters do not seem very friendly because they do not back down from anyone. That caused a little consternation!

Other times I would put animals in drawers, like that white squirrel I had for a pet. It always made things interesting. But it didn't end there. To get back at me, some of the employees got together and cooked up a plan. When I came to work one morning, there was an orangutan sitting on my desk. They had gotten it from the zoo and brought it to my office. I never gave them a reaction. I went over and talked to it, but he never responded.

Another time I came to work and there was a 12-foot python on my desk. Pat was in on that one. She called my office and told them when I was on the way to work so they could get the snake out and have it ready for me.

For a period in Winnipeg, we had a chimpanzee as the team mascot. He would go to birthday parties for the kids, that type of thing.

Well, one day we came up with the idea to have the chimpanzee at the football game. He got more pictures taken of him than the players did! Our trainer was walking around with him, and all of a sudden the chimp became interested in the footballs; he was fascinated by the balls flying through the air during our warm-ups. Pretty soon, the trainer brought the chimp over by the goal post and let him climb onto the crossbar. As the balls were kicked, he would wave at them, trying to knock them down. Before long he was up near the top of the goal post, trying to knock down those footballs. The fans went nuts!

It was so popular, we did that before the games for two years. By the time we got out on the field for our pregame warm-ups, the stands would be full. Everyone came early to watch our chimpanzee try to knock down the field goals. It was a huge hit.

I love almost all animals, but I have tried everything possible to be friendly to seagulls, to no avail. I raised them, fed them, did everything for them, and as soon as they were raised, they said, "The heck with you," and off they would go. Ravens, on the other hand, are very different. They want to be your buddy. Ravens will sit on your shoulder, look you in the eye, and even come when you call them. They're really amazing animals.

Many years ago, at our lake place, I had two ravens. They were around all the time. I would call them and they would come down to get something to eat. They were wild, but they hung around all the time. They also used to go over to the neighbors' place. Sometimes they got into a little trouble. "Yeah, they were here this morning. They pulled the clothespins right off my clothesline," they would tell me. But other than that they were really good.

One week one of the neighbors let some of their relatives use their cabin for the weekend, and the ravens ended up in their back-yard. The lady had come out to hang up some wash and those two big ravens came right up to her. Bear in mind, ravens are large. They have a wingspan of probably six feet, which can be pretty intimidating. As soon as they landed, she went screaming into the house. Her son was there and thought she was being attacked by these huge black birds, so he grabbed a shotgun and went out and killed both of them. I couldn't blame the family. No one had told them that the ravens would come to visit in the morning. But it was a tragic ending for a couple of great pets.

Another time we had three ravens, a male and two females. The male raven would sit on top of the garage. He was really large and boisterous—typical of a male. One night I heard a big commotion. A great horned owl had come and picked that raven right off the garage roof. There were feathers everywhere. And that was the end of him.

Another time we had a raven at our home in Bloomington, and it stayed with us year-round. Ravens are awfully hardy, and this one roosted outside on top of the dog kennel. We fed him, so he stayed around. Ravens are awfully good mimics. This one could bark like a dog! He was so good, you really could not tell the difference. I mean he was that clever.

The neighborhood kids never paid much attention to the raven except for one kid. For whatever reason, this kid did not like the raven. One day he came over to play basketball. In order to get to the basketball court, the kid had to walk by the dog kennel in our backyard. The raven was perched on the kennel. As he walked by I saw him pick up a rock and make a big detour around the dog kennel. The raven was just sitting on top of the kennel, not paying any attention to the kid, but I was thinking, *I wonder what he is going to do with that rock.*

As the kid got behind the kennel, near the basketball court, he suddenly turned around and threw the rock right at the raven. I suppose he was maybe 15 or 20 yards away. He hit that raven right in the head and knocked him over. I could have given that kid another 5,000 rocks to throw and he would never have hit that raven again, but this one hit it square in the head. I took him to the vet, but it was too late. Our raven died. That was another tragic ending for one of our pets. And they all hurt.

One of the most unusual pets we had was a monkey named Chico that Pat got me for my birthday one year. He looked like one of those organ-grinder monkeys—the ones with the long tails. We built him a big pen for him in the basement. At night we would bring him upstairs and he would come and sit on my lap. He was really friendly. I would be sitting watching television or reading the paper and he would sit there, picking imaginary fleas out of my hair. I would hide things in my pockets and he would go in and out of my pockets looking for things. He would search in and around my collar and down my neck; he was always looking for something. We had a good time together, but Chico was the jealous type.

He did not like our younger son Dan. Chico perceived Dan as a threat to him because he got a lot of attention that Chico wanted for himself. The monkey would go nuts when he wasn't the center of attention. It got to the point where Dan became terrified of Chico and his tantrums, and it came down to making a choice between Chico and my son. Guess who won. Luckily, the guy who bought Chico was a bachelor, and it ended up being a nice home for Chico. That was a good ending.

MY PASSION FOR ANIMALS has led me to pursue many great causes over the years. At the University of Minnesota, before they had the Raptor Center, they were in a serious budget crisis. They were going to have to close the building where they had kept the birds of prey. Their funding was in jeopardy, and I think they needed $50,000 to keep it open.

I had a friend in the state legislature named Bob Lessard. I told him about the problem and asked him if he could help out. He told me that with all the bills that went through the legislature, he was hopeful he could attach a rider to one of them. Well, he did just that. Bob Lessard was able to get the funding, and today it is one of the leading centers of raptor study in the United States. As a result of my intervention, the center invited me to come out and release some eagles back into the wild, which was a huge thrill for me.

I have been fortunate to have had a great family and so many great pets. I'm sure I left out quite a few of them because there have been so many over the years. Like an extended family, they have all brought me lots of love and joy.

Life is pretty good. If I'm sitting at my lake home by the fireplace reading the paper or looking out the window, I know one thing for sure: Boom will be right there next to me, just waiting for me to make my next move.

15   CHANGES TO A GREAT GAME

WHEN LOOKING AT POSSIBLE changes to the game of professional football, it is difficult to say that the game needs any changing at all. Where it comes to popularity, it is the greatest sport ever. Just look at television ratings, the marketing of the game, fantasy football, and even the way people talk about it. The game has become bigger than anyone could have imagined.

I think the reason it is so successful has to do with the nature of the competition itself. That it is a team sport, that the players demonstrate an unparalleled athleticism, and that the game moves so fast. And the marketing has been tremendous. The National Football League has managed the game well over the decades, and overall it has been a tremendous success.

One aspect that has enhanced the game and made it what it is today has to do with rule changes. The new rules have not only improved the game, but they have also heightened the fans' interest. Take the holding rule, for example. You used to have to keep your hands inside the opposing player's shoulders. Now offensive players can extend their arms wide and push their opponents. If you look at the size of some of these defensive tackles and ends, some of them have a seven-foot wingspan. That's absolutely huge! The rule change has really helped the offense keep these giants under control.

Another rule is that you can no longer chuck or hit a player more than five yards downfield. That change in the rules has freed up the receivers and made the game more exciting from a passing perspective. Back in the days when I played, you were taking your life in your hands when you went over the middle of the field on a pass route. There were linebackers there just waiting to tear your head off. It used to be that you could hit the receiver at any time until the ball was in the air; now you cannot hit him at all. Both of these changes have really opened up the offensive game and made it a more pass-friendly situation for players.

There have been additional rule changes made solely for safety reasons—things like eliminating the chop block and the cut block. In my mind, all of these changes have been good for the game for the most part.

A dramatic change that I see when compared to previous eras is today's instant replay and the coaches' challenges. I'm sure the game officials are not very pleased with that aspect, but it all contributes to making the best on-field decisions.

I think the game has come a long way, but I also feel there is a lot more room for improvement. I propose some more changes that would further enhance fan interest and make the game more entertaining—and even more competitive—than it already is. The time to make a change is when something is at the height of success. Change can be difficult to acclimate to under any circumstances. I think now is the right time to do it.

THE EXTRA POINT

I think you can start with the extra point after a touchdown. There is no intrinsic entertainment value in watching the extra point. Sure, anything can happen, but for the most part it is automatic. You rarely see a kicker miss that extra point. So for fans watching the game at home or at the stadium, it is generally the time to leave your seat and use the bathroom, get something to eat, or let the dog out.

During the 2012 season there were only six extra points missed—out of 1,235 attempts. That's a 99.5 percent accuracy rate! Field goals attempted inside 20 yards in 2012 were even better; not a single one was missed.

At one time, the kick was made from 10 yards out because the goal posts were then on the goal line, rather than the back of the end zone and yet the point after touchdown is still for the most part automatic at 20 yards, the distance at which it is kicked today. Teams do have the option to go for the two-point conversion but rarely exercise it unless that additional point is truly needed. I think that by moving the extra point distance you could make the game more interesting. If you moved the line of scrimmage from the 3-yard line to perhaps the 20-yard line, this would mean the ball would be kicked from the 27-yard line, making the kick 37 yards. In 2012, the percentage of kicks made from 30 to 39 yards was at 88—not quite so automatic.

The percentages would still be high with the quality of kickers we have today, but it would heighten the interest level after the touchdown score. I guarantee people would not be so anxious to leave their seats then. Plus, it would bring another entertaining segment to the game because the extra point would become a more valuable aspect of the game as a whole.

Consider a game where one team scores at the end and needs the extra point to win or tie. Even though the extra point is a game clincher, no one even gives a thought to the fact that the kicker might miss it. But if the kick is coming from the 37-yard line, that would be a big deal.

I'm not sure what the exact distance should be—maybe the 20- or perhaps the 25-yard line; that's for others to decide. But the key is for it to be from a distance where the percentage of success decreases. I think it would be a fantastic rule change. I'm sure it would be hard for the traditionalists to adopt, but I definitely think it would make things more interesting. As far as I can tell, in discussing it with fans, no one has disagreed yet.

THE FIELD GOAL

Another change to the game that I submit would be worthy concerns field goals. The field goal is worth three points, no matter how long it is. If you kick the field goal with the ball starting on the 3-yard line, which would represent a 20-yard field goal, you get three points. That particular kick, like the extra point, is an automatic kick. If the ball is on the 40-yard line, making for a 57-yard field goal, you still only get three points.

The longer the kick, the more challenging it becomes, but the points remain the same. I propose that field goals should be graduated. Take the field and divide it up. Kicks from the 1- to the 10-yard line: one point. From the 11- to the 30-yard line: two points. From the 31-yard line or longer: three points. There was a time when football players had a chance to block field goals, but today that rarely ever happens. Matt Blair blocked 22½ kicks for us! No one in today's game even comes close.

Another variable that could make the kicking game more interesting would be to narrow the goal posts. Then there would be some strategy involved. If your team is driving down the field and needs to kick a game-winning field goal, and you only get one point for a short kick or two beyond a certain yard line, you will have to decide from where on the field to attempt the kick. Do you want to go inside the 10-yard line, or do you want to move back for a longer kick that nets you more points? Maybe you will want to go for a touchdown, or back up in yardage for the longer kick. This would open up a whole new aspect of the game of football. I'm certain coaches would absolutely detest this because everyone in the stands would want to make the call. But the fact is, they already do that anyway!

I think it would be a revolutionary change. Depending on the score of the game or the time left on the clock, there would be some really significant decisions to be made. Let's say you are on the 3-yard line and it is fourth down. Is it better to go for a touchdown from the 3-yard line or kick a one-point field goal?

The commentators would love it. They'd be bubbling over with their thoughts about the scenarios, what ought to be occurring on the field. It would be entertaining, no doubt about it. Right now kickers are so proficient that it makes many aspects of the game dull. Dull spots in the game exist. If your team drives down the field to the 10-yard line and then makes the field goal to win the game, what is exciting about that? In fact, you'll see people leaving the game at that point, more concerned with the postgame traffic than the probability that such a kick could be missed. It gives all the prognosticators and all the postgame guys something to talk about that is interesting. I'm not talking controversy. I'm talking interest. It would make a good game better.

I mentioned that coaches would not like this, but if it did become a part of the game, they would work out all the percentages and figure it all out. It would not be as easy a decision as it is today but a more entertaining decision that comes with a lot of strategy. And what do most coaches love, if not the strategy of the game?

Certainly you would see some different scores, so the gamblers would go nuts. You wouldn't see the 21–14 or the 24–10 games as often. You would see the 22–16 or the 25–19 games more often. I submit that it would be tremendous change for the better.

THE KICKOFF

Speaking of the kicking game, another tremendously dull part of the game is the kickoff. Today it is kicked out of the end zone, or so deep in the end zone that most of the time there is no return at all. What used to be one of the most exciting parts of the game has become almost a nonfactor.

Many like to make the point that there are more injuries that occur during the kickoff return than in other aspects of the game, so the lack of returns is better for the game from that respect. Well, that may be true. But from the entertainment side of things, it is a dead play. You line up 22 players and they run up and down the field…and nothing happens. The ball is kicked out of the end zone. Cue commercial.

When I was a coach, I felt that the kickoff was an integral part of the game; now it is reduced to meaninglessness. So what can you do about it? Well, you can force the opponent to bring the kickoff out of the end zone, for one thing. You can move the kickoff spot back so the ball will not be kicked all the way through the end zone. You can mandate that the kick cannot be downed. You could make a rule that if the ball is not returned out of the end zone, the team gets the ball on the 5-yard line, or something to that effect. Or you could introduce a penalty stating that if the kick rolls out of the end zone, the ball comes out to the 25- or the 30-yard line, keeping the kicker from booming it. This would take the dead wood out of the game. It would make the game more entertaining. Concessions personnel might not be as happy because people would have to stay in their seats, but who else would protest?

THE FAIR CATCH

Let's stay with the kicking game and take a look at punting and the fair catch. The fair catch is the worst play we have in the game. Again, we have 22 guys running around and *nothing* happens.

The Canadian game does not have the fair catch rule. Now heaven forbid that here in America we would ever copy something from the Canadian Football League, but the fact is football was played professionally in Canada long before it became an American game. Those against this change will be quick to say, "Well, the poor return man is going to get injured." If you look closely at the Canadian game, the return man rarely is injured. It is a skill position in the CFL and helps players develop dramatically.

The way it works is that the punting team cannot be within five yards of the return man. The defenders must keep five yards from the receiving player when he catches the ball. Right there you take the problem of a "defenseless receiver" out of the equation. And here's where things get interesting. If you give some of these exceptional athletes five yards to catch the ball and run, believe me, it'll make those punts worth tuning into. Institute the same thing in the NFL, and you have changed the game and kept it safe.

Today, we put the best players with the best hands on the field to catch the kick, but only so they can fair catch the ball and establish possession. It doesn't make any sense to me. This change would actually make the game safer, I'd argue, because under the current rules, when the return man opts not to call for a fair catch, he really puts himself in a vulnerable position. Those receivers often do get killed after they catch the ball.

Eliminating the fair catch and modifying the rules with a five-yard safe zone would make the punting aspects of the game safer, and extremely entertaining to boot.

RUNNING OUT THE CLOCK

Another really dead part of the game can come in the last two minutes. If the team that's behind is on defense and has no timeouts left, the game is essentially over. They are helpless to stop the clock from running. The team in the lead will snap the ball, take a knee, and then everyone stands around while the clock runs down. Where's the fun in that? If a game is so close that the teams are within one score of each other in the final minutes, the end of the game should be the most exciting part!

I'd propose a rule change stating that if a team does not gain a yard on a down in the last two minutes of the game, the clock stops. If you gain a yard, the clock keeps running. This forces the team that's ahead to run a legitimate play, which would in turn bring suspense at the end.

A small percentage of the time, there may be a fumble. Or the defense would stop the offense for a loss or no gain. It would give the trailing team a fighting chance.

With this simple change, the fans get their money's worth in the last few minutes of the game. The "victory formation" has to be taken out of football. The game is worthy of being exciting all the way down to the end.

I doubt I will ever see changes like this in my lifetime, but I really advocate for them. I know this for sure: it would certainly create a lot of discussion, and it would strengthen what is already the greatest team sport of all time.

16 A RETURN TO THE PURPLE?

I HAVE NEVER TOLD this story to anyone. A few years ago, during the 2005 football season, I was offered the opportunity to return to the Minnesota Vikings as the head football coach. At the ripe old age of 78! And I came very close to taking the job.

Mike Tice was the current head coach of the Vikings when I received a call from Red McCombs, the team owner. I was on the road when Red called, en route to South Dakota to do some pheasant hunting with my friend Marty Davis.

The Vikings had finished the 2004 season with a respectable 9–7 record but missed the playoffs. The 2005 season had been full of ups and downs; it was well into the season when Red called. When he asked me if I would consider returning to coaching, I asked him, "Where?"

When he told me Minnesota, I said to him, "Red, you already have a coach."

He told me he was planning to get rid of Tice. I said, "Red, you have a coach, and I am not going to talk to you about this while Mike is coaching the team."

He tried a different tack. "Well, let me put it another way: we are going to make a change, now would you be interested?"

I said again, "Red, you have a coach," and that was the end of our conversation.

It wasn't long before he called me back. The team was playing in Detroit in early December, and Red told me that he had asked Rob Brzezinski, one of the team vice presidents, to return to Minneapolis after the game. Rob was from Detroit and had planned to stay for a few days, but Red needed him back in the Twin Cities. The plan was to fire Tice after the Detroit game.

Red said to me, "Okay, now Tice is going to be gone. Would you be interested in coaching the team?" I told him I would consider it.

At the time of these calls, I was in Marty Davis' car, talking on his cell phone, so he was privy to what was going on. This was all very intriguing to Marty, and I can guarantee you that he can give chapter and verse of what happened. In fact, it might be best here to get Marty's version of what was going on as we rode in his car:

> Bud was using my cell phone, talking with Red McCombs about coming back to coach the Vikings. It was an incredible conversation. Red was planning on firing Mike Tice and hiring Bud as the new head coach—right then, during the season.
>
> I just listened as the calls went back and forth, on and off, for several hours. Between calls, Bud told me he enjoyed negotiating with Red, knowing that he had been a used-car salesman.
>
> I think McCombs offered something like a million dollars to Bud, and Bud just winked at me and told Red to refer to his Blue Book to see what Bud was worth. It was incredible! The added value was that it was all the truth.

So Red says, "Get back here to Minneapolis, because right after the Detroit game we are going to get rid of Tice and we want to name you as coach. It's a done deal."

Well, the Vikings beat Detroit in an exciting finish to the game, which changed things as far as I was concerned. I mean, the Vikings had just won a tough game, and the organization and the fans were feeling pretty good. To me, it was not the time to change head football coaches. But nevertheless Red called again.

I told him, "Red, timing is everything. You can't fire a coach after that emotional win the team just got in Detroit. This is not good timing. You just won a football game. Everyone is happy and now you are going to fire the coach?"

Red said they were going forward anyway. I knew that naming me the head coach was going to be a really big deal. This would be "Bud Grant coming back to coach the Vikings for the third time." We talked about how I would take over the team and what I would do. I told him that I would only be a figurehead for the first year. He wanted to give me a two year deal that would be to finish out the season and then coach the next year. I reiterated that for the first year, I would only be a figurehead. After all, we couldn't fire the coaches at this juncture; I would have to keep most of what was going on intact. It was nuts to start over that late in the season—that would be disaster in the making.

Red had a sidekick who was with him during all of the conversations named Gary Woods. Gary was kind of his financial guy. Red was a promoter and Woods was the money guy. We talked about a lot of things, and as we talked I could hear Woods in the background talking to Red.

And then I heard Woods say to Red, "salary." So Red then came back with, "Okay, we will pay you what Tice is making this year and then we will have a new salary for you to coach next season." I said, "Red, Tice is the lowest-paid coach in the National Football League. I am not going to accept that."

And just like that, Woods got into the picture. I could hear him in the background conferring with Red. So they offered me something like $150,000 a game. I told the two of them, "When I left the Vikings after the 1985 season, I turned down what would have been the highest salary among coaches in the NFL. I would have been the highest-paid coach in the league. You know what the coaches make at this time. I will take a dollar less than the highest-paid coach in the league. I was a head coach for 28 years and we won many championships and went to four Super Bowls, so that's my counteroffer."

I could faintly hear Woods talking to Red in the background while Red had his hand over the phone, saying, "No, no, no. We can't pay him anything like that."

I remained firm. "Red, you know what the coaches are making. If you can pay me one dollar less than what the highest-paid coach in the league is making, then we can talk business."

He said, "I'll call you back."

I'm not sure who the highest-paid coach was at that time but he was probably making $4 to $5 million a year. Well, they called back a little later with another offer that wasn't even close. I told them, "Red, now this is a big move that you are going to make. You have to think this through. If you want me to coach, you know what I am asking. And I have more experience than any coach that is out there. That's why you are talking to me."

They had a press conference all set to announce me as the head coach, but Gary Woods wouldn't let Red pay me the money, so the deal fell through. It was over just that fast.

I would have come back. I thought the Vikings had a pretty good team, and returning to coaching was kind of an exciting thought. The money would have been good, and I thought it might be fun to come back to coaching—for a short time, anyway. It certainly would have been exciting to do at 78 years old.

Sometime later I had a conversation with Mike Tice. I recall him saying to me, "Bud, I hear you almost took my job." I said to him, "Mike, I don't know what you know, but don't believe all that you hear. You knew that you were on the hot seat around here, but you survived."

It was an interesting thought. I would have brought Jerry Burns on again as my offensive coordinator, and I bet John Michels would have come back with me, too. I wonder if we could have found a way to have Tarkenton return as our quarterback. I know Bill Brown and Jim Marshall would have been ready to go.

17 CANTON

OBVIOUSLY, ONE OF THE great passions of my life has been coaching. I would never have been involved in it for 28 years if it hadn't meant a lot to me. And without question, one of the major highlights of my coaching career was the recognition that I received in my election into the Pro Football Hall of Fame in Canton, Ohio.

The Hall of Fame was not something that I ever gave a whole lot of thought about while I was involved in professional football. We played a couple of preseason games in Canton during my tenure with the Vikings so I knew something about it, but it was never something I gave regular thought to.

But my history with Canton didn't start out quite so rosy. Back in those days, players got paid to play in those Canton exhibition games, but the coaches did not receive any compensation. I didn't like that. I went to someone who had authority in the games and asked him about it. I was told, quite simply, "No, the coaches don't get paid, just the players."

"Wait a second," I said. "The players get paid for this game and it is an extra game on the schedule for the coaches, too. So why don't we get paid?" They had never been paid before, was the only reasoning I got in return.

I didn't give up. I went to a higher authority who was involved in the Hall of Fame game and said, "Well, maybe if we don't get paid, then maybe we don't coach the game in Canton." I then went to the league. I also went to the opposing coach in the game; he was with me completely.

It wasn't long before this edict got everywhere. The players heard about it and the league was not happy. They started looking for another team to play in the game, but it was too late. The schedule had already been set.

When the players got wind of what was going on, they decided that if the coaches were not going to be paid, they were not going to play the game themselves. This really put the league into a snit because this was a televised game. So, the commissioner of the National Football League, Pete Rozelle, called Max Winter, who then called me. Max pleaded with me not to go through with it. I told him we didn't have a coaches' union, and we were well within our rights to do it. And I told him that if I didn't coach, my players didn't want to play.

Max said, "Okay. I will pay you. Don't make this a league matter."

It was too late. "No, Max, this is bigger than that. The league is going to have to pay us."

Max was upset, to say the least. It wasn't every day that the commissioner called Max for a favor; being unable to grant it was even worse.

In the end, the league agreed to pay coaches the same amount that the players got. And from then on, coaches were compensated for the Hall of Fame Game. I must have received a dozen or more calls from other coaches and assistant coaches thanking me for taking the stand on behalf of everyone. I knew the position we were in—we coaches held all the cards. By taking the stand before the game, we had a good chance to get pay for the coaches and that in the end it would become a permanent resolution to a long-term problem. If we had tried to get this done at a league meeting or in the off-season, it never would have happened. Simple as that.

The least important part of a football team in the eyes of the league is the coach. We were made to feel as if we were the most dispensable, and that was an issue to me. Which is why I took a stand and proved the point.

Back to the Pro Football Hall of Fame. It was never something that I thought actively about reaching. Today you see players actually lobbying to get in! They have people write letters of support. I have had players come to me and ask if I would write letters extolling how great they were.

I never did anything to promote myself. I never asked anyone to do a single thing for me. Every city had a sportswriter on the voting committee, and Sid was the Twin Cities' representative. I know that Sid pushed for me some, and I'm sure that helped, so I'm grateful for his support. But I certainly never would have asked for it.

When I got elected, it was certainly an honor—but I didn't realize at the time how significant an honor it was. Being a part of the Pro Football Hall of Fame is tremendous, and I'm tremendously grateful. The treatment that we received at the Hall of Fame exceeded all expectations. It is the highest honor one can receive in our business of professional football. I appreciated when I went to Canton and saw firsthand how everything was handled and saw firsthand how all of the Hall's honorees were revered.

The Vikings organization rented a Greyhound bus for me to travel to Canton and bring my family and friends along. One of the fellows that we took was Lute Pettis, who was my baseball manager many years back at Osceola, Wisconsin, and his wife. And we brought other friends with as well, along with our large extended family.

Canton was, quite simply, the highlight of my career. To go there and be a part of it all was big time. There were six of us being enshrined in the Class of 1994, and we were the focus of everything and treated like kings. It was a wonderful experience.

I wanted someone who knew me well to do the introduction, so I chose Sid. We have known each other a very long time and he is my very best friend. He knows more about me than anyone I could think of. Some of the other guys had a family member or a coach, but no one had ever had a sportswriter introduce him. So that was a first.

It was a very emotional time for me. I had my family with me, and looking around there were so many great players and football men who all were there to honor us. And then you had a chance to go through the Hall and see all the greats of the past. It was extremely humbling. To be in that inner circle was just incredible.

To be elected is a culmination of a career. By describing my background in my speech, I was told later that I captured the heart of what the Hall was all about for honorees. I began with my background, starting right at the beginning when I was a "practice rat" for the New York Giants when they trained at Superior.

It made me so proud to be elected to the Pro Football Hall of Fame and it sure would have made my dad proud, too. He would have been looking around for Steve Owen to tell him, "See the Kid over there? He made it."

MY HALL OF FAME induction speech was very personal to me, and I believe it sums up my career and all it stood for. Which is why I chose to reprint it here, as a last word in this book on my life in football.

July 30, 1994

This is a great day for Sid and me. We have come a long way. You know, as a coach you don't get here because you can kick or catch or tackle or run or throw. You get here because you had the help of a lot of people. You reflect on what a lot of people have done.

I would first like to say that Max Winter—who was president of the Vikings when I arrived and also worked with the Lakers when I played professional basketball—was very instrumental in me coming to the Minnesota Vikings. He and general manager Jim Finks convinced me to come from Canada and join the organization. They did me a great service and I am forever indebted to them.

Sid mentioned Jim was one of the great general managers and a model for all general managers in the National Football League.

After Jim it was Mike Lynn, who I felt in his era and my time was the finest general manager in the NFL. He helped us tremendously with everything he did, ran a happy ship, made it possible for us to do things, and to go on and win some football games.

As a coach you reflect, as I mentioned, on the players and what they do. The players you see behind me, the great players you see sitting over there—as coaches like Tom Landry and me, we reflect with everything they do. Sometimes maybe we shouldn't, but we do.

I am sorry to say that there are not a lot of Vikings in the Hall of Fame yet. I hope that this is something that will be corrected in the near future because the Vikings have some record setters that are out there. I am thinking of Paul Krause, who holds the record for 81 interceptions, and should be in here very soon. Jim Marshall, 19 years as a starter, 270 starts. He will be here, too. Mick Tingelhoff, our center: 240 starts, played many years. Carl Eller has been nominated; I am sure you will see Carl in here. Ron Yary played many years, as did Matt Blair.

There are many others who I think are deserving and will eventually be here enjoying this tremendous feeling. I only mention a few, but there are many others, many that will never be included or considered for an honor like this. Players who worked diligently, and I am here on behalf of them. There are so many I couldn't mention them all, but I will say that Roy Winston, a 15-year player for us probably will never be considered. He was very instrumental, along with a lot of other players. The Hilgenbergs, the Warwicks, the Sharockmans, the Bryants, Siemons, Hannons, Sundes, Kramers, Osborns, Rashads, Voigts, Whites, Aldermans, Browns, all familiar names that I hope will be remembered.

No coach is ever successful without a great staff. I was very fortunate. I didn't have a lot of assistant coaches, and the reason was because they stayed with us for a long time. Jerry Burns—17 years, a wonderful friend and coach—certainly gets credit for many of the things we did offensively. A trainer by the name of Fred Zamberletti came to the Vikings in 1961 and is still there. No coach can exist without a close association with a trainer. John Michels was with me for 27 years, starting in Winnipeg. John should be standing here today with me for all he has done, and I thank him.

And, of course, you can't get by in this business without support from home. My family is here today. This is probably the finest vacation and family gathering we have ever had. My wife, Pat, is sitting here. When I needed support and understanding and love, she was there. All my children are here, Kathy and Steve, grandchildren; Kelly, Rickie, Gretchen; my daughter Laurie, son-in-law Bob, grandchildren Ben and Chris; Pete, wife Joan, Jennifer, Bryan; three-month-old Elaina is at home and couldn't make it. Maybe next time. Mike, wife Colleen, and Taylor and Ryan are here with them. Bruce, wife Terry are here and the next time they are here they will have another with them because they are working on it. It is in the hopper now. My son Dan—I don't think he got the message yet—but he is here having a great time along with a lot of other friends and relatives, too many to mention at this time.

Also, I would just like to say something about the fans in Minnesota. They have been great. It is a great place to play, a great place to live, and a great place to work. It has been one of the finest places to raise a family and coach a football team in the National Football League. They contributed so much to my success.

With all the thank-yous out of the way, one of the questions that I am asked the most is "What does it mean to be here today?" Well, maybe I can give you a brief history. I have answered it a number of times but I don't know if I can come up with the right answer. When I was born my name was Harry. My father's name was Harry, and you can't run around the house with two Harrys. So my mother nicknamed me and called me Buddy Boy; my dad called me Kid. The Buddy Boy was shortened to Bud. If I would have been a boxer I would have been Kid Grant, because my dad always referred to me as Kid.

My father was very important in my life and was interested in sports and got me interested. I remember Joe Lewis, I remember the night he knocked out Max Schmeling. My dad and I jumped up and down as we listened to the radio. It was great. He loved baseball, the stars, heroes, football, and boxing, but something changed in 1939, when the New York Giants came to Superior to train. They trained in 1939, 1940, and 1941.

As a kid I hung around the New York Giants. My dad had a concession stand at the ballpark and got to know Steve Owen, the Giants head coach. My dad kept saying, "Hey, my kid is going to play for you someday." Every year Steve Owen would come back and measure me and I would be a little bit bigger. My dad would say, "The Kid is going to make it. He is going to play for the Giants." Steve would say, "Keep working on him. Keep feeding him." Well, the war came and a few years went by [without the Giants in Superior], but the Giants came back in 1948. Now "the Kid" was a little bigger and Steve was looking at me a little more convincingly that someday I might play in the National Football League. And my dad said, "The Kid is going to make it."

My dad used to tell me stories about the NFL, because as I mentioned earlier today, [there are] two players born in Superior who played in the NFL and are presently in the Hall of Fame. Tuffy Leemans came from Superior, played with the New York Giants, and is in the Hall of Fame. Ernie Nevers, one of the original Hall of Famers, came from Superior and he is in here. So there was a background even in a town of 30,000 way up in Northern Wisconsin on Lake Superior.

The radio didn't carry the games and we would get the Chicago paper once in a while. My dad would tell me the stories of Red Grange and Johnny "Blood." I asked him, "Where did Johnny "Blood" get a name like that?" He said he was a tough guy. He broke his nose every game and the blood would stream down his face. Johnny "Blood" McNally is here. George Trafton, a great center for the Bears is here. These guys were the toughest guys in football. George had a finger missing. I asked my dad how he lost his finger. My dad said they bit it off in the bottom of a pile. I didn't believe that, so I asked George one day how he lost his finger. He said, "I stuck it in a .45 in Chicago and they blew it off," so I didn't know what to believe.

Bronko Nagurski was from Minnesota and there were many stories my dad would tell me about Bronk. *There* was a tough cookie. Of course living close to Green Bay, Curly Lambeau was a legend. Don Hutson, "the greatest receiver of all time," my dad would tell me. "If you ever want to be a receiver, do what Don Hutson did," he would say. Of course, we didn't have any film so we really didn't know what Don Hutson did. We just read about it. Sammy Baugh was another. There are many stories about Sammy Baugh. I was raised on all that. Those were my dad's heroes.

Then it came to be my turn, so I could identify with some heroes of my own. Tony Canadeo, Green Bay, is here. A great athlete, Otto

Graham is another. I envied him because of his athletic ability. "Crazy Legs" Hirsch from Wisconsin, almost as good as Hutson. "Night Train" Lane always wanted people to call him Night Train. "Bulldog" Turner from the Bears is here. These were all the names that I followed. Chuck Bednarik, one of the great all time players, he is here. And then Paul Brown, who I had a chance to play for and coach against. Paul may have had more influence on my life in coaching than anyone. He is here. And Marion Motley, my all time hero. He is here.

Those are all my heroes, my dad's heroes. So I go back a long way, back to the 1930s following NFL players. And I am here with Tuffy and Red, Johnny "Blood," Bronko, Curley, Crazy Legs, Night Train, and Bulldog. You can't imagine what an honor it is.

If my mother were here today, I would look at her face and see the pride she would have. She is 93 years old and couldn't make it. And if my father was here, that would be special. He was different than I was. He was a very gregarious guy. He would stand up and he would say, "The Kid made it! He finally made it!"

Well, I am here and they can't take it away. And one other thing my father told me a long time ago: If you are ever asked to speak at such an auspicious occasion with so many great speakers, make sure you stand up good and tall so they all can see you. Talk good and loud so they all can hear you. Make a short speech so they all will listen to you, and then sit down so they all will like you. Thank you, Dad.

18 LOVES AND PASSIONS OF MY LIFE

HAVING TALKED ABOUT LIFE, my career, the Hall of Fame and all
that goes with it, I have saved the last segment of my autobiography
to underscore the importance of my family. In each segment of my
career I have emphasized that family is number one. And although
football has occupied many hours, days, weeks, months, and years
of my life, always on the front burner in my heart and my soul has
been my wife and children.

Pat and I had a shared philosophy of how we were going to
live our lives and raise our family. Maybe we just got lucky, but our
viewpoints meshed. There are others who spend their lives trying to
achieve their hopes and dreams and it never works out. For us, it did.

We both came from lower-middle-class backgrounds. We could
survive on a little and never needed to live a lavish lifestyle. As long
as we could put food on the table for ourselves and our six kids, we
were happy. And happily, we enjoyed the same things.

We talked about many things as we looked forward to our
future. We began by agreeing that we wanted to have a family.
We wanted to get married and have several children. We wanted a
home and we decided that Pat would be a homemaker; raising our
family right was paramount. We talked about where we wanted to
live and all of the other things that we knew would be important
to our lives.

When Pat and I first started going together back in college, I was aware that both of her grandparents were ministers. She was raised in that type of environment and all of her relatives had some type of connection to church. We didn't avoid the topic of religion, but we never had much discussion about it. Neither of us had strong feelings one way or another. I was not convinced, even growing up, about God. My dad was Catholic, so I was certainly exposed to the church it and had a first communion, but even at that time I had questions that could not be answered.

Pat had similar experiences. She did have religious overtones in her family, but not necessarily from her mother and father. In our talks, we decided that we could get along fine without religion being a part of our lives.

Basically, I don't believe in a lot of the teachings, but I do believe in church. I think that churches are invaluable. They serve needs of so many people and are a wonderful thing. They provide so much to so many.

We knew the kids would someday ask about religion, and they did. We told them that we didn't go to church, that we were nondenominational. We did not have any baptisms, confirmations, or any Sunday school for the kids. It never presented a problem for any of us. The only time we went to church was when someone else got married or buried. It wasn't as if we preached against it; we just weren't actively involved.

Today, some of our kids are involved with their spouses, and that's wonderful, but it's not for me. Paraphrasing Carl Sagan, if there is no scientific proof in something, it does not exist. I am not a believer in miracles; miracles are explainable.

We can replace virtually all parts of our body, our lungs, our hearts, hips, legs, arms, and kidneys but we cannot replace our mind—and that's where most of the miracles come from. If someone can come to me with proof of something, I will believe it. I am an agnostic in the Webster's sense which in part reads "a person who holds that the existence of the ultimate cause, as God, and the essential nature of things are unknown or unknowable, or that human knowledge is limited to experience." To me the Bible is not proof. The Bible is not scientific. It is all prophets. For this reason, I am not a believer in God, and therefore religion has not been a part of my life or part of raising our family.

Pat was a master at keeping things at even keel. She could handle Dan when he was a little guy and Kathy when she was in college. She easily took care of the age differences between our children. She made sure that everyone was healthy, happy, and at the same time became independent and free-thinking. Pat was a great listener and kept it together for each of us. She is the one who made it all work for our family. In addition to her dedicated volunteer commitment at Fairview Southdale Hospital.

Having said all that about Pat, it doesn't leave me much of a role here, does it? But I was the provider. I put the food on the table and made sure that we all had what we needed. I was the coach, and Pat was the general manager.

We had a very happy family. Pat and I got along extremely well. I cannot remember Pat hardly ever raising her voice. She had two things—I suppose we can call them expletives—that she used. One was "Whoa!" We learned quickly that when she said, "Whoa," that was about as tough as it gets and you better stop what you are doing right now! Now, I will say one other thing about that. If Pat stomped her foot and said, "Whoa," that was the total end. It was the toughest she would get and she did it very well. We all knew to take heed. The other thing that she would say was, "Oh, darn!" If she spilled something, "Oh, darn," would come out. But I never heard her use a swear word. Just the "Oh, darn." That was about as bad as it got for her.

We had so many great years together. If she were still with me, I know she would have a few things to say about this autobiography of mine. I know she would be able to add a few things like, "Nothing ever happened when you were home. If the furnace went out, you were on a trip. If the plumbing started to leak, you were hunting or in Green Bay."

Bruce was born on December 31ˢᵗ. I was planning on going moose hunting; I went every year between Christmas and New Year's. This particular year, Bruce was due on the 31ˢᵗ. Before I left on the 26ᵗʰ, Pat reminded me, "Now, you know I am due to have the baby on the 31ˢᵗ."

I told her, "Pat, don't have the baby until I get home. Well, I left on the 26ᵗʰ, got home on the 29ᵗʰ, and she had the baby right on schedule. I can't help but think Pat has something to do with it. She knew how to handle things really well. I was lucky that time—and I got a moose, too.

We never had a true philosophy of life. For the most part, we kind of took it as it came along. Pat steered the ship and always kept us on course.

Losing my beloved Pat several years ago was a devastating time for all of us. It was an extremely difficult time for me. We had been married for 60 years. With her passing, part of me was lost forever.

I have been fortunate in my life, however, to have met two Pats. After six decades of an exceptional marriage, I felt a deep void in my life, as does everyone who loses a spouse. Everybody handles the experience differently, I suppose, but I didn't just go out and look for another companion; at least I was not thinking in those terms at all. And then I met Pat.

To meet somebody who is compatible to all aspects of your life is almost a miracle. Now, I do not believe in miracles, but to have that happen has to be considered almost a miracle. I met someone who had similar values, similar interests, and similar tastes. At this stage of my life my meeting my second Pat has made my days very enjoyable the last few years.

We like many of the same things and have basically the same temperament. We have a great relationship and have a lot of fun together. Another thing that has been remarkable is the acceptance she has gotten from my family and vice versa. My family is quite large, and she has accepted them and they have accepted her more than can be imagined. My children and grandchildren are in communication with Pat oftentimes more than they are with me. Pat is a very gregarious person and has truly become a big part of our large family. She reaches out to all of them and has been fully accepted in every respect. She tells me more of what is going on in their lives than even I get directly from the kids.

Our relationship has meant a great deal to me. Even from a health standpoint it has been tremendous. She has brightened my spirit again and made my days enjoyable. She has not replaced my wife, but she has filled an emptiness in me. She has enhanced my life and I hope I have enhanced hers as well.

The other good thing is she owns her own house, has her own car, her own teeth, and is very self-sufficient—besides being a caring and loving human being! An additional side benefit is that the kids, who lost their mother, have felt the responsibility to take care of their father. In the beginning, after Pat died, I literally had a banquet at my house every night. The kids kept bringing food over all the time and felt an overwhelming need to take care of me. Pat has taken on so much of that role. Now the kids don't feel like they have to be my caregiver every day.

Older people like independence, and I feel like I have that with Pat in my life. She really takes care of me, makes sure I am doing okay, and keeps the kids up to date on what is going on in our lives. Pat has strengthened our family's connection, no doubt about it.

With respect to my kids, each of them has met and exceeded all of my expectations. I don't live through my children and never did. I have my own life, and once they reached the point where they had all become self-sufficient, I have made sure that I do not intrude in their lives. That said, I like to think that I have been available for them if they have wanted or needed anything. I know Pat would be happy where they are; I certainly am. I'm so happy with my children, grandchildren, and great-grandchildren. I'm happy with the mates they have chosen, how their lives have gone. I have no expectations that were not met by them. They have reached their various levels in life and have all been successful. I could not be more proud of each of them.

To know my children are happy is a feeling like none other. There are people who feel that they may have failed their children or failed in their upbringings. I don't feel that way at all.

As you grow older, you enjoy different things with your family. I have all kinds of pictures and records of when and where we went on family vacations, when we came home for Christmas from Winnipeg, when we went to the lake and to places like Disneyland. As you get older, they start their own families. They have spouses, children, grandchildren, and extended families of their own. The family tree is now split off in several directions. Keeping it all together becomes more difficult.

We don't do all of the things that we used to do together anymore because each of the kids has their own families, and that's okay. You cannot live vicariously through your kids and I think the transition has been good. I don't feel like they have to look after me any more than I have to look after them, but yet we still enjoy each other and communicate on a regular basis. All of our children, grandchildren, and great-grandchildren live within a half an hour of our home.

I feel the real proof of our relationship as parents to our children centers around the fact that when each of our children got married and began their own lives, they all came back to live near their mother. They wanted to be by their mother. Now, whether they were cognizant of it at the time, I don't know. Regardless, it was a great tribute to what Pat meant to each of them.

I mentioned a little about having no religion in our family. Often, when the question of religion popped up, I would hold up Pat as an example to our children. I would say to them, "Look at your mother. If you want to emulate anybody or anything, look at your mother. If you want to be like someone or believe in someone, believe in your mother, because your mother is the finest person on this earth. She is better than anyone you will ever meet or will ever know in your lifetime."

Pat was a good person and lived by a creed, something that she always carried in her purse. It was a message of sorts that exemplified her life. It read:

To laugh often and love much

To win the respect of intelligent people and the affection of children

To appreciate beauty

To find the best in others

To give of oneself

To leave this world a better place.

Pat didn't preach it. She lived it.

She never said a word about goodness. She lived it.

I told our kids, "You look at your mother. Whatever she does or says, watch and listen. She is the best, and you will never have anything better in your life."

AFTERWORD: THE GRANT LEGACY

AS A SON OR daughter of Bud Grant you are asked often about what life was like growing up with a father in the spotlight. The questions revolve around the great Vikings years and Super Bowl trips. To most Minnesotans, the legacy our father has left encompasses championships and the stone-faced stare on the frozen sidelines of Met Stadium. As the children of this Minnesota icon we know his legacy is much more.

Our dad was part of a great partnership with our mom, Pat, whose legacy will live on for years to come. Between them they have influenced three generations of Grant families, always guiding and teaching and loving their children, grandchildren, and great-grandchildren.

My dad always set aside time for family. Our family outings and trips growing up in Winnipeg will always be fond memories. Our family dinners were a priority, with all of us waiting patiently "until your mother sits down" before we could begin. Our time at the cabin was always precious. Our dad continues to enjoy these gatherings, and you can see the pride he has when all of us are together, with grandchildren and great-grandchildren running all over and the babies being passed from one relative to another. Our family life created a stability that we have all benefited from.

The influence of our parents has crossed over into the next generations. All of us have raised great families with wonderful children and grandchildren. We teach just as we were taught. We want our kids to be thoughtful and caring. We were taught to be independent and to have high expectations. Raising a child can be done without yelling and with respect, letting them each have setbacks but knowing that the family will be there for them in the end.

We watched as our father showed us how to deal with loss when our mom passed away. His devotion to her in her final years was a true lesson on how to deal with life and death.

Vikings fans know Bud Grant as a great leader of men and a producer of championships. We the children of Bud Grant have been blessed to have had him as a father and leader of our family whose influence will be seen for years to come. Our families and all the future generations will carry Bud and Pat Grant's legacy forward. The Hall of Fame recognizes a career that was well done. Our hope is that as our families continue to grow and expand, we are all part of a legacy to our dad of a job well done.

Kathy
Laurie
Pete
Mike
Bruce
Dan

APPENDIX: CAREER STATISTICS

HUMBLENESS PREVENTS BUD FROM listing his superlatives himself, but this coauthor has no such reservation. Below is a short list of his accomplishments in a long football career.

+ Won nine letters at the University of Minnesota from 1946 to 1949: four in football, three in basketball, and two in baseball.
+ Was named to the 1949 All-American Football Team.
+ Won an NBA championship with the Minneapolis Lakers in 1950.
+ Was a first-round NFL draft pick in 1950, selected 14th overall by the Philadelphia Eagles.
+ Ranked second in the league among NFL receivers in 1952 with 57 catches.
+ Played four CFL seasons with the Winnipeg Blue Bombers, with whom he caught 216 passes and led the league in receptions three times.
+ Holds professional football record of five interceptions in one game.
+ Was the Blue Bombers' top pass receiver and starting cornerback before retiring to become the head coach.

+ Coached the Blue Bombers for 10 years to a regular-season record of 102–56–2.
+ Earned a playoff record at Winnipeg of 20–10–1

- Coached the Blue Bombers to six Western Conference titles and four Grey Cup championships in the CFL with Winnipeg.
- He was the first CFL coach to win 100 regular-season games in his first decade of coaching.
- Coached the Vikings to a regular-season record of 158–96–5.
- His Vikings teams advanced to the playoffs 12 times, won 11 Central Division titles, and won the NFC championship three times (in 1973, 1974, and 1976) and the NFL title in 1969.
- Coached the Vikings to four Super Bowls.

- Voted Minnesota Athlete of the Half-Century in 1950.
- Elected to the Minnesota Sports Hall of Fame in 1987.
- Elected to the Canadian Football League Hall of Fame in 1983.
- Elected to the Pro Football Hall of Fame in 1994.